THE TRINITY AND THE KINGDOM

JÜRGEN MOLTMANN

The Trinity and the Kingdom

THE DOCTRINE OF GOD

1817

HARPER & ROW, PUBLISHERS, San Francisco
Cambridge, Hagerstown, New York, Philadelphia
London, Mexico City, São Paulo, Sydney

Translated by Margaret Kohl from the original German edition, *Trinität und Reich Gottes* (Munich: Chistian Kaiser Verlag, 1980). This translation was originally published in Britain under the title *The Trinity and the Kingdom of God* by SCM Press, Ltd., London 1981.

FIRST U.S. EDITION

Library of Congress Cataloging in Publication Data

Moltmann, Jürgen.
  The Trinity and the kingdom.

  Translation of Trinität und Reich Gottes.
  Includes index.
  1. Trinity. 2. Kingdom of God. I. Title.
BT111.2.M613   1981   231′.044   80-8352
ISBN 0-06-065906-8   AACR1

81 82 83 84 85   10 9 8 7 6 5 4 3 2 1

*To the Reformed Theological Academy of the
Ráday Collegium in Budapest
and
the Collegium Doctorum Ecclesiae Reformatae
in Hungary
in gratitude and brotherly fellowship*

CONTENTS

PREFACE

Moving forward means a continually new beginning; and this is true of theological work too. *Theology of Hope* (1964; ET 1967), *The Crucified God* (1972; ET 1974) and *The Church in the Power of the Spirit* (1975; ET 1977) were programmatic in style and content: in each of them the aim was to look at theology as a whole from one particular standpoint. My aim here is different. What I should like to do now is to present a series of systematic contributions to theology, differing from my earlier books in a number of ways. Here I should like to consider the context and correlations of important concepts and doctrines of Christian theology in a particular systematic sequence. I am not attempting to present a system or a 'Dogmatics', however – which is one reason for choosing the description 'contributions to theology'.

Every consistent theological summing up, every theological system lays claim to totality, perfect organization, and entire competence for the whole area under survey. In principle one has to be able to say everything, and not to leave any point unconsidered. All the statements must fit in with one another without contradiction, and the whole architecture must be harmonious, an integrated whole. Every theoretical system, even a theological one, has therefore an aesthetic charm, at least to some degree. But this allurement can also be a dangerous seduction. Systems save some readers (and their admirers most of all) from thinking critically for themselves and from arriving at independent and responsible decision. For systems do not present themselves for discussion. For that reason I have resisted the temptation to develop a theological system, even an 'open' one.

The common, tried and tested view of what dogmatics is also made me hesitate. In the political language of the Emperor Augustus, dogma meant 'decree' (Luke 2.1). A decree is not supposed to be critically questioned; above all we are not supposed to reject it. The decree is imposed by force if necessary. Of course the theological concept of dogma is far removed from all this. But even here there is the odour – and often enough the attitude – of a judgment which is final and no longer open to appeal. Even if it is not 'dogmatic' in our everyday sense of the word, dogmatic thinking in theology likes to express itself in theses; not in theses for discussion, but in theses that are simply promulgated, which evoke agreement or rejection, but not independent thinking and responsible decision. They enforce their own ideas on the listener; they do not help him to formulate his own.

The expression 'contributions to theology', which I have chosen to indicate the content and style I have in mind, is intended to avoid the seductions of the theological system and the coercion of the dogmatic thesis; but it is not simply meant to be a rhetorical understatement. I have conceived and planned these 'contributions to theology' in a certain order, whose logic will emerge in the course of the series itself. They presuppose an intensive theological discussion, both past and present. They participate critically in this discussion, offering their own suggestions, their aim being to prepare the way for a theological discussion in the future which will be both broader and more intensive.

By using the word 'contributions', the writer recognizes the conditions and limitations of his own position, and the relativity of his own particular environment. He makes no claim to say everything, or to cover the whole of theology. He rather understands his own 'whole' as part of a whole that is much greater. He cannot therefore aim to say what is valid for everyone, at all times and in all places. But he will set himself, with his own time and his own place, within the greater community of theology. For him this means a critical dissolution of naive, self-centred thinking. Of course he is a European, but European theology no longer has to be Euro*centric*. Of course he is a man, but theology no longer has to be andro*centric*. Of course he is living in the 'first world', but the theology which he is developing does not have to reflect the ideas of the dominating nations. On the contrary, it will try to help to make the voice of the oppressed heard. We normally presuppose the absolute nature of our own standpoint in our own context. To abolish this tacit presupposition is the intention behind the phrase 'contributions to theology'.

Behind all this is the conviction that, humanly speaking, truth is to be found in unhindered dialogue. Fellowship and freedom are the human components for knowledge of the truth, the truth of God. And the fellowship I mean here is the fellowship of mutual participation and unifying sympathy. What is meant is the right to the liberty of one's own personal conviction and one's own free assent. This free community of men and women, without privilege and without discrimination, may be termed the earthly body of truth. And this of course means that the converse is true as well: that only truth can be the soul of a free community of men and women like this. Theological systems and assertive dogmatics can hardly bring out this aspect of truth. They exert coercion where free assent can be expected and given. They leave the individual mind little room for creative fantasy. They allow no time for individual decisions. But it is only in free dialogue that truth can be accepted for the only right and proper reason – namely, that it illuminates and convinces *as* truth. Truth brings about assent, it brings about change without exerting compulsion. In dialogue the truth frees men and women for their own conceptions and their own ideas. In liberating dialogue teachers withdraw into the circle of sisters and brothers. The pupil becomes the friend. Christian theology would wither and die if it did not continually stand in a dialogue like this, and if it were not bound up with a fellowship that seeks this dialogue, needs it and continually pursues it.

So we have to ask ourselves: in what fellowship did these contributions to theology develop? For what fellowship are they written? As we all know, the community of theologians can be a very narrow one; for every theologian also likes to be someone on his own, someone unique. But if we cease to take the special and fortuitous features of our own subjectivity too seriously, that community reaches far beyond particular periods and natural frontiers. The fellowship in which theological contributions are expected and offered, reaches back over the centuries to the biblical testimonies themselves; for these testimonies were the beginning of an unbroken, still incomplete, and uncompletable *dialogue in history*. There are unsettled theological problems for which every new generation has to find its own solution if it is to be able to live with them at all. No concept within history is ever final and complete. Indeed in the history of Christian theology the openness of all knowledge and all explanations is actually constitutive; for it is their abiding openness that shows the power of their eschatological hope for the future. If we consider theology's task and its problems, then the historical intervals are unimportant, and Athanasius, Augustine, Luther or Schleiermacher enter into the theological discussion of the present day. We have to come to terms with them as we do with contemporaries. What we call 'tradition' is not a treasury of dead truths, which are simply at our disposal. It is the necessary and vitally continuing theological conversation with men and women of the past, across the ages, in the direction of our common future.

But theological fellowship always reaches beyond our own present denominational, cultural and political limitations too. As the present contribution hopes to show, today Christian theology has to be developed in *ecumenical fellowship*. We can no longer limit ourselves merely to discussions with our own tradition without being quite simply 'limited'. As far as is humanly possible, we must take account of the other Christian traditions, and offer our own tradition as a contribution to the wider ecumenical community. Then, as I have said, we recognize our own whole to be part of a greater whole, and by recognizing our own limits we can step beyond them. Then we begin to get the better of self-centred, particularist ways of thinking.

'Particularist' is the name we give to isolating, sectional thinking, which is hence self-complacent and anxiously self-justifying. Because it only recognizes its own premises and only wants to have its own conclusions accepted, it comes forward with an absolute claim. In Christian theology particularist thinking is schismatic thinking. The divisions of the church are its premise, and it deepens these divisions through controversial 'distinctive' doctrines. In the age of ecclesiastical divisions – an age reaching to the present day – it is this denominational absolutism that has been practised. The differences are used to stabilize our own limited identity. To think ecumenically means overcoming this schismatic thinking, to which we have become so accustomed that many people do not even notice it any more, and beginning to think in the coming ecumenical fellowship. It means no longer thinking contrary to the others, but thinking with them and for them. It requires us to invest our own identity in this coming ecumenical fellowship. But how can we get away from particularist schismatic thinking, to thinking that is universal and ecumenical?

The theological testimonies of the Christian faith can be viewed in the light of their particularity. Then there are Orthodox, Catholic, Anglican, Lutheran and many other theological testimonies. But they can also be investigated and interpreted in the light of their universality. Then they can be seen as the testimonies of the one church of Christ, and we can interpret them as contributions to the theology of this one church of Christ. Then, whatever denominational stamp a text may have, the important thing is simply its contribution to the truth to which all together are subject. Truth is universal. Only the lie is particularist.

Because today the growing ecumenical fellowship has already to be seen as the earthly body of Christ's truth, in these 'contributions to theology' I am trying to take up Protestant and Catholic, Western and Eastern traditions, to listen to what they have to say, and to come to terms with them critically and self-critically. This work on the doctrine of the Trinity is dedicated especially to an overcoming of the schism between the Eastern and Western churches which has so tragically burdened the whole life of the Christian faith ever since 1054. I owe many ideas to the conferences on the Filioque question, which at my suggestion were held by the ecumenical Commission for Faith and Order in 1978 and 1979; but I am indebted to these conferences even more for the hope that this question may be solved and that the schism may be healed.

In addition to this I have been particularly concerned to bring Judaism and the testimonies of the biblical Jewish faith into the discussion with the biblical Christian faith. The first schism in the history of the kingdom of God began with the separation between Christianity and Judaism. Even if we are not free to annul that first schism all by ourselves, we can still overcome its fateful effects and arrive at the common ground crossed by paths which are indeed still divided but which none the less run parallel to one another. This is enjoined on us by our common commitment to the scriptures and our common hope for the kingdom. It is time to extend our theological conversations in the ecumenical fellowship to theological conversations with Israel. The testimonies of the biblical Jewish faith may also be interpreted as the testimonies to a fellowship that goes beyond Judaism, for God's people are *one* people.

Since 1975 I have discussed the basic ideas of this contribution to the doctrine of the Trinity in many groups, with many colleagues and post-graduate students. I should like to thank all of them here

for the work we have done together. A draft of some chapters of
the book formed the basis for the Warfield Lectures, which I
delivered in October 1979 at Princeton Theological Seminary. This
invitation forced me to concentrate my ideas, and I am grateful for
it. Finally I should like to express my warmest thanks to Dr Michael
Welker for the criticism with which he has accompanied the writing
of this book. I am also extremely grateful to Mr Siegfried Welling
for his laborious work on the proofs.

Here too, as in other theological work, there has been a picture
in front of me. It is Andrei Rublev's wonderful fifteenth-century
Russian icon of the Holy Trinity. Through their tenderly intimate
inclination towards one another, the three Persons show the profound unity joining them, in which they are one. The chalice on
the table points to the surrender of the Son on Golgotha. Just as
the chalice stands at the centre of the table round which the three
Persons are sitting, so the cross of the Son stands from eternity in
the centre of the Trinity. Anyone who grasps the truth of this
picture understands that it is only in the unity with one another
which springs from the self-giving of the Son 'for many' that men
and women are in conformity with the triune God. He understands
that people only arrive at their own truth in their free and loving
inclination towards one another. It is to this 'social' understanding
of the doctrine of the Trinity that this book is an invitation.

Tübingen   JÜRGEN MOLTMANN
April 1980

I

Trinitarian Theology Today

What do we think of when we hear the name of the triune God? What ideas do we associate with the Trinity? What do we experience in the fellowship of the Father, the Son and the Holy Spirit?

The answers will vary greatly, if indeed an answer is attempted at all. Some people will think of the traditional rituals and symbols of Christian worship, baptism, the Lord's Supper and the blessing. Other people are reminded of passionate disputes in the early church. Some will see in their mind's eye the pictures of Christian art depicting three divine Persons, or two Persons and the Holy Spirit in the form of a dove. Many people view the theological doctrine of the Trinity as a speculation for theological specialists, which has nothing to do with real life. That is why modern Protestants like to content themselves with the young Melancthon's maxim: 'We adore the mysteries of the Godhead. That is better than to investigate them.'[1] It is difficult enough to believe that there is a God at all and to live accordingly. Does belief in the Trinity not make the religious life even more difficult, and quite unnecessarily? Why are most Christians in the West, whether they be Catholics or Protestants, really only 'monotheists' where the experience and practice of their faith is concerned?[2] Whether God is one or triune evidently makes as little difference to the doctrine of faith as it does to ethics. Consequently the doctrine of the Trinity hardly occurs at all in modern apologetic writings which aim to bring the Christian faith home to the modern world again. Even the new approaches made by fundamental theology do not begin with the Trinity. In the attempts that are being made to justify theology today – whether it is hermeneutical theology or political

theology, process theology or the theological theory of science –
the doctrine of the Trinity has very little essential importance.

In this chapter we shall try to demolish some explicit objections
and some tacit inhibitions, and shall try to uncover ways of access
to an understanding of the triune God. After we have discussed
the question of the experience of God, the practice and the knowledge or perception of faith, we shall go on to look at the three
conceptions of God which have been developed in Western history:
God as supreme substance; God as absolute subject; the triune
God. We shall see these ideas as steps along a path. And in the
course of this discussion we shall have to consider critically different views about what reason is, theologically speaking.

§1 RETURN TO TRINITARIAN THINKING

1. *Experience as a Means of Access?*

The first group of express objections and tacit reservations towards
the doctrine of the Trinity come from experience; they are related
to the limitations of the experience open to us. By experience the
modern person means perceptions which *he himself* can repeat and
verify. They are perceptions, moreover, which affect *him himself*,
because they crystallize out in some alteration *of* his self; that is to
say, they are related to his subjectivity. Must not truth be something we can experience? Can we experience God? Is it possible to
talk about the triune God out of personal experience?

It was Friedrich Schleiermacher who first understood the way in
which this modern concept of experience and truth was related to
actual existence, and it was he who consistently remoulded 'dogmatic theology' into 'the doctrine of faith'. The piety which is
faith's expression is 'neither knowledge nor action, but a determination of feeling or immediate self-consciousness'. By this
Schleiermacher does not mean psychologically ascertainable emo-
tions; he means that the whole human existence is affected. That
is why he talked about '*immediate* self-consciousness'.[3] In this
immediate self-consciousness we experience ourselves as 'quite simply dependent', that is to say, we become aware of ourselves in
relation to God, the reason and the ground of our own selves. For
Schleiermacher, therefore, the experience of the self in faith points
towards God. God is indirectly experienced in the experience of

the absolute dependency of our own existence. This means that all statements about God are bound to be at the same time statements about the personal existence determined by faith. Statements about God which do not include statements about the immediate self-consciousness of the believer belong to the realm of speculation, because they are not verifiable by personal experience. It was therefore quite consistent for Schleiermacher to put the doctrine of the Trinity at the end of his doctrine of faith: the doctrine of the triune God is 'not a direct statement about Christian self-consciousness, but only a web of several such statements' – i.e., a construction which gathers together a number of different statements of faith.[4] As the transcendent ground of our sense of absolute dependence, God is *one*. Schleiermacher therefore understood Christianity as a 'monotheistic mode of belief'. The church's doctrine of the three divine Persons is secondary, because it is a mere web of different statements about the Christian self-consciousness; it does not alter Christianity's monotheism at all. Consequently it is enough to talk about the one God, by talking about one's own Christian self-consciousness. The doctrine of the Trinity is superfluous. Assuming the presuppositions of our modern, subjective concept of experience, the transformation of dogmatics into the doctrine of faith, and the conversion of the church's doctrine of the Trinity into abstract monotheism, is inescapable.

But can faith's experience of God be adequately expressed in this concept? Must not faith for its part fundamentally alter the concept? If faith is a living relationship, then faith conceived of as 'a determination of feeling or immediate self-consciousness' can only grasp one side of the matter. The other side of the relationship, the side we term 'God', remains unknown if we ascribe to it no more than the reason behind the definition of one's own self. Even if we relate 'experience' to the experiencing subject, concentrating it solely on the experience of the self *in* experience, it will still be permissible to ask, not only: *how do I experience God?* What does God mean for me? How am I determined by him? We must also ask the reverse questions: *how does God experience me?* What do I mean for God? How is he determined by me?

Of course the relationship between God and man is not a reciprocal relationship between equals. But if it is not a one-sided relationship of causality and dependency either – if it is a relationship of covenant and love – then for man's experience of himself this question is not merely valid; it is actually necessary. Can a person experience 'himself' in his relationship to God as person if God is certainly supposed to mean everything to him, but if he is not supposed to mean anything to God? In faith the person experiences God in God's relationship to him, and himself in his relationship to God. If he experiences God in this, then he also thereby experiences the way God has 'experienced' – and still 'experiences' – him. If one were only to relate the experience of God to the experience of the self, then the self would become the constant and 'God' the variable. It is only when the self is perceived in the experience which God has with that self that an undistorted perception of the history of one's own self with God and in God emerges.

The expression 'experience of God' therefore does not only mean our experience of God; it also means God's experience with us. Consequently we are not using the concept of experience in quite the same way in both cases. God experiences people in a different way from the way people experience God. He experiences them in his divine manner of experience. The Bible is the testimony of God's *history* with men and women, and also the testimony of God's *experiences* with men and women. If a person experiences in faith how God has experienced – and still experiences – him, for that person God is not the abstract origin of the world or the unknown source of his absolute feeling of dependency; he is *the living God*. He learns to know himself in the mirror of God's love, suffering and joy. In his experience of God he experiences – fragmentarily, indeed, and certainly 'in a glass, darkly' – something of God's own experience with him. The more he understands God's experience, the more deeply the mystery of God's passion is revealed to him. He then perceives that the history of the world is the history of God's suffering. At the moments of God's profoundest revelation there is always suffering: the cry of the captives in Egypt; Jesus' death cry on the cross; the sighing of the whole enslaved creation for liberty.[5] If a person once feels the infinite passion of God's love which finds expression here, then he understands the mystery of the triune God. God suffers with us – God suffers from us – God suffers for us: it is this experience of God that reveals the triune God. It has to be understood, and can only be understood, in trinitarian terms. Consequently fundamental theology's discussion about access to the doctrine of the Trinity is

carried on today in the context of the question about God's capacity or incapacity for suffering. That is why here we have put
chapter II, on the passion of God, before our account of the
doctrine of the Trinity in the narrower sense.

From time immemorial, experience has been bound up with
wonder or with pain. In wonder the subject opens himself for a
counterpart and gives himself up to the overwhelming impression.
In pain the subject perceives the difference of the other, the contradiction in conflict and the alteration of his own self. In both
modes of experience the subject enters entirely into his counterpart.
The modern concept of experience, which has discovered and
stressed its subjective components, threatens to transform experience into experience of the self. But the justifiable perception of
the determinations of the individual self in any objective experience
must not lead to obsessedly preoccupied interest in mere experience
of the self; that would be narcissism. The only experiences perceived would then be those which confirmed the self and justified
its condition; and interest in experience of the self is then in fact
fear of experiencing the other. This means that the capacity for
wonder and the readiness for pain are lost. The modern culture of
subjectivity has long since been in danger of turning into a 'culture
of narcissism',[6] which makes the self its own prisoner and supplies
it merely with self-repetitions and self-confirmations. It is therefore
time for Christian theology to break out of this prison of narcissism, and for it to present its 'doctrine of faith' as a doctrine of the
all-embracing 'history of God'. This does not mean falling back
into objectivistic orthodoxy. What it does mean is that experience
of the self has to be integrated into the experience of God, and
that experience of God has to be integrated into the trinitarian
history of God with the world. God is no longer related to the
narrow limits of a fore-given, individual self. On the contrary, the
individual self will be discovered in the over-riding history of God,
and only finds its meaning in that context.

2. *Practice as a Means of Access?*

A second group of objections and reservations towards the doctrine
of the Trinity come from the sphere of practical application and
are connected with the practicability of the truth. The modern
world has become pragmatic. What does not turn into act has no

value. It is only practice that verifies a theory, for reality has become identical with the historical world. People understand themselves as historical beings. For them the only possible correspondence between being and consciousness is to be found in actual historical practice. For them truth only comes about in what is truly act. Hence for men and women today the truth, as Brecht says, must 'always be concrete'. And that means it must 'be performed'. That is the modern turn from the pure theory of truth to the practical theory of it. But is truth, which under certain given circumstances is incapable of realization, therefore to be despised and thrown away simply because of that? Is the truth which God himself is, so 'practicable' that people have to 'realize God', 'put God into practice'? Is the doctrine of the Trinity a practical truth?

It was Kant who elevated moral practice into the canon by which the interpretation of all biblical and ecclesiastical traditions is to be judged. The interpretation is to be ruled by practical reason, for interpretation also means application:

> Passages of Scripture which contain certain *theoretical* doctrines, proclaimed as sacred but going beyond all the concepts of reason (even the moral ones) *may* be interpreted to the advantage of the latter; and those which contain statements contradictory to reason *must* be so interpreted.[7]

The first example he takes is the doctrine of the Trinity:

> From the doctrine of the Trinity, taken literally, nothing whatsoever can be gained for practical purposes, even if one believed that one comprehended it – and less still if one is conscious that it surpasses all our concepts.[8]

Whether we have to worship three or ten persons in the deity is unimportant, Kant claimed, because 'it is impossible to extract from this difference any different rules for practical living'. For theoretical reason God is unknowable, because he exceeds the limits of any possible experience; so it is only in the postulates of practical reason that Kant brings God to the fore, together with 'liberty' and 'immortality'. Here the transcendental definition 'God' is sufficient; for moral monotheism is enough to provide the foundation for free and responsible conduct.

Given the presupposition of the modern comprehensive, moral, political or revolutionary concept of practice, the transformation of theological dogmatics into ethics or politics is quite understandable. But do the experience and practice of the Christian faith find adequate expression in this modern concept of practice? Does not this faith have to burst apart that concept, changing it fundamentally, if it wants to bring out its own truth?

The modern understanding of the Christian faith as a practice of living which tries to conform to the life of Jesus, in order to carry on his cause, is only half the truth, because it only perceives one side of what the believer has to give.

The person who acts has God behind him and the world in front of him, so to speak. For him, the world is the domain to which he is sent, the domain where the gospel is to be proclaimed, where we are to love our neighbour and liberate the oppressed. The future is the domain of open potentialities. It depends on him, ultimately, which of these potentialities he realizes and which he rejects. He thinks in the movement of God to the world and is himself part of this movement. He works in the movement from potentiality to reality and is himself the realizer. Whether it is a question of ethical theology or political theology or revolutionary theology, it is always *the theology of action*. In this theology practice takes precedence over reflection and theory. 'The first thing is the obligation to love and serve. Theology only comes *after* this, and is a second act.'[9] The practical act which is necessary in today's misery is the liberation of the oppressed. Theology is hence the critical reflection about this essential practice in the light of the gospel. It does not merely aim to understand the world differently; it wants to change the world as well. It sees itself as one component in the process through which the world is liberated. That is the fundamental idea underlying the new theology of liberation. Today it is the best ethical and political theology, because it tries to do, and teaches us to do, what is needful today for the needs of the oppressed.

But Christian love is not merely a motivation, and Christian faith is more than the point from which action takes its bearings. Being a Christian is also characterized by gratitude, joy, praise and adoration. Faith lives in meditation and prayer as well as in practice. Without the *vita contemplativa* the *vita activa* quickly becomes debased into activism, falling a victim to the pragmatism of the modern meritocratic society which judges by performance. Of course there is a speculative trivialization of the concept of God. But it can be pragmatically trivialized too.

In meditation and contemplation man turns to the God in whom he believes, opening himself to his reality. Without any alibi in what he does, he stands before what Barth called 'the all transforming fact' and surrenders himself wholly to it. 'To know God means to suffer God' says a wise old theological saying. To suffer God means experiencing in oneself the death pangs of the old man and the birth pangs of the new. The Old Testament already tells us that 'He who looks upon God must die'. The closer people come to the divine reality, the more deeply they are drawn into this dying and this rebirth. This becomes vividly present and experienceable in the figure of the crucified Jesus. Christian meditation and contemplation are therefore at their very heart *meditatio crucis*, the stations of the cross, meditation on the passion. The person who turns to the God who encounters us visibly in the person of the crucified Jesus, accepts this transformation. In the pain of repentence and a new beginning he experiences the joy of God's fellowship. The practice of his own life is thereby changed, and changed much more radically than is possible within the potentialities open to the 'active' person. The man or woman who suffers God in the fellowship of the crucified Jesus can also praise God in the fellowship of the Jesus who is risen. The theology of the cross becomes the theology of doxology.

Action and meditation are related to one another in many different ways. The point of intersection emerges from the situation in which the individual finds himself. But the one always conditions the other. Meditation can never lead to flight from the Christian practice required of us because, being Christian meditation, it is *meditatio passionis et mortis Christi*. Practice can never become the flight from meditation because, as Christian practice, it is bound to discipleship of the crucified Jesus. Consequently theology in action and theology in doxology belong together. There must be no theology of liberation without the glorification of God and no glorification of God without the liberation of the oppressed.

The modern world's devotion to what is ethical and pragmatic has led to the disintegration of the doctrine of the Trinity in moral monotheism. The reduction of faith to practice has not enriched faith; it has impoverished it. It has let practice itself become a matter of law and compulsion.

If we are to be freed for practice – not from it! – it is important for meditation, contemplation and doxology to be rediscovered. It is only together, not each for itself, that practice and adoration lead men and women into the history of God. The rediscovery of the meaning of the doctrine of the Trinity begins when the one-sidedness of a merely pragmatic thinking is overcome, and when practice is liberated from activism, so that it can become a liberated practice of the gospel. This has consequences for the nature of knowing itself – for the way in which we arrive at knowledge.

In the pragmatic thinking of the modern world, knowing something always means dominating something: 'Knowledge is power.' Through our scientific knowledge we acquire power over objects and can appropriate them. Modern thinking has made reason operational. Reason recognizes only 'what reason herself brings forth according to her own concept'.[10] It has become a productive organ – hardly a perceptive one any more. It builds its own world and in what it has produced it only recognizes itself again. In several European languages, understanding a thing means 'grasping' it. We grasp a thing when 'we've got it'. If we have grasped something, we take it into our possession. If we possess something we can do with it what we want. The motive that impels modern reason *to know* must be described as the desire to conquer and to dominate.

For the Greek philosophers and the Fathers of the church, knowing meant something different: it meant knowing in *wonder*. By knowing or perceiving one participates in the life of the other. Here knowing does not transform the counterpart into the property of the knower; the knower does not appropriate what he knows. On the contrary, he is transformed through sympathy, becoming a participator in what he perceives. Knowledge confers fellowship. That is why knowing, perception, only goes as far as love, sympathy and participation reach. Where the theological perception of God and his history is concerned, there will be a modern discovery of trinitarian thinking when there is at the same time a fundamental change in modern reason – a change from lordship to fellowship, from conquest to participation, from production to receptivity. The new theological penetration of the trinitarian history of God ought also to free the reason that has been made operational – free it for receptive perception of its Other, free it for participation in that Other. Trinitarian thinking should prepare the way for a liberating and healing concern for the reality that has been destroyed.

§2 ON THE WAY TO THE TRIUNE GOD

The question about the reality of God has been answered in various different ways in the history of Western theology. One answer was given by Greek antiquity, continued to be given in the Middle Ages, and still counts as valid in the present-day definitions of the Roman Catholic Church: God is the supreme substance. The cosmological proofs of God claim to offer sufficient grounds for this assumption at every period. The other answer springs from the special tradition of the Old Testament and, by way of mediaeval nominalism, passed down to the Idealist philosophy of the nineteenth century. According to this answer, God is the absolute subject. The biblical testimonies of salvation history and the present experience of the world as history force us to think of God, not merely as the supreme substance but as the absolute subject as well. The specific answer given by Christian theology goes beyond these two answers: God, it claims, is the triune God. But what does this characteristically Christian answer mean in relation to those other concepts of God, which theology took over for itself in the course of its history? How are we to understand the reality of the world if we are to understand God, not as supreme substance and not as absolute subject, but as triunity, the three-in-one?

1. God as Supreme Substance

The cosmological proofs of God proceed from the finitude of the world and contrast this with infinite being. Because finitude has several definitions, there are several cosmological proofs. Their common starting point is the finitude of the world, and this can be so classified that they follow one another as steps on a single path. According to Aquinas there are 'five ways' of cosmological proof.[11] Some neo-Thomist theologians believe that they are the only convincing proofs of God at all; all the others are either fallacies or proofs which can be traced back to the 'five ways'.[12] In 1871 the First Vatican Council defined the fundamental demonstrability of God for Roman Catholic theology by stating 'that God, the origin and goal of all things, can be known with certainty from created things, with the help of the natural light of human reason'.[13] In 1907 the anti-modernist oath restricted this to 'the five ways', with the declaration 'that God can be known with certainty and can hence also be proved, as cause can be proved from effects'.[14]

The cosmological proofs of God start from the world and presuppose that the world is cosmos, not chaos, well ordered by means of eternal laws, and beautiful in its protean forms. The proofs derive from Greek philosophy, and Greek philosophy of course presupposes the spirit of the Greek religion, for it grew up out of the Enlightenment of this religion. In Greek 'God' is a predicate, not a name. The Divine Ones are present in all wordly happenings. They need no special revelations. Consequently life in the eternal orders of the cosmos is a plenitude of all that is divine. Human life is led in the presence and in the fellowship of the gods if it is in correspondence with the orders and movements of the cosmos. Πάντα πλήρη θεῶν, said Thales, in a phrase frequently quoted by Plato and Aristotle. It was on the basis of this cosmic religion that Greek religious philosophy grew up, a philosophy which enquires about the origin of the gods and about their divine nature. The divine nature, the Deity, τὸ θεῖον is one, necessary, immovable, infinite, unconditional, immortal and impassible. What is divine is defined by certain characteristics of the finite cosmos, and these are marked by negation. That is the *via negativa*. Because the Divine is *one*, it is the origin and measure of the Many in the cosmos.

This philosophical inference about the nature of the divine presupposes a divinely ordered cosmos. The existence of the divine essence is not in question. It is already presupposed by the existence of the cosmos. The divine essence is indirectly manifested in the mirror of that cosmos. The deity can be known from the world, by a process of deduction. Conversely, the world as cosmos, which reflects the divine essence and the divine wisdom, is comprehended from the presence of the divine. Here deity and cosmos provide mutual evidence for one another, thereby opening up a space for living in the chaos of the world, and order in the terrors of time. The cosmological proof of God based on the world is always at the same time the theological proof of the world based on God. That is why the concept of the world as cosmos is fundamental.

Aquinas's 'five ways' go back to Aristotle and Cicero. They presuppose the Greek concept of a cosmos which is a hierarchical order, graduated into different strata of being. The proofs are so ordered that each demonstration explains what the preceding one had implicitly presupposed; so the 'five ways' belong together in a single demonstrative process. They start from general phenomena in the world and enquire about their ultimate foundation, beyond which nothing can be asked at all. The first starts from movement in the world and arrives at the concept of the *primum movens*; the second proceeds from effects in the world and arrives at the concept of the *causa prima*; the third starts from the potential being of all things and arrives at the concept of the *ens per se necessarium*; the fourth begins with the gradations of being in the world and arrives at the concept of the *maxime ens*; the fifth, finally, starts from the order of the world and arrives at the concept of the highest *intellectus*. To these five definitions Aquinas adds in each case: '*et hoc dicimus Deum*'.

The cosmological proof of God was supposed by Thomas to answer the question *Utrum Deus sit*? But he did not really prove the *existence* of God; what he proved was the *nature* of the divine. The divine nature is the moving, causing, necessary, pure and intelligent Being for being that is moved, caused, possible, inter-mingled and ordered: that was how he understood the *via eminentiae*. In this way Aquinas answered the question: 'What is the nature of the divine?', but not the question: 'Who is God?'. With the help of his proof, God as the supreme essence or being has become conceivable, although we are not compelled to call this highest substance 'God'. The fact that 'all' human beings call this substance 'God' is due to the *consensus gentium* which Aquinas himself says is not conclusive, but merely provides the general linguistic rule, which may in certain circumstances be relative.

The five ways of the cosmological proof of God are certainly cogent on the basis of the cosmology and metaphysics they pre-suppose. But is this cosmology itself convincing? If the human understanding of reality changes fundamentally, these proofs of God lose their power, like all other proofs as well. They are irre-futable from the standpoint of their own premises; but these prem-ises can quite well be cut from under their feet. What separates modern thinking from Greek and mediaeval metaphysics is a changed view of reality as a whole.

2. *God as Absolute Subject*

The method of the cosmological proofs of God rests on the premise that there is an ordered cosmos. The perceiving person finds himself existing *in* this order as a living being endowed with soul and spirit. The 'house of being' is his wordly home. This thinking in terms of being was superseded by the rise of modern, European subjectivity. Once man makes himself the subject of his own world by the process of knowing it, conquering it and shaping it, the conception of the world as cosmos is destroyed. Descartes split the world into *res cogitans* and *res extensa*; and this modern dichotomization has made the ontological order of being obsolete, and the monarchy of the highest substance obsolete at the same time.[15] Reality is no longer understood as the divine cosmos, which surrounds and shelters man as his home. It is now seen as providing *the material* for the knowledge and appropriation of the world of man. The centre of this world and its point of reference is the human subject, not a supreme substance. There is no higher reality encompassing man, the sphere of his experience and the realm of his awareness. It is *he himself* who opens up reality and makes it accessible. So the unity of what is real is determined anthropologically, no longer cosmologically and theocentrically. The cosmos shows no 'traces' of the deity; on the contrary, it is full of traces of man. This transition to modern time has been called 'the anthropological turning point' (Martin Buber), 'the uprising to subjectivity' (Martin Heidegger) and the path 'from ontocracy to technocracy' (A. T. van Leeuwen). It was out of this transition that Western atheism grew up. A world which has in principle become man's object proves only the existence of man and no longer the existence of a God. Is this the beginning of European nihilism?

What did we do when we unchained this earth from its sun? Where is it moving to now? Away from all the suns? Do we not continually stumble and fall? Backwards, sideways, forwards, in all directions? Is there still an above and a below? Are we not wandering through an infinite nothingness? Do we not feel the breath of empty space? Do we not continually encounter night and still more night? Do we not have to light our lanterns before noon? . . . God is dead! God remains dead! And we have killed him.[16]

If man can no longer understand himself in the light of the world and its cohesions, but has to comprehend the world and its cohesions in the light of his own plans for its domination, then it would seem the obvious course for him to look for the mirror in which knowledge of God is to be found in his own subjectivity. But of course in the same degree to which he discovers his subjectivity in its superiority to the world, he also discovers that subjectivity's finitude. So he will enquire about an infinite, absolute and perfect subjectivity which lends his own subjectivity bearings, thus sustaining it and giving it permanence. The proof of God drawn from the world gives way to the proof of God drawn from existence, from the soul, from the immediate self-consciousness. That is not an objective proof; it is a subjective one. It is not theoretical; it is practical. People no longer need God in order to explain the world, but they do need him in order to exist with self-confidence, with self-certainty and with self-respect.

This notion of God has a long history. We find the first theological traces of it in Augustine: knowledge of the self is no longer part of knowledge of the world, but is related exclusively to knowledge of God. 'O eternal God, could I but know who I am and who thou art.' 'My desire is to know God and the soul. Nothing else? No, nothing else.'[17] The subject becomes directly certain of itself. Certainty of God becomes the correlative of direct certainty of the self. This means of access to God has a biblical foundation. The world is God's work, but man is God's image. That means that every human being finds in himself the mirror in which he can perceive God. The knowledge of God in his image is surer than the knowledge of God from his works. So the foundation of true self-knowledge is to be found in God.

It was Descartes who finally stripped the world of God, making it an affair of mathematics; and it was he who made this idea the basis of his philosophy of subjectivity: a person can doubt all the experiences mediated by the senses, but not the fact that it is he himself who doubts. In the process of thinking he becomes directly conscious of himself. This certainty of the self is the *fundamentum inconcussum*. But he is conscious of himself as a finite being. Consequently the notion of a finite being is already presupposed and inherent in the notion of his self-consciousness: 'The mere fact that I exist and that a certain idea of a completely perfect being ... is within me is the most convincing demonstration that God

exists.'[18] The more, therefore, man experiences himself as subject
– even if finite subject – over against the world of objects he has
subjected, the more he recognizes in God, not the supreme substance of the world, but the infinite, perfect and absolute subject,
namely the archetype of himself. God is for him no longer the
ground of the world, but the ground of the soul. He is sought, not
as the secret of the world, but as the secret of his own soul.

It was only after Kant had confuted the proofs of God from the
world through his critique of pure reason that Protestant theology
began to concern itself seriously with reflections about subjectivity.
Influenced by Kant and Schleiermacher, the ethical theology grew
up – in Protestantism particularly – for which faith means moral
certainty of God; and the theology of experience, for which God
is experienced in the believing person's experience of his own self.
God is not to be found in the explicable world of things; he has to
be sought for in the experienceable world of the individual self. It
is only possible to talk about God when one talks about man or,
to be more precise, about oneself, and out of one's own experience
of the self: this, Rudolf Bultmann declared, is the fundamental
principle of existential theology. 'For if the realization of our own
existence is involved in faith and if our existence is grounded in
God and is non-existent outside God, then to apprehend our existence means to apprehend God.'[19]

But it was Fichte and Hegel who went over to a consideration
of God's absolute subjectivity for the first time. If, for the anthropological reasons we have mentioned, God has to be understood
as the absolute, perfect subject, then we must also think of God as
the subject of his own revelation and as the subject of man's
knowledge of him. Consequently his revelation can only be 'self-
revelation' and man's knowledge of him can only be man's own
'self-knowledge'. Really, there can be no indirect communication
of God by way of his works in the world or through his image in
man; there can only be his direct 'self-communication'. God understood as absolute subject presupposes free will in God, which is
not necessary in the concept of the supreme substance. God reveals
himself where and when he likes. He reveals himself in a certain
person and a certain history, determined by him.

God, thought of as subject, with perfect reason and free will, is
in actual fact the archetype of the free, reasonable, sovereign person, who has complete disposal over himself. That is why, in the

bourgeois world of the nineteenth and twentieth centuries, this concept of God was developed further into the concept of '*absolute personality*' and, in simpler phraseology, to the idea of '*the personal God*'. The starting point and the goal of this modern concept of God was and is the interpretation of the person as subject, and stress on the subjectivity of all his knowledge and all his relationships.

3. The Triune God

The churches' traditional doctrine of the Trinity derives from the specifically Christian tradition and proclamation. In order to comprehend the New Testament's testimony to the history of Jesus Christ, the Son of God, theology had to develop the trinitarian concept of God. The history of Jesus the Son cannot be grasped except as part of the history of the Father, the Son and the Spirit. We shall be showing this in chapter III. Here we shall simply ask how the specifically Christian doctrine of the Trinity fits in with the general concepts of God as supreme substance and absolute subject, and what problems emerge at this point; and we shall ask too whether the doctrine of the Trinity itself cannot provide us with the matrix for a new kind of thinking about God, the world and man.

Ever since Tertullian, the Christian Trinity has always been depicted as belonging within the general concept of the divine substance: *una substantia – tres personae*. The one, indivisible, homogeneous, divine substance is constituted as three individual, divine persons. Consequently the converse also applies: the three persons are certainly different from one another, but they are one in their common divine substance. It is understandable that for Augustine and Thomas Aquinas this one, common, divine substance counted as being the foundation of the trinitarian Persons and was hence logically primary in comparison. Augustine proceeded from the one God, whose unity he apprehended in the concept of the one divine essence, only after that arriving at the concept of the trinitarian Persons. According to Aquinas, when we generalize, or abstract, from the trinitarian Persons, what remains for thought is the one divine nature.[20] It is this, he claimed, which is in general to be called 'God', not the three Persons, or only one of them.

This presentation of the trinitarian Persons in the one divine substance had considerable consequences for Western theology, and even for Western thinking in general. In theological textbooks ever since Aquinas, the article on God has been divided into the treatise *De Deo uno* and the treatise *De Deo trino*. Even Protestant orthodoxy took over this two-fold division. First of all comes the proof and the assurance that there *is* a God and that God is *one*. Only after that is the doctrine of the triune God developed. First of all we have general, *natural theology*; the special *theology of revelation* comes afterwards. Natural theology, accordingly, provides the general framework within which the theology of revelation draws the special Christian picture of God. The framework makes the picture possible, but it also restricts it. The metaphysical characteristics of the supreme substance are determined on the basis of the cosmological proofs of God. The divine being is one, immovable, impassible, and so forth. The specifically Christian doctrine of God can change nothing about all this, even though it has to talk about the triune God and the sufferings of the Son of God on the cross. Natural theology's definitions of the nature of the deity quite obviously become a prison for the statements made by the theology of revelation. That is clearly evident in the definition of God's unity. If natural theology's article *De Deo uno* is put before the article *De Deo trino*, then what is really being taught is a double divine unity – a unity of the divine essence, and the union of the triune God. The result is that the first unity forces out the second. Consequently, not only is there undue stress on the unity of the triune God, but there is also a reduction of the tri-unity to the One God. The representation of the trinitarian Persons in a homogeneous divine substance, presupposed and recognizable from the cosmos, leads unintentionally but inescapably to the disintegration of the doctrine of the Trinity in abstract monotheism.

Ever since Hegel in particular, the Christian Trinity has tended to be represented in terms belonging to the general concept of the absolute subject: *one subject – three modes of being*. The one, identical, divine, subject can only be thought of as perfect subject if it can relate to itself. If it relates to itself this must be viewed as an eternal process of self-differentiation and self-identification of the absolute subject. It is only on the basis of the presupposed self-differentiation of the absolute subject that we can talk about God's 'self'-revelation and 'self'-communication. The reflection process of the absolute subject has – like the reflection process of every finite subject as well – this triadically conceivable structure of self-distinction and self-identification.

A Christian doctrine of the Trinity which is to be presented in the medium of the modern concept of God as absolute subject must renounce the trinitarian concept of person, because the concept of person also contains the concept of the subject of acts and relationships. It must surrender the concept of person to the one, identical God-subject, and choose for the trinitarian Persons another, non-subjective expression. For this, Western tradition would seem to offer the neuter concept of 'mode of being'. Out of the necessity of its being, the one identical divine subject reflects on itself in three modes of being, communicating itself in this triadic way: God reveals himself through himself. The Father is assigned to the 'I', the Son to the 'self', and the Spirit to the identity of the divine 'I-self'; and this becomes the basic structure of modern doctrines of the Trinity. What the traditional doctrine of the Trinity meant, is supposed to be reproduced by talking about 'the self-relationships and self-mediations of the one, united God'.[21]

The later notion of 'absolute personality' does at least take us a step further.[22] The human personality is the result of a historical maturing process of the person; and in a similar way the absolute personality of God must be seen as the result of his eternal life process, eternally present in himself. The absolute personality of God fulfils its eternal being in three different modes of being. The effect of its triadic life on earth is therefore a process of self-emptying and re-appropriation of absolute personality.

Here the problems for the doctrine of the Trinity resemble those we discovered in the earlier Trinity of substance: the unity of the absolute subject is stressed to such a degree that the trinitarian Persons disintegrate into mere aspects of the one subject. But the special Christian tradition and proclamation cannot be conceived of within the concept of the absolute subject. To represent the trinitarian Persons in the one, identical divine subject leads unintentionally but inescapably to the reduction of the doctrine of the Trinity to monotheism.

A new treatment of the doctrine of the Trinity today has to come to terms critically with these philosophical and theological traditions. A return to the earlier Trinity of substance is practically impossible, if only because the return to the cosmology of the old way of thinking about being has become impossible too, ever since the beginning of modern times. To carry on with the more modern 'subject' Trinity is not in fact very fruitful either, because modern thinking in terms of 'subject' is increasingly losing force and significance. Anthropological thinking is giving way to the new, relativistic theories about the world, and anthropocentric behaviour is being absorbed into social patterns. 'The belief that the most important thing about experience is the experiencing of it, and about deeds the doing of them, is beginning to strike most people as naïve.'[23] The world of growing interdependencies can no longer be understood in terms of 'my private world'. Today the appeal to pure subjectivity is viewed as an inclination towards escapism.

The present book is an attempt to start with the special Christian tradition of the history of Jesus the Son, and from that to develop a historical doctrine of the Trinity. Here we shall presuppose the unity of God neither as homogenous substance nor as identical subject. Here we shall enquire about that unity in the light of this trinitarian history and shall therefore develop it too in trinitarian terms. The Western tradition began with God's unity and then went on to ask about the trinity. We are beginning with the trinity of the Persons and shall then go on to ask about the unity. What then emerges is a concept of the divine unity as the union of the tri-unity, a concept which is differentiated and is therefore capable of being thought first of all.

In distinction to the trinity of substance and to the trinity of subject we shall be attempting to develop a social doctrine of the Trinity. We understand the scriptures as the testimony to the history of the Trinity's relations of fellowship, which are open to men and women, and open to the world. This trinitarian hermeneutics leads us to think in terms of relationships and communities; it supersedes the subjective thinking which cannot work without the separation and isolation of its objects.

Here, thinking in relationships and communities is developed out of the doctrine of the Trinity, and is brought to bear on the relation of men and women to God, to other people and to mankind as a whole, as well as on their fellowship with the whole of creation. By taking up panentheistic ideas from the Jewish and the Christian traditions, we shall try to think *ecologically* about God, man and the world in their relationships and indwellings. In this way it is not merely the Christian *doctrine* of the Trinity that we

II

The Passion of God

If, in the manner of Greek philosophy, we ask what characteristics are 'appropriate' to the deity, then we have to exclude difference, diversity, movement and suffering from the divine nature.[1] The divine substance is incapable of suffering; otherwise it would not be divine.[2] The absolute subject of nominalist and Idealist philosophy is also incapable of suffering; otherwise it would not be absolute. Impassible, immovable, united and self-sufficient, the deity confronts a moved, suffering and divided world that is never sufficient for itself. For the divine substance is the founder and sustainer of this world of transient phenomena; it abides eternally, and so cannot be subjected to this world's destiny.[3]

But if we turn instead to the theological proclamation of the Christian tradition, we find at its very centre the history of Christ's passion. The gospel tells us about the sufferings and death of Christ. The delivering up of God's Son for the reconciliation of the world is communicated to us in the eucharist in the form of bread and wine. When the passion of Christ becomes present to us through word and sacrament, faith is wakened in us – the Christian faith in God. The person who believes owes his freedom to Christ's representation. He believes in God for Christ's sake. God himself is involved in the history of Christ's passion. If this were not so, no redeeming activity could radiate from Christ's death. But how is God himself involved in the history of Christ's passion? How can Christian faith understand Christ's passion as being the revelation of God, if the deity cannot suffer? Does God simply allow

Christ to suffer for us? Or does God himself suffer in Christ on
our behalf?[4]

Christian theology acquired Greek philosophy's ways of thinking
in the Hellenistic world; and since that time most theologians have
simultaneously maintained the passion of Christ, God's Son, and
the deity's essential incapacity for suffering – even though it was
at the price of having to talk paradoxically about 'the sufferings of
the God who cannot suffer'.[5] But in doing this they have simply
added together Greek philosophy's 'apathy' axiom and the central
statements of the gospel. The contradiction remains – and remains
unsatisfactory.

Right down to the present day the 'apathy' axiom has left a
deeper impress on the basic concept of the doctrine of God than
has the history of Christ's passion. Incapacity for suffering apparently counts as being the irrelinquishable attribute of divine perfection and blessedness. But does this not mean that down to the
present day Christian theology has failed to develop a consistent
Christian concept of God? And that instead – for reasons which
still have to be investigated – it has rather adopted the metaphysical
tradition of Greek philosophy, which it understood as 'natural
theology' and saw as its own foundation.

The ability to identify God with Christ's passion becomes feeble
in proportion to the weight that is given to the 'apathetic' axiom
in the doctrine of God. If God is incapable of suffering, then – if
we are to be consistent – Christ's passion can only be viewed as a
human tragedy. For the person who can only see Christ's passion
as the suffering of the good man from Nazareth, God is inevitably
bound to become the cold, silent and unloved heavenly power. But
that would be the end of the Christian faith.

This means that Christian theology is essentially compelled to
perceive God himself in the passion of Christ, and to discover the
passion of Christ in God. Numerous attempts have been made to
mediate between apathy and passion in a christological sense, in
order to preserve the apathetic axiom; but – if we are to understand
the suffering of Christ as *the suffering of the passionate God* – it
would seem more consistent if we ceased to make the axiom of
God's apathy our starting point, and started instead from the
axiom of God's passion. The word 'passion', in the double sense
in which we use it, is well suited to express the central truth of
Christian faith. Christian faith lives from the suffering of a great

passion and is itself the passion for life which is prepared for suffering.[6]

Why did the theology of the patristic period cling to the apathy axiom, although Christian devotion adored the crucified Christ as God, and the Christian proclamation was quite capable of talking about 'God's suffering'?

There were two reasons:

1. It was his essential incapacity for suffering that distinguished God from man and other non-divine beings, all of whom are alike subjected to suffering, as well as to transience and death.

2. If God gives man salvation by giving him a share in his eternal life, then this salvation also confers immortality, non-transience, and hence impassibility too.

Apathy is therefore the essence of the divine nature and the purest manifestation of human salvation in fellowship with God.

The logical limitation of this line of argument is that it only perceives a single alternative: either essential incapacity for suffering, or a fateful subjection to suffering. But there is a third form of suffering: active suffering – the voluntary laying oneself open to another and allowing oneself to be intimately affected by him; that is to say, the suffering of passionate love.

In Christian theology the apathetic axiom only really says that God is not subjected to suffering in the same way as transient, created beings. It is in fact not a real axiom at all. It is a statement of comparison. It does not exclude the deduction that in another respect God certainly can and does suffer. If God were incapable of suffering in every respect, then he would also be incapable of love. He would at most be capable of loving himself, but not of loving another as himself, as Aristotle puts it. But if he is capable of loving something else, then he lays himself open to the suffering which love for another brings him; and yet, by virtue of his love, he remains master of the pain that love causes him to suffer. God does not suffer out of deficiency of being, like created beings. To this extent he is 'apathetic'. But he suffers from the love which is the superabundance and overflowing of his being. In so far he is 'pathetic'.

In the patristic period Origen seems to have been the only one to recognize and employ this distinction.[7] Of all the Greek and Latin Fathers he is the only one who dares to talk theologically about 'God's suffering'. Writing about the text 'He who did not spare his own Son but gave him up for us all' (Rom. 8.32), he says:

> Tradidisse eum dicitur hoc ipso, quod cum in forma Dei esset, passus est eum exinanire seipsum, et formam servi suscipere.[8]
>
> In his mercy God suffers with us (συμπάσχει); for he is not heartless.[9]
>
> He (the Redeemer) descended to earth out of sympathy for the human race. He took our sufferings upon Himself before He endured the cross – indeed before He even deigned to take our flesh upon Himself; for if He had not felt these sufferings [beforehand] He would not have come to partake of our human life. First of all He suffered, then He descended and became visible to us. What is this passion which He suffered for us? It is the passion of love (*Caritas est passio*). And the Father Himself, the God of the universe, 'slow to anger, and plenteous in mercy' (Ps. 103.8), does He not also suffer in a certain way? Or know you not that He, when He condescends to men, suffers human suffering? For the Lord thy God has taken thy ways upon Him 'as a man doth bear his son' (Deut. 1.31). So God suffers our ways as the Son of God bears our sufferings. Even the Father is not incapable of suffering (*Ipse pater non est impassibilis*). When we call upon him, He is merciful and feels our pain with us. He suffers a suffering of love, becoming something which because of the greatness of his nature He cannot be, and endures human suffering for our sakes.[10]

When Origen talks about God's suffering, he means the suffering of love, the compassion which is at the heart of mercy and pity. The merciful, the pitiful person participates in the suffering of another, he takes the other's sufferings on himself, he suffers for others. For Origen this suffering is divine suffering. It is the suffering of God, who bears the world by bearing its burdens. It is the suffering of the Father who in giving up his 'own Son' (Rom. 8.32) suffers the pain of redemption. It is the suffering of God's Son, who takes our sins and sicknesses upon himself. Origen, that is to say, talks about a divine passion which Christ suffers for us, and at the same time points to a divine passion between the Father and the Son in the Trinity. The suffering of love does not only affect the redeeming acts of God outwards; it also affects the trinitarian fellowship in God himself. In this way the extra-trini-

tarian suffering and the inner-trinitarian suffering correspond. For
the divine suffering of love outwards is grounded on the pain of
love within. It is significant that Origen has to talk about God in
trinitarian terms at the moment when his text makes him begin to
talk about God's suffering. For we *can* only talk about God's
suffering in trinitarian terms. In monotheism it is impossible. Both
Aristotelian philosophy and the religion of Islam make this clear.

In this chapter we are trying to develop a doctrine of *theopathy*.[11]
So let us first of all look at the theologians who – contrary to the
main stream of theological tradition – start from God's passion
and not from his apathy. These theologians are rare and difficult
to find, so we shall consider them in some detail. We shall be
looking at the rabbinic and kabbalistic doctrine of the Shekinah;
an Anglican theology of 'the sacrifice of eternal love'; a Spanish
mysticism of 'the pain of God'; and a Russian-Orthodox philosophy of religion, 'the divine tragedy'.

§2 THE 'PATHOS OF GOD'

One of the first people explicitly to contest the theology of the
apathetic God was Abraham Heschel.[12] In a dispute with the Hel-
lenestically influenced Jewish philosophies of religion that had been
developed by Philo, Jehuda Halevi, Maimonides and Spinoza, he
called the theology of the Old Testament prophets a 'theology of
the divine pathos'.[13]

In his *pathos* the Almighty goes out of himself, entering into the
people whom he has chosen. He makes himself a partner in a
covenant with his people. In this *pathos*, this feeling for the people
which bears his name and upholds his honour in the world, the
Almighty is himself ultimately affected by Israel's experience, its
acts, its sins and its sufferings. In the fellowship of his covenant
with Israel, God becomes capable of suffering. His existence and
the history of the people are linked together through the divine
pathos. Creation, liberation, covenant, history and redemption
spring from the pathos of God. This therefore has nothing to do
with the passions of the moody, envious or heroic gods belonging
to the mythical world of the sagas. Those gods are subject to
destiny because of their passions. But the divine passion about
which the Old Testament tells us is God's freedom. It is the free
relationship of passionate participation.[14] The eternal God takes

men and women seriously to the point of suffering with them in their struggles and of being wounded in his love because of their sins.

Of course the images of Yahweh as Israel's friend, or father, or mother, or her disappointed lover are just as anthropomorphic as the notions of an ardent, jealous, angry, or erotically craving God. But what these images are trying to express is missed by the person who holds 'apathy' to be the only characteristic that is 'appropriate' for the deity. Jehuda Halevi did this when he maintained that sympathy and compassion were signs of spiritual weakness and hence inappropriate for God:

> He ordered poverty for the one and riches for the other without any alteration in his nature, without any feeling of sympathy with the one or anger with the other. He is the just judge.

Maimonides did the same when he declared that no predicate indicating physical nature and suffering must be applied to the Eternal One:

> God is free from passions; He is moved neither by feelings of joy nor by feelings of pain.

Spinoza followed the same line when he propounded the thesis that 'God neither loves nor hates'. For a long time the divine apathy was a fundamental principle for Jewish theologians too. It was Abraham Heschel who perceived for the first time that the divine pathos is the appropriate hemeneutical point of reference for the anthropomorphic utterances of God in the Old Testament.[15]

If we start from the pathos of God, then we do not consider God in his absolute nature, but understand him in his passion and in his interest in history. This means understanding the historical nature of God. In his criticism of Philo, Heschel showed that the terms and concepts of philosophical monotheism cannot express the Jewish experience of God, because that is the experience of divine pathos, not a realization of the apathy of the divine being. Because human beings continually unfold their own living character in the sphere of their experience of God, we can follow Heschel when he talks about the Stoic idea of the *homo apatheticus* and about the Jewish existence of the *homo sympatheticus*[16] The experience of the divine pathos throws a person open to the joy and pain of life. He loves with God's love; he is jealous for God's honour; and he suffers with the sufferings of his God, in order finally to rejoice in God's joy.

On the ground of the Jewish experience of God, Heschel developed *a bipolar theology* of the covenant. God is in himself free and not subject to any destiny; yet through his pathos God has at the same time committed himself in his covenant. He is the God of gods; and at the same time for his little people of Israel he is the God of the covenant. He reigns in heaven; and at the same time dwells with the humble and meek.

This conceals a second bipolarity.

The sympathy of man responds to the experience of the divine pathos. That too is determined by God. That is why the prophet is called an *ish ha-ruach*, a man filled with the spirit of God. The sympathy of the spirit which comes from God responds to the pathos in which God goes out of himself. This makes a second *self-differentiation* in God perceptible. God the Lord is a 'single' God. He is the 'only' God. But that does not mean that he is one (*monas*) in the monistic sense. On the contrary, the experience of the divine pathos inevitably leads to the perception of the self-differentiation of the one God.[17]

These insights are deepened if we take up early rabbinic theology and the kabbalistic doctrine of the Shekinah.[18] What Heschel called the divine pathos is described here as 'God's self-humiliation'. The history of the world develops out of a series of *divine self-humiliations* and it is these that it represents: the creation, the choosing of the patriarchs, the covenant with the people, the exodus and the exile are all forms of this self-humiliation on God's part. The rabbis interpreted Psalm 18.35 (RSV: 'Thy right hand supported me, and thy help made me great': Luther's version: 'When thou dost cast me down, thou makest me great') as meaning: 'Thou showest me thy greatness through thy humiliation of thyself.' The Almighty humiliates himself to the end of the world. He is high and lifted up – and looks upon the lowly. He reigns in heaven – and dwells with widows and orphans. Like a servant he bears the torch before Israel in the desert. Like a slave he carries the people with their sins. In this way the One who is high and lifted up encounters men and women in what is small and despised. These self-humiliations are to be understood as God's *accommodations* to human weakness. But as the accommodations of eternal love they are at the same time already *anticipations* of the universal indwelling of God's eternal glory.

The idea of the Shekinah includes these three aspects: the present *indwelling* of the Lord in Israel; the form assumed by the *condescension* of the Eternal One; and the *anticipations* of the glory of the One who is to come.

Through his Shekinah God is present in Israel. Together with Israel he suffers persecutions. Together with Israel he goes into exile as a prisoner. Together with the martyrs he experiences the torments of death.

> Since God's sufferings in exile were taken completely seriously, Israel's deliverance from exile was logically bound to be seen as God's deliverance too ... In this intimate bond of common suffering God and Israel wait together for their deliverance. Israel knows that it will be delivered, since God will deliver himself and his people with him ... The suffering of God is the means by which Israel is redeemed: God himself is 'the ransom' for Israel.[19]

Through this belief Israel's suffering is embedded in God's suffering, and the glorifying of God in the world is linked with Israel's redemption. This faith in the God who suffers with Israel is the inexhaustible source of the power which saves the persecuted people from despair and paralysis, and keeps its assailed and disappointed hope alive.

In order to see how the idea was developed further, let us look at certain concepts in Jewish mysticism. Here the Shekinah was thought of in hypostasized and personified form.[20] But if the Shekinah is viewed, not merely as one of God's characteristics, but as God in person, then it is necessary to assume a profound self-differentiation in God himself. As Gershom Scholem has shown,

> From this time on there has been a mysterious fissure, not indeed in the substance of Divinity, but in its life and action. This doctrine has been completely hedged round with reservations, but its basic meaning for all that is clear enough. Its pursuit led to the conception of what the Kabbalists call 'the exile of the Shekinah'. Only after the restoration of the original harmony in the act of redemption, when everything shall again occupy the place it originally had in the divine scheme of things, will 'God

be one and His name one', in Biblical terms, truly and for all time.[21]

It was these ideas which Franz Rosenzweig was evidently taking up when he explained:

> Mysticism builds its bridge between 'the God of our fathers' and 'the remnant of Israel' with the help of the doctrine of the Shekinah. The Shekinah, the descent of God to man and his dwelling among them, is thought of as a divorce which takes place in God himself. God himself cuts himself off from himself, he gives himself away to his people, he suffers with their sufferings, he goes with them into the misery of the foreign land, he wanders with their wanderings ... God himself, by 'selling himself' to Israel — and what should be more natural for 'the God of our Fathers'! — and by suffering her fate with her, makes himself in need of redemption. In this way, in this suffering, the relationship between God and the remnant points beyond itself.[22]

But if this history of evil and suffering is determined by God's differentiation between himself and his Shekinah, and by the rift which cuts off the Shekinah from God himself, how is this estrangement overcome? It is overcome through *prayer* and acknowledgment of 'the one God'. According to Franz Rosenzweig, to pray the *Shema Israel* in the historical experience of God, in the experience of the Exile, means:

> To acknowledge God's unity — the Jew calls it *uniting God*. For this unity is, in that it becomes; it is a Becoming Unity. And this Becoming is laid on the soul 'of man and in his hands.[23]

Through the prayer of acknowledgment the persecuted Shekinah will be united with God and God with his estranged Shekinah. This comes about in this hostile world and is a sign of hope for the coming glory in which God 'will be all in all' in the world which he has put to rights. The estrangement is overcome too through the acts of the good, which are directed towards the overcoming of evil and the establishment of the future harmony of the one world. That is the meaning of the Hebrew word *tikkun*.[24]

Of course the doctrine of theopathy we have described is only one of the ways of understanding God on the basis of fundamental

Jewish experience. But we see here too that to start from God's pathos and compassion means coming to accept a self-differentiation or 'rift' in God. If God suffers with Israel in his passion for her, then he must be able to confront himself, to stand over against himself. The doctrine of the Shekinah is the logical result of making God's pathos the starting point.

But if in history the Shekinah is so far removed and estranged from God that it is unrecognizable, so that it has to be 'united' with God through prayer and the acts of the good, why has God withdrawn his indwelling in the world so far from himself, and what caused the 'rift' in God's life and activity? The answer can really only be: the dichotomy in God which is experienced here is based on the pathos and the initial self-humiliation through which the Almighty goes out of himself and becomes involved with the limited world and with the freedom of his image in that world. Love seeks a counterpart who freely responds and independently gives love for love. Love humiliates itself for the sake of the freedom of its counterpart. The freedom towards God of the human being whom God desires and loves is as unbounded as God's capacity for passion and for patience. Love of freedom is the most profound reason for 'God's self-differentiation' and for 'the divine bipolarity', for 'God's self-surrender' and for the 'rift' which runs through the divine life and activity until redemption.

The most moving potentiality of this theology is that it allows us to comprehend the Jewish people's history of suffering and the story of its martyrs as the history of the suffering of the tortured divine Shekinah. 'When man suffers torment, what does the Shekinah say? "My head is heavy, my arm is heavy" ', says a Mishnah, talking about the way God suffers with the torments of the hanged.[25]

§3 'THE ETERNAL SACRIFICE OF LOVE'

In the nineteenth and twentieth centuries it was English theology which carried on the theological discussion about God's passibility. Continental theology passed it by unheedingly. J. K. Mozley expounded it in detail in his book, *The Impassibility of God. A Survey of Christian Thought*, expressing surprise in his preface that there was no classic German monograph on the subject 'to lighten the labours of other students'.[26]

It is true that the German theology of the same period can show nothing comparable with the wealth of literature in English on this subject. This is all the more surprising since many theses which were introduced into theological discussion by the dialectical theology of the twenties are already to be found in the Anglican theologians who made God's passibility their starting point.

The reason for the resolve to start from the idea of God's capacity for suffering, contrary to the whole theological and philosophical tradition, was evidently the Anglican idea of the eucharistic sacrifice. One basic concept runs through the whole literature on the subject: the necessity of seeing the eucharistic sacrifice, the cross on Golgotha and the heart of the triune God together, in a single perspective. The immediate occasion for developing the power of God's suffering theologically was the apologetic necessity for providing a reply to Darwin's theory of evolution. In what sense are we to understand God's almighty power?

One of the most remarkable books about God's capacity for suffering is *The World's Redemption* by C. E. Rolt.[27] The outbreak of the First World War prevented the book from being as widely discussed as it deserved.[28]

Rolt starts from the assumption that Darwin's theory of evolution calls the doctrine of God's almighty power in question. He answers with a concept of omnipotence which is derived from the cross of Christ.[29] The sole omnipotence which God possesses is the almighty power of suffering love. It is this that he reveals in Christ. What was Christ's essential power? It was love, which was perfected through voluntary suffering; it was love, which died in meekness and humility on the cross and so redeemed the world. This is the essence of the divine sovereignty. The passion is the final victory of the Son of God.[30] Rolt then goes on to deduce the eternal divine nature from Christ's passion. What Christ, the incarnate God, did in time, God, the heavenly Father, does and must do in eternity. If Christ is weak and humble on earth, then God is weak and humble in heaven. For 'the mystery of the cross' is a mystery which lies at the centre of God's eternal being.[31]

This is the fundamental idea of the whole Anglican theology of God's suffering: the cross on Golgotha has revealed the eternal heart of the Trinity. That is why we must trace the thread back from the historical, earthly cross to the eternal nature if we are to perceive the primordial heavenly image.[32]

The oldest writings which Mozley cites for this theology argue like this:

> It is as if there were a cross unseen, standing on its undiscovered hill, far back in the ages, out of which were sounding always, just the same deep voice of suffering love and patience that was heard by mortal ears from the sacred hill of Calvary.[33]

The thoughtful and widely circulated devotional writing *The Mystery of Pain* (it was published anonymously but the writer was in fact James Hinton) takes up the Johannine principle: 'He who has seen me has seen the Father' in order to say:

> If God would show us Himself, He must show us Himself as a sufferer, as taking what we call pain and loss. These are His portion; from eternity He chose them. The life Christ shows us is the eternal life.[34]

If we follow through the idea that the historical passion of Christ reveals the eternal passion of God, then the self-sacrifice of love is God's eternal nature. There is no definition of the divine nature which could avoid including this in its concept. The sacrifice of love is not, either, merely a divine reaction to man's sin. Nor is it a free decision of will on God's part, in the sense that it need not have been made. For the cross of Christ is not something that is historically fortuitous, which might not have happened. God himself is nothing other than love. Consequently Golgotha is the inescapable revelation of his nature in a world of evil and suffering.

The theological argument which thinks along these lines begins with the eucharist, from there moves to the historical cross on Golgotha, and from that point draws a conclusion about *God's eternal nature*. God is love; love makes a person capable of suffering; and love's capacity for suffering is fulfilled in the self-giving and the self-sacrifice of the lover. Self-sacrifice is God's very nature and essence. C. E. Rolt develops his doctrine of the Trinity from this axiom: God sacrifices himself in eternity, and his whole nature is embodied in this act. He is the lover, the beloved and the love itself.[35] But because his being is absolute, there is nothing outside himself which he can sacrifice in eternity. So it follows that what God eternally sacrifices is himself. His whole being is the eternal sacrifice of *self-love*. But because God, as perfect love, is at the same time perfectly *selfless*, he loves himself in the most extreme and complete self-forsakenness.[36] God lays God open for his future.

Through his understanding of God's self-love as his self-sacrifice, Rolt's trinitarian interpretation of God's eternal self-love leads to a doctrine of the Trinity which is open to the world. Love has to give, for it is only in the act of giving that it truly possesses, and finds bliss. That is why God has to give himself; and he cannot possess himself apart from this act of serving. God has to give himself completely; and it is only in this way that he is God. He has to go through time; and it is only in this way that he is eternal. He has to run his full course on earth as servant; and it is only in this way that he is the lord of heaven. He has to be man and nothing but man; and it is only in this way that he is completely God. So God's divinity is not cut off from his humanity, and his humanity is not cut off from his divinity: 'It was necessary for God to be Man, for only so could He be truly God.'[37]

In order to be completely itself, love has to suffer. It suffers from whatever contradicts its own nature. But if God is love and nothing but love, can there be anything which contradicts his being, so that he suffers from it and has to endure it as part of his own self-sacrifice? What is this? It is evil. 'God loves himself unselfishly, and therefore He must suffer evil.'[38] By suffering evil he transforms evil into good.

Rolt shows very well how in world history God's suffering love transforms 'brute force' into 'vital energy'. Suffering love overcomes the brutality of evil and redeems the energy in evil, which is good, through the fulfilment which it gives to this misguided passion. Rolt sees this principle as acting at all stages of evolution. In the chapter on 'Redemptive Creation' he tries to show that the process of evolution is the process of redemption through suffering love. He means by this the continuous transformation of deadly violence into vital energy. The Beatitude 'blessed are the meek, for they shall inherit the earth' is for him the principle of a humane society capable of survival; moreover he holds that scientifically speaking it is also demonstrably nature's 'method of creation' and 'the path of evolution'. Through openness and capacity for suffering, the divine love shows that it is life's pre-eminent organizing principle in the deadly conflicts of blind natural forces.

But if God is already in eternity and in his very nature love, suffering love and self-sacrifice, then evil must already have come into existence with God himself, not merely with creation, let alone with the Fall of man. It is only if there is a tension within God himself that we can talk in a way that makes sense about God's eternal self-sacrifice. But is there an 'opposition' within God himself? In this connection Rolt points to mystical theology; and we are reminded here of Jakob Böhme.

Rolt himself, however, restricts his argument at this point to God as the single source of good and evil: 'Brute force . . . comes from God and He is responsible for it. Good and evil come from the same source and are therefore precisely the same thing.'[39] How are we to interpret this? Rolt maintains the bold thesis that evil does not exist because God created it; it exists just because he refused to create it. He puts it in paradoxical terms: 'Evil exists precisely because He commands it not to exist.'[40] A statement like this only makes sense if 'non-existence' has the power of nullity as whatever is shut out from God. But then the statement makes very good sense indeed. Because God creates order and excludes chaos, chaos (as what has been excluded by creation) is an ever-present threat to that creation. If, now, God endures this evil in suffering love, then he transforms its deadly power into vital energy. The power of the negative is caught up into the process of the becoming of being. His patient, suffering love is the creative power which 'gives life to the dead and calls into existence the things that do not exist' (Rom. 4.17). The evil which God suffers is the condition of his eternal bliss because it is the presupposition for his triumph. 'This is the mystery of the Cross, a mystery which lies at the centre of God's eternal Being.'[41]

This means that God's eternal bliss is not bliss based on the absence of *suffering*. On the contrary, it is bliss that becomes bliss through suffering's acceptance and transformation. In the eternal joy of the Trinity, pain is not avoided; it is accepted and transmuted into glory. The eternity of the God who is love, suffering love, and self-sacrifice can only be the consummation of this very history of suffering. 'God must, therefore, pass through time to attain to his eternal being. And in this passage He must experience the pain as untransmuted pain. Only thus can he transmute it, and, by it, attain to his own perfect bliss.'[42]

In the First World War the great preacher and writer G. A. Studdert Kennedy gave a popular and practical form to this theology of the suffering God. His book *The Hardest Part*[43] has a prophetic and radical force rather like that of Barth's *Epistle to the Romans*, which came out at about the same time. In fact it deserved even greater attention than Barth's book, for the theology of the suffering God is more important than the theology of the God who is 'Wholly Other'. What was able to stand the test of the battlefields of Flanders and created faith even in the hells there was the discovery of the crucified God:

> It's always the Cross in the end – God, not Almighty, but God the Father, with a Father's sorrow and a Father's weakness, which is the strength of love. God splendid, suffering, crucified – Christ. There's the Dawn.[44]

Studdert Kennedy acquired this profound intuition or impression of the suffering God revealed in Jesus, and his conviction of the necessity of this truth, when he was working as an Anglican priest in the narrow streets and dark homes of the English slums. His experiences as chaplain to the forces only deepened this 'essential truth' for him. Studdert Kennedy also perceived the eminently political importance of the theology of the suffering God. 'God Almighty' is for him nothing other than the religious myth of power and the injustice on earth which cries out to high heaven. He is the world's tyrant, God the oppressor, the imperial, the 'Prussian' God.

> In their hearts all true men worship one God – the naked, wounded, bloody, but unconquered and unconquerable Christ. This is the God for Whom the heart of democracy is longing, and after Whom it is blindly, blunderingly, but earnestly groping.[45]

For him the war was a struggle between the God who is suffering love and 'the Almighty' who blesses the violence and the weapons.

> I want to win the world to the worship of the patient, suffering Father God revealed in Jesus Christ . . . God, the Father God of Love, is everywhere in history, but nowhere is He Almighty. Ever and always we see Him suffering, striving, crucified, but conquering. God is Love.[46]

Studdert Kenney called his book after his poem 'The Hardest Part':

The sorrows of God mun be 'ard to bear,
if 'e really 'as Love in 'is 'eart,
And the 'ardest part i' the world to play
Mun surely be God's Part.

§4 'THE SORROW OF GOD'

A year before C. E. Rolt's book was published, a work appeared in Spain entitled *Dei Sentimiento Tragico de la Vida en los Hombres y en los Pueblos*.[47] The author was Miguel de Unamuno (1864–1936), one of the great Spanish writers and philosophers of this century.[48] The book, which was translated into English in 1921, appeared in German in 1925 (with an introduction by E. R. Curtius). In Germany too it made an enduring impression. It fitted the mood of the twenties and lent support to the Roman Catholic parallel to the Luther Renaissance of the period with its catchword of 'consoled despair'. Reinhold Schneider was the writer who was most profoundly affected by Unamuno: 'It must have been about this time that the fame of Miguel de Unamuno reached me . . . He lifted me out of my life like a landmark which can never be put back in the same place. What stirred me, comforted me and sustained me, in my innermost pain especially, was the idea of existence as a death struggle and the passionate conflict with time, existence as ceaseless challenge.'[49]

In 1897, during a profound crisis in his life, Unamuno discovered Spanish passion mysticism. Through it he came to understand the mystery of the world and the mystery of God. Christ's death struggle on Golgotha reveals the pain of the whole world and the sorrow of God. Hegel, Kierkegaard ('the brother from the North'), Schopenhauer and Jakob Böhme helped him to formulate this insight of his.

'The tragic sense of life' is a fundamental existential experience, for it is the experience of the death of human existence. 'Life is a tragedy, and a tragedy is a perpetual struggle without victory or hope of victory – simply a contradiction.'[50] Everything living is involved in this contradiction and is only alive as long as it is involved in it. Since death is inescapable, life itself is a contradiction, for life wants to live, not die. The thirst for living is the thirst for eternity. Unamuno wants to affirm this contradiction, which is inherent in life, since life is incapable of fulfilment. He wants to affirm it in order to cling to the profound experience of disagreement: it is man's sharpest pain to try very hard and not achieve anything. Unamuno calls this painful experience of life *congoja*, which means pain, sorrow, anguish, oppression (angor, anxietas, co-angustia).

Congoja is also the quintessence of his picture of Christ. The Christ despairing in his agony on the cross is for him the only true picture of Christ.[51] He captured this image in his poem 'The Christ of Velázquez': 'The crucifixes, the Spanish images of Christ, are images of appalling tragedy. They reflect the cult of the Christ in his death agony, the Christ who is not yet dead.'[52] For Unamuno this crucified Christ in his dying torment became the revelation of the universal *congoja* contradiction of the world and every individual life. 'Agony then, is a struggle. And Christ came to bring us agony; struggle, not peace ... "And what about peace?" we shall be asked ... But the point is that this peace is the fruit of war and that war is the fruit of peace. And herein lies the agony.'[53] According to Unamuno's dialectic it is not a question of war or peace, contradiction or correspondence. What we are faced with is the contradiction in the correspondence and the correspondence in the contradiction. It is that which is the agony that is insoluble. It is that which is the conflict that finds no peace.

Out of the existential experience which he calls the tragic sense of life, and out of this contemplation of the crucified Christ in his dying torments, Unamuno developed his theology of the infinite *sorrow of God*.

He is quite aware of having to break with a tradition lasting for more than two thousand years: 'This God of the logician, arrived at by the *via negationis*, knew neither love nor hate. He was a God without sorrow (*congoja*) and without glory – an inhuman God. His very justice was only a mathematical, logical justice, and so really an injustice.'[54] 'It is only the logical and frozen *ens realissimum*, the *primum movens*, that does not suffer because it does not love. It is incapable of suffering anything and is hence a pure idea.'[55] The modern concept of God shares this defect too: 'The "categorical" neither suffers nor lives, nor does it exist as subject at all. But how is the world supposed to emanate from this? Such a world would be merely the idea of a world. But the real world suffers. In suffering it feels the very material of reality, feels in its physical existence the spirit and itself, the immediate presence of what is.'[56]

Unamuno therefore breaks with 'natural theology' as philosophical defence of the Christian faith in God: 'The God of so-called natural theology cannot, however, be conceived of as suffering.'[57] This natural theology is an illusion. It prevents people from recognizing the crucified Christ, from perceiving the contradiction of their own existence, and from understanding God's sorrow. At the same time Unamuno does preserve 'natural theology's' universal claim; he applies that claim to the theology of the cross, using it to evolve his universal theology of pain, which we might describe as panentheistic.

A God who cannot suffer cannot love either. A God who cannot love is a dead God. He is poorer than any man or woman. Unamuno agrees with the Browning lines which he quotes:

> For the loving worm within its clod
> Were diviner than a loveless God
> Amid his worlds, I will dare to say.[58]

The living God is the loving God. The loving God shows that he is a living God through his suffering. 'For to us in our suffering God reveals himself as the suffering God. As sufferer, he demands our compassion, and on other sufferers he confers his own compassion. He envelops our anguish with his immeasurable anguish, which knows no end.'[59]

The truth of the suffering God has been revealed to us through Christianity:

> All this constituted the scandal of Christianity among the Jews and Greeks, among the Pharisees and the Stoics; and from that time it has been a scandal even among many Christians too: the scandal of the cross, the scandal that God should become man in order to suffer and die and rise again, that God should suffer and should experience what death is. Yet this truth, the truth of the suffering God, which so appals the mind of man, is the revelation emerging from the very matrix and mystery of the universe. It was revealed to us when God sent his Son so that he might redeem us by suffering and dying. It was the revelation of the divine nature of suffering, since only that which suffers is divine . . . Only what is dead, inhuman, does not suffer.[60]

Unamuno concedes to tradition that:

> This may sound like a blasphemy of God, because suffering
> includes an incompleteness, a limitation. And certainly God is
> limited by the coarse matter in which he dwells, by the lack of
> awareness out of which he seeks to draw both himself and us.
> So we must strive to do the same work of liberation for God.
> God suffers in all and in each individual awareness of transitory
> matter, and we all suffer in God. Religious suffering is simply
> this two-sided divine suffering.[61]

In these sentences Unamuno's theological vision of the world
emerges with particular clarity. In his boundless love God interpenetrates everything living. This means that God imposes a limitation on himself, since in this way the Infinite One enters into his
finite creation. If he enters into his finite creation, then he also
participates in its evolution. God and the world are then involved
in a common redemptive process. In this process God participates
in the world's pain and suffers in all who suffer. That is why we
participate in God's pain. It is not only that we need God's compassion; God also needs ours. What evolutionary process is meant
here? For Unamuno all living things are striving to arrive at an
awareness of themselves. This process of developing awareness
comes about through the experience of pain. Awareness means
knowing-with, feeling-with and suffering-with. It is only through
pain that living things arrive at awareness of one another and of
themselves. By arriving at awareness through pain, the living become free, and God himself becomes free in the process. 'The soul
of each one of us will not be free so long as anything is enslaved
in God's world; and even God himself will only be free when our
souls are free.'[62]

The deliverance of the world from its contradiction is nothing
less than God's deliverance of himself from the contradiction of
his world. Through the experience of death, man participates in
God's pain over his world: 'Sorrow (congoja) teaches us about
God's sorrow, his sorrow at being eternal and surviving his creatures. Sorrow teaches us to love God.'[63] The God who is love, and
who loves every one of his creatures with a love that is infinite, is
bound to experience sorrow and loss at the death of every one of
the beings he has created. Our sorrow and our loss are experienced
participation in his pain. That is why in our pain our hope is

directed towards that divine future in which God will have all his creatures beside him to all eternity. That is to say, our hope is for the day when all things will be restored and gathered in a new, eternal order.

The question of *theodicy* is the explicit background to this theology of God's universal sorrow. Unamuno's idea is a simple one: either God lets people suffer, or he suffers himself. The God who lets the innocent suffer is the accused in theodicy's court. The God who suffers everything in everyone is his only possible defending counsel. But are the two – the God who is so accused, and the God who suffers – not one and the same? Face to face with Velázquez' crucifix, Unamuno had an idea that reaches the limit of radical boldness: 'Is this the atoning God, who wants to clear his conscience of the guilt, the reproach of having created man, and at the same time evil and suffering?'[64] For him at all events the crucified God is the only possible divine answer to the universal theodicy question, which is the tormenting sting in every agony. That is why, in the history of the world's suffering, the crucified Christ is our sole means of access to knowledge of God.

Anyone who starts from the experience of suffering and who perceives the mystery of the world in God's own sorrow is compelled to talk about God in christological terms. And he inevitably thinks of God in trinitarian ones: 'The Father is only known by means of the Son, the Son of Man who suffers the blood anguish of fear and torment of heart, who awaits death in darkness of soul – death and the pain that kills and makes resurrection possible.'[65] The *congoja* contradiction in God cannot be understood at all except in trinitarian terms. For the contradiction which Unamuno sees God himself as suffering is not merely the contradiction of God's world. It is bound up with that; but it is also a contradiction in God himself. This forbids us to think of God's unity in the sense of a logical identity, whether it be of a substance or a subject.

But how does the *congoja* contradiction in God himself come about, and what is its real nature? At this point Unamuno is silent. He contents himself with a pointer to Jakob Böhme's idea about there being a 'dark side' to God.

What does this theology of God's sorrow mean for *the development of man's humanity*? Life does not become a specifically human life through the suppression of suffering, pain and contradiction. Life does not become happy life in a world without suffering, without pain, without conflict and contradiction. On the contrary, that would be the necrophil world of petrification and death. 'The capacity for pleasure is impossible without the capacity for suffering, and the faculty of pleasure is the same as the faculty for pain. He who does not suffer does not enjoy, just as he who does not perceive cold does not perceive heat either.'[66] The deeper man's capacity for suffering, the greater his experience of happiness. So there is no happiness without pain. Anyone who seeks for happiness without pain becomes 'incapable of loving or of being loved'. He really lives 'without great joy or suffering'.[67] Pleasure and pain, happiness and suffering are the two sides of a life that loves and is loved; they condition one another and corresponds to one another. But for Unamuno sorrow goes beyond both. 'Sorrow is something deeper, something more intimate and more spiritual than mere pain. Sorrow often penetrates right into what we call happiness, and even into what truly is happiness – happiness which is yet not sufficient for the person who sorrows, and before which he even trembles.'[68] Why? Because the sorrow of God and the agony of Christ do not find an end when my pain ends. In the divine sorrow which goes beyond true happiness, our own pain finds an eschatological dimension. That is why Unamuno says finally: 'The more man is capable of suffering – which means capable of sorrow in this profounder sense – the more he is truly man.'[69]

If this theology of God's sorrow did not have this eschatological dimension it would be on the very edge of masochism, and pain would be an expression of personal dissatisfaction. Sorrow without hope can make a person just as inarticulate and apathetic as the suppression of suffering and pain. The experience of pain is not in itself any deeper or more profound than the experience of true happiness. It is only participation in the pain of the world and in God's pain over the world that gives our own limited experience of pain the religious dimension of sorrow. But the eschatological direction and outlook which is inherent in this universality turns this sorrow into sorrow in hope for the infinite bliss of the world and of God himself in the world.[70]

To submerge the self mystically in the dying torments of the crucified Jesus would mean giving these torments eternal validity if the submergence were not bound up with a hidden, inner, joyful exaltation over the risen and transfigured Christ. A theology of the cross without the resurrection is hell itself. That is why Unamuno's wonderful insight into the universal *sorrow of the Father* of the crucified Christ seems to me to be only one side of a hidden hope – the side that faces us and which we can experience. And this hidden hope is hope for the redeeming *joy of God* which overcomes the world. How could we participate in God's sorrow and feel compassion with God's pain if this unquenchable hope for the reversal of all things and for the divine redemption were not involved?

The fellowship of the God who is love has these two sides: it leads us into God's sufferings and into his infinite sorrow; but it will only be consummated in the feast of God's eternal joy and in the dance of those who have been redeemed from sorrow. For true love bears all things, endures all things and hopes all things in order to make the other happy, and thereby to find bliss itself.

§5 'THE TRAGEDY IN GOD'

Berdyaev was neither a professional theologian nor a professional philosopher, so he has often been apostrophized as a 'thinker'. It is certainly true that his very originality makes it hard to fit him into any particular category.[71] Here we shall be considering the basic ideas of his philosophy of history, which might be described as a theosophy of human destiny.[72]

According to Berdyaev, the inner reason for the existence of the world and its history is *freedom*: 'The origin of the world springs from the freedom willed by God in the beginning. Without His will or longing for freedom no world process would be possible.'[73] History exists because man is free. But because man continually misuses and suppresses his freedom, human history is a tragedy. It is a tragedy of freedom, not a tragedy of doom.[74] Because God himself wants man to be free, the tragedy of human history is God's own tragedy too. God desires the freedom of his image on earth, and yet cannot force freedom on him; he can only create it and preserve it through the suffering of his eternal love. Consequently the history of man's freedom is simply the side of the history of God's passion which is open to our experience and perception. God's suffering stands at the centre only because God wants freedom.

Why does God want freedom? If the reason for history lies in the tormenting mystery of freedom, then the foundation of this mystery of freedom is to be found in God himself. It is not just that man longs for God. *God also longs* for man. 'A longing for the beloved, the one who freely loves and, in response to it, the genesis of man in God.'[75] This longing of God's is a movement in God himself, which leads him out of himself and brings him to his counterpart, his 'Other' – man. So the tragedy of human freedom is at the same time the passion history of this longing of God's for men and women. Berdyaev therefore calls the true tragedy of human history the tragedy of God, who wants freedom, and can only create and preserve it through the suffering of his love. God wants only the free manifestation of men and women and their free creative activity. It is only these which respond to and reciprocate the longing God has for human beings he has created.

But if, then, the reason for the mystery of human freedom is to be found in God himself, then we must assume a movement, a passion, a history – yes, even a 'tragedy in God' himself. That is why Berdyaev, pointing to Jakob Böhme's idea about a 'dark nature in God', talks about 'the possibility of tragic destiny for the divine life':

> When in the divine life a passion tragedy is played – a particular divine destiny in the centre of which stands the suffering of God himself and of his Son – and if in this suffering the redemption and liberation of the world is fulfilled, then this can only be explained by saying that the profoundest source of such a tragic conflict, such a tragic movement, and such a tragic passion is present in the depths of the divine life itself.[76]

Here Berdyaev deliberately departs from the philosophical statement and turns to the mythological one, for he sees the profoundest reason for the existence and history of the world in a *theogonic process*: 'The divine life itself in a deep and mysterious sense is history. It is a historical drama, a historical mystery play.'[77] In saying this he takes up Schelling's attempt to translate the concept of theogonic process out of mythology into philosophy.

Berdyaev knows what philosophical tradition he is challenging with these ideas. He calls it *monism*; and it is 'logical and . . . abstract monism'[78] that he wants to confute. Monism thinks of the deity as something immovable, beyond history, beyond conflicts and processes, and hence beyond the tragedies of passion too. It thinks of movement as applying merely to the imperfect world with its multifarious manifestations and defines the deity by denying mobility. Monism thinks of the world of movement merely as a 'seeming' world, a world of appearance, which has no real being. The deity stands in unique contrast to the contradictions of this empirical world: it is the One in contrast to the Many, it is the Immovable in contrast to the Moved, it is eternally the Same in itself, in contrast to everything that is not identical with itself. Berdyaev believes that this monism is based on an inner contradiction:

1. It remains incomprehensible how the depths of the absolute life of the one, immovable deity can be the source and the moving force of the multifarious, moved and non-identical world: 'No form of abstract monism is therefore capable of explaining inwardly the origin of the plural world.'[79]

2. Consistent monism must fall a victim to acosmism: it can only recognize the being of the one, absolute, unmoved deity, but not the being of the movable world in its diversity. In other words, in order to describe the deity, it must eliminate what it denies: movement. Berdyaev believes that it is an irony of thought that the 'disciples of consistent monism' should fall victims to dualism instead of escaping it. They permit a radical breach between the unmoved deity and the moved world, and describe the simple being of the deity by way of contradictions. In actual fact, therefore, without dualism it is impossible to state the monistic position at all. Anyone who wants to remove the deity from the conflicts of movement by denying movement, is actually bringing God into that very conflict with movement. And to define the deity by denying the world makes the dualism of God and the world insurmountable. If this is true and unavoidable, then the only possibility left to us is to fuse the monistic and dualistic elements into a *dialectic of history*, so that we understand the meaning of world history 'in relation to the destiny of the Absolute itself and the interior drama implicit, predetermined and fulfilled in its depths'.[80]

Berdyaev too is well aware of the *theological* tradition he has to get over in saying this: 'There exists, indeed, a widespread Christian doctrine which denies that the principle of movement and of tragic destiny can affect the nature of the Divine Being.'[81] He considers that the 'Christian doctrine of the immobility and inertia of God and the Absolute, and of the effectiveness of the historical principle only in the created and relative world' is in the first place an 'exoteric doctrine' which 'ignores what is most inward and mysterious, the esoteric truth implicit in the doctrine of the Divinity'. But this doctrine really stands in glaring contradiction to the most fundamental mystery of the Christian faith: 'to the Christian doctrine of the Divine Trinity, to the Christian doctrine of Christ as the centre of that divine life, to the Christian mystery of Golgotha.'[82] We must not tolerate it – even as 'natural theology's' doctrine of God – in the forecourts of the Christian doctrine of the Trinity; though it is here that it has sheltered, ever since Aquinas, in the article *de Deo uno* of the Western church's theology. We cannot simultaneously claim that God is immovable and moved, impassible and suffering, beyond history and historical: 'For it is impossible to assert the tragic destiny of the Son of God and his expiatory death without at the same time admitting movement in the divine life.'[83]

Anyone who denies movement in the divine nature also denies the divine Trinity. And to deny this is really to deny the whole Christian faith. For according to Berdyaev, the secret of Christianity is the perception of *God's triune nature*, the perception of the movement in the divine nature which that implies, and the perception of the history of God's passion which springs from this. Christian faith is the experience of the boundless freedom of which this is the source.

This movement in God is made possible and determined by the fact that 'in the depth of that life emerges the divine mystery, the inner suffering thirst of the Godhead, its inner longing for its "Other", which for God is capable of being the object of the highest, most boundless love.'[84] In his heart God has this passionate longing, not just for any, random 'Other' but for '*his*' Other – that is, for the one who is the 'Other' for him himself. And that is man, his 'image'.

If he longs for this other, it is not out of *deficiency* of being; it is rather out of the superabundance of his creative fullness. If we talk about this divine longing, then we do not mean any 'imperfection of the Absolute' when we transfer the principle of historical movement in this way. On the contrary, *the lack of any creative movement would mean an imperfection in the Absolute*. 'For creative movement, indeed . . . is a characteristic of the perfection of being.'[85] God longs for his Other, in order that he may put his creative love into action. So the objection that any movement in God represents a deficiency of divine perfection falls to the ground. On the contrary, the drama of divine love and human freedom, which begins in the innermost heart of the Godhead and constitutes its life, is the very proof of divine perfection. Yet there is a tension inherent in this which effects God himself: it is not merely something which he causes to operate outside his own self. This tension is to be found in God's longing for 'his Other', the Other whom he loves and for whose responding love he thirsts. For Berdyaev, this 'thirst of God's' is the key to the riddle of world history. But what justification can we find for it in God himself?

In the tri-unity, the Father eternally loves the Son. That is the love of like for like, for someone that is one's own. It is not love for the Other. But does the love of like for like not always presuppose love for the 'Other' too? And is the love of like for like *and* for the Other not more than simply the love of like for like?

Berdyaev did not pursue this question any further, although he seems to presuppose this idea: 'The world therefore appears to Christian awareness as created, because God was the Son. The creation of the world by God the Father is a moment of the deepest mystery in the relationship between God the Father and God the Son.'[86] He finds the ground for the creation of the world within the Trinity, not outside it. This means that there must be something in the relationship of the Father to the Son which potentially goes beyond this relationship and actually leads to the creation of the world. To use Berdyaev's own language: the love of God for his Other must already be presupposed as a matter of course in the love of God for his Son. The creation of the world is nothing other than 'a history of the divine love between God and his Other self'. This means that God's love for the Son also potentially presupposes the Son's *incarnation*. The incarnation of God's Son is not an answer to sin. It is the fulfilment of God's eternal longing to become man and to make of every man a god out of grace; an 'Other' to participate in the divine life and return the divine love.

The greatness of Berdyaev's metaphysic of history lies in the fact that by accepting a 'history in God' he can place heavenly and earthly history in the reciprocal historical relationship of divine laws and human freedom. Human history is essentially the history of freedom. As the history of freedom, it is at the same time the history of God's passion. The centre and pivot of the divine-human history is the cross of the incarnate God on Golgotha. 'It was not only the most just of men who was thus crucified, but also the Son of God. Unjust suffering is divine suffering. And unjust divine suffering brings about the expiation of all human suffering.'[87] The cross is at the centre of human freedom, and at the centre of God's suffering at the same time. Perception of Christ's cross makes 'the metaphysical historical' and 'the historical metaphysical'. Our earthly history of freedom is grasped as an element in the heavenly history, for the tragedy of human freedom is the history of the sufferings of the divine love. Berdyaev presents the theology of history as the theology of freedom, and vice versa. His theology of the cross is the answer to the theodicy problem, which arises from the theology of history and freedom:

> Evil and suffering exist because freedom exists; but freedom has no origin; it is an ultimate frontier. But because freedom exists, God Himself suffers and is crucified. The Divine love and sacrifice are God's answer to the mystery of freedom wherein evil and suffering have their origin. Divine love and sacrifice are likewise freedom.[88]

§6 GOD AND SUFFERING

The theology of God's passion which we have described presupposes the theodicy question as the universal background to its understanding and as its particular point of relevance. Consequently we must, in conclusion, consider this underlying foundation in more detail.

It is in suffering that the whole human question about God arises; for incomprehensible suffering calls the God of men and women in question. The suffering of a single innocent child is an irrefutable rebuttal of the notion of the almighty and kindly God in heaven. For a God who lets the innocent suffer and who permits senseless death is not worthy to be called God at all. Wherever the suffering of the living in all its manifold forms pierces our consciousness with its pain, we lose our childish primal confidence and our trust in God. The person who is torn by suffering stands alone. There is no explanation of suffering which is capable of obliterating his pain, and no consolation of a higher wisdom which could assuage it. The person who cries out in pain over suffering has a dignity of his own which neither men nor gods can rob him of. The story of Job makes this evident; and since that time no theology can fall below Job's level. The theology of 'Job's friends' is confuted. Does Job have any real theological friend except the crucified Jesus on Golgotha?

The protest atheism of modern times also has something of Job's dignity:

> Ged rid of the imperfect; that is the only way you can demonstrate God. Spinoza tried. You can deny evil but not pain. Only reason can prove the existence of God. Feeling revolts against it. Mind this, Anaxagoras: why am I suffering? That is the rock of atheism. The faintest quiver of pain, even in an atom, rends creation from top to bottom.[89]

These sentences of Georg Büchner's are a classic description of the problem: suffering *is* the rock of atheism, for it is on this rock that every theism runs aground which lives from the illusion of 'an unscathed world'.

But can atheism hold its ground on this rock of suffering if it is only the indictment against *God* which turns suffering into pain, and makes of pain so flinty a rock? That is the other side of the experience of suffering. If it were not for their desire for life, the living would not suffer. If there were no love of justice, there would be no rebellion against innocent suffering. If there were no 'longing for the Wholly Other', we should come to terms with the here and now, and accept the absence of what does not exist. If there were no God, the world as it is would be all right. *It is only the desire, the passion, the thirst for God which turns suffering into conscious pain and turns the consciousness of pain into a protest against suffering.* But the atheism for which this world is all there is, runs aground on the rock of suffering too. For even the abolition of God does not explain suffering and does not assuage pain. The person who cries out in pain over suffering has his own dignity, which no atheism can rob him of. The story of Job makes this evident too. His atheistic wife's advice, 'Curse God and die' (Job 2.9), does not reach the soul of the righteous man at all. He rejects it from the outset. Since that time no atheism can fall below Job's level. Beneath this level there is no atheism that deserves to be taken seriously; there is merely triviality.

The theism of the almighty and kindly God comes to an end on the rock of suffering. On the rock of suffering the atheism of the godless person who is left to himself ends too. But then what begins on that rock of suffering, in the pain which cannot find a divine answer, and which atheism cannot abolish? What begins is the dialectic of *theodicy's open question*: if suffering calls in question the notion of a just and kindly God, then conversely the longing for justice and goodness calls suffering in question and makes it conscious pain. The old theodicy question used to be: *Si Deus justus – unde malum*? The sting in the question, *unde malum*? is the just God. If we did not long for him, we should not ask the question at all. On the other hand the sting in the question, *an Deus justus sit*? – is there a God? a just God? – is the experience of suffering in all its manifold forms.

God and suffering belong together, just as in this life the cry for God and the suffering experienced in pain belong together. The question about God and the question about suffering are a joint, a common question. And they only find a common answer. Either that, or neither of them finds a satisfactory answer at all. No one can answer the theodicy question in this world, and no one can get rid of it. Life in this world means living with this open question, and seeking the future in which the desire for God will be fulfilled, suffering will be overcome, and what has been lost will be restored. The question of theodicy is not a speculative question; it is a critical one. It is the all-embracing *eschatological question*. It is not purely theoretical, for it cannot be answered with any new theory about the existing world. It is a practical question which will only be answered through experience of the new world in which 'God will wipe away every tear from their eyes'. It is not really a question at all, in the sense of something we can ask or not ask, like other questions. It is *the open wound of life* in this world. It is the real task of faith and theology to make it possible for us to survive, to go on living, with this open wound. The person who believes will not rest content with any slickly explanatory answer to the theodicy question. And he will also resist any attempts to soften the question down. The more a person believes, the more deeply he experiences pain over the suffering in the world, and the more passionately he asks about God and the new creation.

Human suffering takes multifarious forms. That is why we can also find such diverse attempts at an explanation in religious theory. The Fathers of the church consistently followed the rabbinic

and Pauline doctrine: suffering and death are the divinely appoint-
ed *punishment for human sin*. 'The wages of sin is death'
(Rom. 6.23). Since all human beings have to die, death proves the
universality of sin. This reduction of suffering and death to sin
means that the beginning of salvation is seen as being the forgiveness of sins. Human redemption then takes place in two steps: sin
is overcome through grace, in Christ's sacrificial death on the cross;
the consequences of sin – suffering and death – are overcome by
power, through the future resurrection of the dead.

The causal derivation of suffering and death from sin did give
rise to misgivings among some of the Fathers, however.[90] Clement
of Alexandria, Origen and Theodore of Mopsuestia disputed the
causal connection. They taught that death belonged together with
the creation of man as finite being. It is therefore not a consequence
of sin, and not a divine punishment either. This means that for
them death is by no means 'natural' death. They believed that
Christ will overcome not merely sin but death as well, for eternal
life is bound to be a life that is immortal. Through his sacrificial
death on the cross, Christ redeems us from sin and its moral
consequences. Through his resurrection and through his kingdom,
Christ consummates creation-in-the-beginning by overcoming
death as a part of creation and by leading mortal men and women
into the immortality of the divine glory. The doctrine of physical
redemption embraces the suffering and death of the created being.
Augustine and the Latin Fathers, on the other hand, traced all
forms of suffering and death back to sin, reducing the doctrine of
redemption to juridicial form in the doctrine of grace.

Of course there is a connection between sin and suffering. The
Old Testament already held guilt and destiny to be so closely linked
that it is impossible to distinguish them as if they were two distinct
things. Misery is the lot of anyone who sins against God. This
misery is already inherent in the sin itself. That is why the sinner
is not really a wrongdoer who has to be punished in addition. He
is someone pitiable, and we must have compassion on him. Of
course there is a connection between evil and suffering, in personal
relationships and in what people do to one another. The suffering
of one person is the guilt of another. But this moral and judicial
interpretation of suffering in the context of evil acts against God
and man is a limited one. It is not well adapted to offer a universal
explanation of suffering in the world. We cannot say, 'if there were

no sin, there would be no suffering'. Experience of suffering goes far beyond the experience of guilt and the experience of grace. It has its roots in the limitations of created reality itself. If creation-in-the-beginning is open for the history of good *and* evil, then that initial creation is also a creation capable of suffering, and capable of producing suffering.

What hurts far more than the connection between guilt and suffering is *innocent suffering*, the suffering of the righteous, the suffering of the poor, and the suffering of children. Anyone who has once perceived the limitations of the moral and judicial link between suffering and guilt, finds elements of 'innocent' suffering even in the suffering of the guilty. For to say that guilt has to be punished through the infliction of suffering is not a view designed to lessen and overcome suffering in the world; on the contrary: the guilt-expiation complex increases suffering and gives it permanence through the archaic religious idea of a world order that has been spoilt and has to be restored.

The moving psalms of lament in the Old Testament are the outbursts of pain of the innocent who are persecuted, and the righteous who suffer. Job's suffering too is suffering that goes beyond any conceivable measure of punishment and hence does not even allow the search for some hidden guilt to begin at all. In the pain over the loss of beloved children the question of guilt becomes completely obsolete. A possible desire for self-punishment cannot be satisfied by pain of this kind. On the contrary, it makes the desire utterly nonsensical. The suffering of Cain may perhaps be seen as punishment for his fratricide. But Job's sufferings no longer have anything to do with punishment. Even the customary phrase about 'innocent suffering' still actually presupposes that we could accept 'guilty suffering'. But in actual fact the experience of suffering goes far beyond the question of guilt and innocence, leaving it behind as totally superficial.

The experience of suffering reaches as far as love itself. The love which creates life and quickens it is the positive thing; it is against this that the negativeness of suffering and death shows up and is perceived. What people call 'innocent suffering' is – if we put it positively – the suffering of love, and the suffering of those who are loved. For love there *is* only 'innocent' suffering, because any-one who loves cannot look on at the other person's suffering any longer – he wants to overcome it. So his love suffers with the sufferings of the other, and experiences its own death when the other dies.[91]

Suffering as *punishment for sin* is an explanation that has a very limited value. The desire to explain suffering is already highly questionable in itself. Does an explanation not lead us to justify suffering and give it permanence? Does it not lead the suffering person to come to terms with his suffering, and to declare himself in agreement with it? And does this not mean that he gives up hope of overcoming suffering?

Suffering reaches as far as love itself, and love grows through the suffering it experiences – that is the signpost that points to true life.

The universal significance of the crucified Christ on Golgotha is only really comprehended through the theodicy question. The history of Christ's sufferings belongs to the history of the sufferings of mankind, by virtue of the passionate love which Christ manifests and reveals. The interpretation of Christ's death on the cross as an atoning event in the framework of the question of human guilt is the central part of this universal significance; but it is not the whole of it, or all its fullness.

§7 GOD'S FREEDOM

The second question which we have to discuss in considering the theology of the divine passion is the question of God's freedom. Is the suffering God free or is he a prisoner of his own history?[92] What is the reason behind the passion of God that makes him suffer with his creation and his people? What freedom can be called divine freedom?

An initial answer is to be found in the nominalist doctrine of decree: God is free. He is compelled to nothing. He can do and leave undone whatever he likes. His creative and suffering love is founded on his groundless decision. Karl Barth tried to get over the nominalist doctrine of *potentia absoluta*, especially in his criticism of Luther. None the less, in his doctrine of God's primordial decision a nominalist fringe still remains:

> He could have remained satisfied with Himself and with the impassible glory and blessedness of His own inner life. But he did not do so. He elected man as a covenant-partner.[93]

This God has no need of us. This God is self-sufficient. This God knows perfect beatitude in Himself. He is not under any need of constraint. It takes place in an inconceivably free over-flowing of His goodness if he determines to co-exist with a reality distinct from Himself, with the world of creatures, ourselves.[94]

God in His love elects another to fellowship with Himself. First and foremost this means that God makes a self-election in favour of this other. He ordains that He should not be entirely self-sufficient as He might be.[95]

What concept of liberty is Barth applying to God here? Is this concept of absolute freedom of choice not a threat to God's truth and goodness? Could God really be content with his 'impassible glory'? Does God really not need those whom in the suffering of his love he loves unendingly?

If God is the truth in that he corresponds entirely to himself, then his revelation can only be true if he entirely corresponds to himself in that revelation. That is to say, not to reveal himself and to be contented with his untouched glory would be a contradiction of himself. And if he himself determines not to be sufficient for himself (although he could be so), then there is after all a contra-diction between his nature before and after this decision; and this would mean a contradiction between his nature and his revelation. The reasoning 'God could', or 'God could have', is inappropriate. It does not lead to an understanding of God's freedom. God's freedom can never contradict the truth which he himself is. 'He remains faithful – for he cannot deny himself' (II Tim. 2.13). God's freedom cannot contradict the highest good which constitutes his essence: 'God is light and in him is no darkness at all' (I John 1.5). But then if God is love, and if he reveals his being in the delivering up of his Son, is he conceivable at all as not-love? Can God really be content to be sufficient for himself if he *is* love? How is the God who suffers in his love supposed to correspond to a God who exists in untouched glory? How can the God who is glorified in the cross of the Son possess an untouched glory at all?

If the eternal origin of the creative and suffering love of God is seen as lying in God's decision of will, then time's 'beforehand – afterwards' structure has to be carried into the divine eternity as well; and we have to talk about a divine nature *before* this decision and a divine nature *after* it. There would be no other way of defining the decision more closely. But that would mean that God has two natures: describing his nature before his self-determination, we would have to say that God is in himself blessed and self-sufficient; whereas describing his nature afterwards, we would have to say that God is love – he chooses man – he is not self-sufficient. 'On the one hand God must be conceived of as self-sufficient, and needing no one – "not having need of anything" (Acts 17.25) – and on the other hand His blessedness must be conceived of as conditional upon the perfecting of His kingdom.'[96] When Hans Martensen wrote these words he was thinking of the kabbalistic idea that 'in the outer chambers is sadness, but in the inner ones unmixed joy'.

Apparently Barth was himself dissatisfied with his nominalist exposition of God's self-determination. Consequently he interpreted God's decree as God's self-determination, and saw in God's self-determination, a free 'over-flowing of his goodness'.[97] The eternal origin of God's creative and suffering love must have these two sides. It is God's free self-determination, and at the same time the overflowing of his goodness, which belongs to his essential nature. His *decision* is a *disclosure* of himself. It is only when we see both sides that God's self-determination ceases to be something arbitrary, and the overflowing of his goodness ceases to be a natural event. That is why the continual polemic against the (originally neo-Platonic) doctrine of emanation – a polemic carried on in the name of God's presumptive liberty – is out of place. If God's self-determination is not an essential emanation of his goodness, it is not self-determination at all. Neither *the fact* of God's self-determination nor *what* he determines himself to be can be viewed as arbitrary, in the sense that it need not have been. God makes nothing out of himself which he was not already from eternity.

The *formalistic* concept of liberty does not lead to a deeper understanding of God. The concept of *absolute power of disposal* derives from the Roman law of property; it is hardly appropriate for the God who is love. Consequently we must look round for a *material* concept of liberty, and one which describes personal relationships, not laws applying to property.

Where his self, his truth and goodness is concerned, God by no means has the choice between mutually exclusive possibilities. For he cannot deny himself. So he does not have the choice between being love and *not* being love. If he is love, then in loving the world he is by no means 'his own prisoner'; on the contrary, in loving the world he is entirely free because he is entirely himself. If he is the highest good, then his liberty cannot consist of having to choose between good and evil. On the contrary, it lies in doing the good which he himself is, which means communicating himself.

Friedrich von Hügel pointed to the stages in the Augustinian doctrine of freedom in order to declare, rightly, that freedom of choice is by no means freedom's highest stage – not even if it is heightened into *potentia absoluta*.[98] The freedom of having to choose between good and evil is less than the freedom of desiring the good and performing it. Man does not already participate in God's eternal freedom in the *posse non peccare* of his primordial condition; he only partakes of it in the *non posse peccare* of grace and glory. This is therefore freedom for the good. The person who is truly free no longer has to choose. A German proverb tells us that 'wer die Wahl hat, hat die Qual' – the person who chooses has the torment of choice. Anyone who has to choose is continually threatened by evil, by the enemy, by injustice, because these things are always present as potentialities. True freedom is not 'the torment of choice', with its doubts and threats; it is simple, undivided joy in the good.

Freedom as it truly is, is by no means a matter of power and domination over a piece of property. So total power is by no means identical with absolute freedom. Freedom arrives at its divine truth through love. Love is a self-evident, unquestionable 'overflowing of goodness' which is therefore never open to choice at any time. We have to understand true freedom as being the self-communication of the good.

Karl Barth tried to mediate between his concept of liberty and the concept of God's goodness by defining God as 'the One who loves in freedom'.[99] He did not want to talk about God's freedom without continually relating it to his love. He saw God's freedom and his love as complementary. But all the same there are still ambiguities in this mediation between liberty and love: either God loves as one who is free, who could just as well *not* love; or his freedom is not distinguished from his love at all, and he is free *as* the One who loves. In the first case there is still an arbitrary element which makes responding love difficult. In the second case there is a tautology.

Which concept of freedom is appropriate to God? As we have seen, the nominalist concepts of freedom of choice and free power of disposal only have a very limited value for our understanding of God's freedom. They derive from the language of domination. In this language only the lord is free. The people he is master of are not free. They are his property, and he can do with them what he likes. In this language freedom means lordship, power and possession.[100] It is this interpretation of freedom as power and lordship over possessions which is being theologically employed if we assume as our starting point that God reveals himself as 'God the Lord'. Then 'God's liberty' means his sovereignty, and his power of disposal over his property – creation – and his servants – men and women.

The other concept of freedom belongs to the language of community and fellowship. Here 'free' has the same etymological root as 'friendly'; its cognates in meaning are 'kind', 'to be well disposed' 'to give pleasure'. The German word for hospitable, *gastfrei* (literally 'guest-free') still shows this meaning even today. If we take this line of approach, freedom does not mean lordship; it means friendship. This freedom consists of the mutual and common participation in life, and a communication in which there is neither lordship nor servitude. In their reciprocal participation in life, people become free beyond the limitation of their own individuality.[101]

Which of these freedoms corresponds to *God's freedom*? The triune God reveals himself as love in the fellowship of the Father, the Son and the Holy Spirit. His freedom therefore lies in the *friendship* which he offers men and women, and through which he makes them his friends. His freedom is his vulnerable love, his openness, the encountering kindness through which he suffers with the human beings he loves and becomes their advocate, thereby throwing open their future to them. God demonstrates his eternal freedom through his suffering and his sacrifice, through his self-giving and his patience. Through his freedom he keeps man, his image, and his world, creation, free – keeps them free and pays the price of their freedom. Through his freedom he waits for man's love, for his compassion, for his own deliverance to his glory through man. Through his freedom he does not only speak as Lord, but listens to men and women as their Father.

§8 GOD IS LOVE

The theology of the divine passion is founded on the biblical tenet, 'God is love' (I John 4.16). So at the end of this chapter let us come back to this statement and develop it in a number of theses.

1. *Love is the self-communication of the good.* It is the power of good to go out of itself, to enter into other being, to participate in other being, and to give itself for other being. If we interpret love as the passionate self-communication of the good, then we have distinguished it plainly enough from destructive passions. Love wants to live and to give life. It wants to open up the freedom to live. That is why love is the self-communication of the good without self-renunciation, and the self-giving of the good without self-dissolution. The loving person enters entirely into the other whom he loves, but in that other he is entirely himself. The unselfishness of love lies in the loving person's communication of himself, not in his self-destruction.

2. *Every self-communication presupposes the capacity for self-differentiation.* The lover communicates himself. He is the one who communicates and the one communicated. In love he is both simultaneously. Love is the power of self-differentiation and self-identification, and it has its source in this process. The greater the self-differentiation of the lover, the more unselfish the self-communication. When we say 'God *loves* the world' (John 3.16), then we mean God's self-communication to the world by virtue of his self-differentiation and his self-identification. When we say 'God *is* love', then we mean that he is in eternity this process of self-differentiation and self-identification; a process which contains the whole pain of the negative in itself. God loves the world with the very same love which he himself is in eternity. God affirms the world with the energy of his self-affirmation. Because he not only loves but is himself love, he has to be understood as the triune God. Love cannot be consummated by a solitary subject. An individuality cannot communicate itself: individuality is ineffable, unutterable. If God is love he is at once the lover, the beloved and the love itself. Love is the goodness that communicates itself from all eternity. The theology of love is a theology of the Shekinah, a theology of the Holy Spirit. This means that it is not patriarchal, but rather feministic. For the Shekinah and the Holy Spirit are 'the feminine principle of the Godhead'.

Thou seest the Trinity
when Thou seest love . . .
For the lover, the beloved and the love
are three.[102]

3. By *deciding* to communicate himself, God *discloses* his own
being; otherwise his decision would not be a self-communication
of the good which he is. If he *discloses* his inner being through his
decision, then his being, his goodness and his own being flow into
this decision, and through that into the world. God communicates
himself to other being, not out of compulsion and not out of some
arbitrary resolve, but out of the inner pleasure of his eternal love:
In this context 'God is love' means: God is self-communication,
and also the desire for self-communication. *Amor extasim facit*:
'Love does not permit the lover to rest in himself. It draws him out
of himself, so that he may be entirely in the beloved' wrote
Pseudo-Dionysius. It is in accordance with the love which is God
that he should fashion a creation which he rejoices over, and call
to life his Other, man, as his image, who responds to him. Not to
do this would contradict the love which God is. In the love which
God is already lies the energy which leads God out of himself –
and in that energy the longing, to use Berdyaev's word. Love not
only has the potentiality for this, but the actual tendency and
intention as well. 'Love as the one that communicates does not yet
find the real place of its activity in God himself, but only where
there is purely free, primal giving, only where there is pure needi-
ness in the receiver.'[103]

In this sense God 'needs' the world and man. If God is love, then
he neither will nor can be without the one who is his beloved.

4. God is love means in *trinitarian* terms: in eternity and out of
the very necessity of his being the Father loves the only begotten
Son. He loves him with the love that both engenders and brings
forth. In eternity and out of the very necessity of his being the Son
responds to the Father's love through his obedience and his surrender to the Father. Father and Son are alike divine beings, but
they are not identical. The Son is other than the Father, but not
other in essence. The inner-trinitarian love is therefore the *love of
like for like*, not the love for one who is essentially different. It is
necessary love, not free love. If this love goes out of itself, then it
is no longer merely engendering and bringing forth, it is creative

too; it is not merely the love which essential nature makes necessary, but free love as well. It is no longer addressed to the Other in the like, but to the like in the Other. Like is not enough for like. If his free and creative love is responded to by those whom it calls to life, then it finds its echo, its answer, its image and so its bliss in freedom and in the Other. God is love. That means he is engendering *and* creative love. He communicates himself to his like *and* to his Other. God is love. That means he is responsive love, both in essence *and* freely. The love with which God creatively and sufferingly loves the world is no different from the love he himself is in eternity. And conversely, creative and suffering love has always been a part of his love's eternal nature. 'The creation of the world . . . is a moment of the deepest mystery in the relation between God the Father and God the Son.'[104] Creation is a part of the eternal love affair between the Father and the Son. It springs from the Father's love for the Son and is redeemed by the answering love of the Son for the Father. Creation exists because the eternal love communicates himself creatively to his Other. It exists because the eternal love seeks fellowship and desires response in freedom. That is why we have indeed to see the history of creation as *the tragedy of the divine love*, but must view the history of redemption as *the feast of the divine joy*.

5. With the creation of a world which is not God, but which none the less corresponds to him, *God's self-humiliation* begins – the self-limitation of the One who is omnipresent, and the suffering of the eternal love. On the one hand the Creator has to concede to his creation the space in which it can exist. He must take time for that creation, and allow it time. He must allow it freedom and keep it free. The creation of a world is therefore not merely 'an act of God outwardly' – an act in an outward direction; it is at the same time 'an act of God inwardly', which means that it is something that God suffers and endures. For God, creation means self-limitation, the withdrawal of himself, that is to say self-humiliation. Creative love is always suffering love as well. On the other hand the Creator participates in his creation, once it has emerged from his love. That is why the creation is:

> at the same time the subjection of God to the sufferings that follow from it . . . If God appoints all these sufferings, they are also sufferings for God himself . . . The idea of divine love is

only complete when we do not surrender to the illusion that God does not suffer. On the contrary, it is an essential point in that holy love of his that He subjects himself to suffering. The problem is not merely an intellectual one: we feel, we experience suffering differently if it is not something fortuitous, but is part of the meaning of the world.[105]

Creative love is ultimately suffering love because it is only through suffering that it acts creatively and redemptively for the freedom of the beloved. Freedom can only be made possible by suffering love. The suffering of God with the world, the suffering of God from the world, and the suffering of God for the world are the highest forms of his creative love, which desires free fellowship with the world and free response in the world.

6. This means that the creation of the world and human beings for freedom and fellowship is always bound up with the process of God's deliverance from the sufferings of his love. His love, which liberates, delivers and redeems through suffering, wants to reach its fulfilment in the love that is bliss. But love only finds bliss when it finds its beloved, liberates them, and has them eternally at his side. For that reason and in this sense the deliverance or redemption of the world is bound up with the self-deliverance of God from his sufferings. In this sense, not only does God suffer with and for the world; liberated men and women suffer with God and for him. The theology of God's passion leads to the idea of God's self-subjection to suffering. It therefore also has to arrive at the idea of God's eschatological self-deliverance. Between these two movements lies the history of the profound fellowship between God and man in suffering – in compassionate suffering with one another, and in passionate love for one another.

III

The History of the Son

§1 TRINITARIAN HERMENEUTICS

The dogma of the Trinity stands at the end of the theological labours of the patristic period over the concept of God. It was finally established in the West through the Athanasian creed:

> Fides autem catholica haec est,
> ut unum Deum in trinitate
> et trinitatem in unitate veneremur
>
> . . .
>
> Qui vult ergo salvus esse,
> ita de trinitate sentiat.

If we turn back from this dogmatic acknowledgment of the Trinity to the proclamation of God as we find it in the New Testament, we feel the hermeneutic difference, and ask: are the seeds of the development that ended in the church's doctrine of the Trinity already to be found in the New Testament? Or is this doctrine merely the result of a subsequent dogmatization on the part of the Christian faith?

It is impossible to overlook this difference. But liberal Protestant scholars and theologians have made an irreconcilable contradiction out of it. They were only able to see the theology of the patristic period as a dogmatization of the Bible's living proclamation of God: 'The living faith seems to be transformed into a creed to be believed; devotion to Christ into Christology.'[1] But in making this judgment they had even to go one step further back still. Paul already obscured 'the religion of Jesus' through his dogmatic acknowledgment of Jesus as the Son of God, replacing the moral discipleship of Jesus by a religious cult of Christ. Jesus proclaimed the kingdom of God: 'He desired no other belief in his person and no other attachment to it than is contained in the keeping of his commandments.'[2] But Paul proclaimed Jesus as the Christ. So even Jesus' apostles falsified his orthopraxy, turning it into the orthodoxy of faith in Christ. Adolf von Harnack summed up this criticism in the famous thesis: 'The Gospel, as Jesus proclaimed it, has to do with the Father only and not with the Son.'[3]

But is the acknowledgment of Jesus, 'the Son of God', really only a later apotheosis of Jesus by the people who worshipped him? Is this confession of faith nothing more than the personal cult of Christians and therefore a superstition that draws people away from Jesus' real concern?

It is not my intention to dispute the critical seriousness of these questions. But they arise out of a preliminary hermeneutical decision which is highly questionable. History means human history, and human history is the sphere of morals. So Jesus has to be understood as a human person. But he is only authoritative as a human person to the extent in which he is able to be a pattern for our own moral actions. All theological statements which the Christian faith makes about God therefore have to be understood and interpreted as the expressions of Christian moral existence. If they cannot be understood as the expression of moral existence then we have to reject them as dogmatistic. Ever since Kant people have held that 'nothing whatsoever can be gathered for practical purposes' from the doctrine of the Trinity.[4] Ever since Schleiermacher we have been told that this doctrine 'cannot count as being the direct statement of the devout personal consciousness'.[5] So it is unbiblical. It does not belong to Jesus himself. It is speculative, superfluous for faith and harmful for morals. This criticism of the church's doctrine of the Trinity has become generally accepted, and it can be traced back to the preliminary decision which led to the moral interpretation of the Bible: faith means being man in the true sense, morally.

If the doctrine of the Trinity in its dogmatic form is not already established in the New Testament, could it not all the same be a way of *interpreting* what the Bible proclaims? In the conflict between different interpretations, it could after all have emerged as the 'true' one. But what is it that the Bible proclaims for which the later doctrine of the Trinity can be viewed as the true interpretation? Here we may take Karl Barth's answer: The Bible is the testimony of God's Word. God's Word is God himself in his revelation. God is in unobliterated unity the revealer, the revelation and the being-revealed.[6] God reveals himself as Lord. This, according to Barth, is the biblical root of the doctrine of the Trinity.[7] What was revealed through Christ is the concrete self-revelation of God. Its content is: 'God reveals himself as Lord.' God's revelation of himself as Lord has a trinitarian structure. Consequently the church's doctrine of the Trinity is the correct interpretation of the self-revelation of God the Lord. What has to be interpreted is the divine lordship, and the interpretation is the doctrine of the Trinity.

This is really a monotheistic conception of the doctrine of the Trinity. Since God's lordship can only be fulfilled by a single subject, identical with itself, it follows that the unity of God himself is to be found in the unified lordship of God.[8] The doctrine of the Trinity is designed to secure and interpret God's sovereignty in every direction. To say that 'God is one in three modes of being' is simply a way of saying that God 'is one God in threefold repetition'.[9] In this way he is the supreme Lord *per se*. This is the way in which he is to be the 'Thou' who in indissoluble unity confronts the human 'I'. In this respect the church's doctrine of the Trinity is nothing other than 'Christian monotheism'.[10]

It is not my intention to dispute the positive significance of this proposition. But it too arises out of a preliminary hermeneutical decision which is in itself questionable, and needs to be tested against the testimony of the New Testament. Is God's lordship really what has to be interpreted, and is the Trinity merely its interpretation? Does the sole sovereignty of the one God precede the divine Trinity? Is it not the reverse which is true? Is the history of the divine lordship not an interpretation of the eternal life of the triune God?

Every monotheistic interpretation of the New Testament testimony finds itself in a similar dilemma to the moral interpretation. It too has to reduce the history to which the Bible testifies to a single subject, and has to interpret it as the work of that one subject. If God is the subject of this history, then this history is his work, his revelation and his rule. He influences everything and is influenced by no one. 'God in Christ' is the subject of this history for Christian monotheism. It therefore has to talk about God's revelation of himself, where according to the testimony of the New Testament it is not God who reveals himself, but the Son who reveals the Father (Matt. 11.27) and the Father who reveals the Son (Gal. 1.16). Consequently Christian monotheism has to talk about 'God's giving of himself', where the New Testament witness tells us that it is God who has 'given up his own Son for us' (Rom. 8.32) and the Son who 'gave himself for me' (Gal. 2.20). This means that Christian monotheism has to reduce the interpretation of Christ's history in a monotheistic sense to the one divine subject. But this does not do justice to the history of Christ.

Basically, both modes of interpretation depend on the same monotheistic premise: history is the work of a single, prevailing subject, whether it be the work of man, in the realization of his moral potential, or whether it be the work of the God who reveals himself. But this premise is not in accordance with the biblical history. According to the witness of the New Testament Jesus is manifested as 'the Son'. His history springs from the co-efficacy of the Father, the Son and the Spirit. His history is the history of the reciprocal, changing, and hence living relationship between the Father, the Son and the Spirit. The history in which Jesus is manifested as 'the Son' is not consummated and fulfilled by a single subject. The history of Christ is already related in trinitarian terms in the New Testament itself. So we start from the following presupposition. *The New Testament talks about God by proclaiming in narrative the relationships of the Father, the Son and the Spirit, which are relationships of fellowship and are open to the world.*

Both the monotheistic ways of interpretation we have described have the same failing: whether we understand the biblical history as the true expression of human faith, or as the unique revelation of the one divine rule, these views coincide if human faith is viewed as unconditional trust, and therefore as the pure sense of dependence, and if God's lordship is viewed as mere sovereignty. These ways of interpretation, which seem so contradictory, are simply two sides of the same shield. If the feeling of absolute dependence corresponds to the unconditional sovereignty of God, then the liberation of man for freedom becomes inconceivable – an unstatable proposition.

We will describe the biblical beginnings of a doctrine of the Trinity in such a way that we shall be able to recognize the trinitarian origin of the biblical history itself. Otherwise the doctrine of the Trinity would remain a problematical approach to the origins of the Christian faith. At the same time, this will bring us face to face with a further task – the task of revising the church's doctrine of the Trinity on the basis of the Bible. For ultimately we must always see to it that the liberating force of the biblical witness is preserved and not obscured.

§2 THE SENDING OF THE SON

In order to grasp the Trinity in the biblical history, let us begin with the history of Jesus, the Son, for he is the revealer of the Trinity. It is in his historical and eschatological history that we can perceive the differences, the relationships and the unity of the Father, the Son and the Spirit. We shall notice the relationships and functions in which the name of the Son is used in the New Testament. Since it is the relationship of Jesus to the Father which we are concerned with here, we have to distinguish between the title 'Son of God' and the name 'the Son', used in an absolute sense. Where the title 'Son of God' is used as a synonym for 'the Son of Man' and 'Lord', it does not fall within our terms of reference. For we have to distinguish between the sonship of Jesus in relation to the Father, and the sonship of Jesus in his exemplary and liberating impact on God's children. Finally, at every stage in the history of the Son we shall be stressing the form of the Trinity that it reveals. In each case we shall be interpreting the individual stages in the history of the Son Jesus in their historical aspect and in their theological one.

1. Jesus' Baptism and Call[11]

It is a well attested fact, historically, that the ministry of John the Baptist preceded Jesus' public ministry; that Jesus belonged for a considerable time to the group round John; that John baptized him; but that he then left the group of John's disciples in order to preach his own message. The baptismal movement was widespread at that time. John the Baptist was lifted out of the ruck and became well known because of his connection with Jesus. Jesus started from John's eschatological message. So this remains the presupposition for Jesus' gospel.

John preached repentance 'in the final hour' before the coming divine judgment: 'Even now the axe is laid to the root of the trees' (Matt. 3.10). In the coming judgment of God's wrath it is only the person who accepts, and accepts now, the chance to repent offered him who will be able to endure. John was not merely a prophet; he was simply 'the Baptist'. He baptized in the River Jordan and proclaimed 'the baptism of repentance for the forgiveness of sins' (Mark 1.4). The place itself had a symbolic significance: it marked the new exodus out of slavery and the entry into the promised land in the End-time; 'Prepare in the desert the way of the Lord' (Isa. 40.3). John apparently did not found any new sect. He worked for repentance as a popular movement. We may assume that his eschatological message was not merely directed towards God's coming wrathful judgment on Israel, but that it also pointed to 'the One who is to come'. According to Isaiah 35.4 'the coming one' is a cypher for God himself, and a cypher too for God's promised Messiah (Matt. 3.11).

Jesus publicly acknowledged and praised the baptism John practised. His baptism was 'from heaven' (Mark 11.30); he came 'in the way of righteousness' (Matt. 21.32); he was 'more than a prophet' (Matt. 11.9), indeed 'there has risen no one greater among those born of women' (Matt. 11.11).

Jesus' baptism by John counts as historical because it must have been a stumbling block for the Christian church that their Redeemer himself should have received baptism for the forgiveness of sins.[12] According to the story in Mark 1.9–11, Jesus' messianic call took place at his baptism. And certainly Jesus' public ministry began after he had been baptized by John. In his baptism, together with many others, he must have experienced the special character of his call. The interpretative accounts talk about 'the Spirit of God descending upon him'. This means first of all his personal inspiration and legitimation as prophet. But it also means the beginning of the messianic era, in which the Spirit will be poured out 'on all flesh'. This messianic (and not merely inspirational) significance of Jesus' baptism is no more than underlined by the vision of 'the heavens opening' and the sound of God's voice. The prophetic-messianic gift of the Spirit to Jesus is bound up with the divine proclamation: 'Thou art my beloved Son, in whom I am well pleased' (Mark 1.11 AV), or 'This is my beloved Son' (Matt. 3.17). When Jesus is declared 'the Son', what does this mean? This form of address is evidently picking up the royal

Israelite ritual in Psalm 2.7: 'You are my son, today I have begotten you.' It is a ritual which itself already displays messianic dimensions ('Ask of me, and I will make the nations your heritage,/and the ends of the earth your possession'). At the moment of enthronement the king is pronounced the 'Son of God'.

We must notice, however, that the synoptic gospels add something: 'Thou art my *beloved* Son.'[13] In the traditions of the Old Testament, the son who is especially 'dear' is always the *only* son – Isaac, for instance. This indicates that Jesus is 'the Son' in a similar way to Israel itself (Deut. 32.6, 18; Isa. 3.4), or the king (II Sam. 7.14ff.), or even the Messiah. He has a special relationship to God, a relationship corresponding to the one between Isaac and his father Abraham. John replaces the 'beloved Son' by the expression 'only begotten Son' (John 1.14 and frequently elsewhere). Paul chooses the expression 'his own Son' (Rom. 8.32). These phrases also point to Isaac, as Hebrews 11.17 shows. This is important for our understanding of the Father's surrender of the Son on the cross.

We must also consider that we do not only have to remember the Son of God of Psalm 2.7; we can also think of the Servant of God in Isaiah 42.1: 'Behold my servant, whom I uphold, my chosen, in whom my soul delights.'[14] The history of Jesus was not the triumphal history of a messianic victor. It was much more like the suffering history of the Servant of God promised in Isaiah 53. But apparently the name of the Son was linked with the passion history of Jesus very early on in Christian tradition, so that the suffering history of the Servant of God also constitutes the majesty of the royal Son of God.

The application of the name of Son in its absolute sense in the story of Jesus' baptism suggests that it is to this baptism that we ought to relate the revelation of Jesus reported in Matthew 11.27:

All things have been delivered to me by my Father; and no one knows the Son except the Father; and no one knows the Father except the Son and any one to whom the Son chooses to reveal him.

Apart from this passage, it is only the Gospel of John in the New Testament which talks about an exclusive and mutual knowing, loving and participating of this kind. At the same time, there is nothing that contradicts the synoptic origin and the Palestinian-

Jewish background of the revelation formula. Its pre-history belongs to Israelite ideas about God's eternal Wisdom – which was
later called the Shekinah. Wisdom was already thought of in hypostatic form as 'the child of God', or as the 'daughter' or 'son'.[15]

Proverbs 8 talk about the Wisdom of God as if it were a person
with its own consciousness and will. It is more than simply one of
Yahweh's 'characteristics'. But Wisdom is probably not yet being
thought of ontologically as a divine 'hypostasis'. This means that
it would be wrong to talk in any way about a 'wisdom speculation'.
Through the Wisdom which God has 'poured out over all his
works' (Ecclus. 1.9), God himself has his mysterious dwelling in
creation (Job 28). In this way Wisdom is identical with God's
'Spirit' which quickens everything that lives. Its indwelling is a
form of God's 'glory', which according to Isaiah 6.3 will fill 'the
whole earth'. If this Wisdom of God's is called 'his delight'
(Prov. 8.30), which he has pleasure in because it 'rejoices always
before him', then it is one with God and yet at the same time it is
a subject of its own, over against God.

We even have to go a step further than this. Really, when Jesus
is called the Son it is Israel as a whole that is being thought of, not
merely individuals in Israel. 'Israel is my first-born son' (Ex. 4.22).
This is the name with which the people are called out of slavery in
Egypt. According to Matthew, Joseph's flight into Egypt, with
Mary and the child, is intended to fulfil the saying: 'Out of Egypt
have I called my Son' (Hosea 11.1; Matt. 2.15). Other features of
the synoptic account of Jesus' history also reflect the history of
Israel as a whole – for example, the forty days' temptation in the
wilderness. The representation of the whole of Israel extends into
the very passion of 'the Son'.

The mutual knowing of the Father and the Son is a mutual
loving. The mutual loving of the Father and the Son is a love of
like for like. Consequently it is exclusive. The opening statement
of Matthew 11.27, signifies the installations of the Son as lord of
the divine kingdom through the Father. The final clause distinguishes the act of revealing from the exclusive mutual knowing of
the Father and the Son, and makes knowledge – by virtue of
revelation – knowledge of the one who is unlike. 'Like is known
by like' applies to the exclusive relationship of the Father and the
Son. 'Those who are unlike know one another' is true of the

revelation to men and women through the Son. This axiom only permits a trinitarian interpretation, not a monotheistic one.[16]

This revelatory saying brings out precisely what distinguishes Jesus from John the Baptist, and makes it clear why Jesus left John; and it indicates the way in which Jesus' message went beyond the eschatological repentance movement of his time.

The external difference is recognizable clearly enough: John proclaims the coming kingdom as God's wrathful judgment on the sin of men and women, and calls for repentance in the final hour, offering baptism as the last hope of salvation; Jesus proclaims the coming kingdom as the kingdom of God's coming grace and mercy. He presents it, not through an accusation of sinners, but through the forgiveness of sins. What John depicts in the baptism in Jordan is messianically implemented in the gospel of Jesus. For Jesus, the gospel of the kingdom is a messianic message of joy, not an apocalyptic threat to the world. The signs that legitimate him are not signs marking the end of the world; they are the tokens of the messianic era: 'The blind receive their sight and the lame walk, lepers are cleansed and the deaf hear, and the dead are raised up, and the poor have the good news preached to them' (Matt. 11.5). But according to Isaiah 35.4 this means: 'Behold your God will come and save you.' Unlike John's disciples, Jesus' disciples do not fast. They do not leave their oppressed country and emigrate into the desert; they go into the villages with Jesus and teach the people. John lived the life of an ascetic, in expectation of judgment. Jesus' life is a festive life, in joy over the dawn of God's kingdom.

What is the inward justification for this difference? The justification is that Jesus knows and proclaims the Lord of the coming kingdom as his Father. This is where his unique authority is to be found. The content of the revelation bestowed on Jesus through his baptism and call must lie in the name for God which he used uniquely and exclusively: Abba, my Father.[17] It was not Israelite tradition to address God like this. What the name 'Abba' stresses is not the fatherly lordship of God, but an unheard-of intimacy. John did not see the Lord of the coming judgment like this either. The revelation of God's name as Father is Jesus' new and unique message. The name of Father stamps his proclamation of the coming kingdom, his turning to the poor and sick, his prayers, and his preparedness for suffering. According to the Christian traditions that have come down to us, Jesus never addressed God simply as

'Father' or as 'our Father', but always exclusively as 'my Father'. He revealed him as 'my Father in heaven'. We have to conclude from this that in the relationship to his God and Father Jesus understood himself as 'the Son', 'the beloved Son', 'the only' or 'the only begotten' Son.[18] This does not mean that he also understood himself as 'Son of God' or allowed himself to be acknowledged as such. He is *the Son of the Father*. The general title 'Son of God' and Jesus' special relationship of sonship to his Father were only fused together later, in early Christian tradition. Consequently here we only have to ask about the significance of the exclusive use of the name of Father and the absolute use of the name of Son in Jesus' own proclamation and behaviour.

What is the relation between the eschatological message of the kingdom of Jesus the Messiah, and this exclusive revelation of the Father by Jesus 'the Son'?

This question is seldom asked, oddly enough, and the description of Jesus' proclamation of the kingdom often does not take Jesus' revelation of the Father into account at all. 'Only in the sphere of the *basileia* is God the Father.'[19] But is it not the very reverse that is true? Jesus did not proclaim the kingdom of God *the Lord*, but the kingdom of God *his Father*. It is not that lordship is the mark of God's fatherhood, but the very reverse: God's fatherhood towards Jesus the Son is the mark of the lordship and kingdom which Jesus preaches. That gives the kingdom he proclaimed a new quality. The *basileia* only exists in the context of God's fatherhood. In this kingdom God is not the Lord; he is the merciful Father. In this kingdom there are no servants; there are only God's free children. In this kingdom what is required is not obedience and submission; it is love and free participation.

How does Jesus manifest the kingdom which he proclaims? He manifests it (as the link with the revelation formula in Matt. 11.28f. shows) by having mercy on the poor, by calling the weary and heavy-laden to himself and refreshing them, by bringing to the poor the joyful message that theirs is the kingdom, and by gathering the oppressed into the liberty of his fellowship. His kingdom is the kingdom of 'compassion'. In Hebrew this word is used for the mother's painful love for the child in her womb. This spontaneous physical impulse is a maternal symbol. If God is called merciful and compassionate, then what is being attributed to him is motherly love in its most elemental form. That is why for Isaiah 49.15

God's compassion is like the compassion of a mother, while Psalm 103.13 compares it with a father's pity for his children. This means that his kingdom is the kingdom of fatherly and motherly compassion, not the kingdom of dominating majesty and slavish subjection. It is the kingdom which 'the Son' manifests through his brotherliness and friendship. God is the Father, not because he is Lord over everything, but because, as the Father of Jesus the Son, he is the Lord of the coming liberty of the universe. The Lord's Prayer shows this too, ultimately speaking. It is *the Father's* kingdom, *the Father's* will and *the Father's* name for whose coming, fulfilment and hallowing we pray in the fellowship of Jesus. By revealing the Father's name, Jesus has given the proclamation of God's kingdom his own unmistakable character. This means that (contrary to what Harnack says) it is not merely the Father who belongs to the gospel which Jesus proclaimed; it is the Son as well. It means that not merely the Father, but the Son too, belongs to the kingdom which Jesus preached. It is impossible to divide Jesus' proclamation of the kingdom from his person. For the kingdom which Jesus proclaims is the kingdom which the Father has made over to the Son. Its structure is not monotheistic, as the word 'rule' or 'kingdom' suggests; it is trinitarian, as the relationship of Jesus the Son to his Father proves; for it is this Father to whom the kingdom belongs and who confers it on the Son, so that it may be manifested and spread. As the later epistle to the Colossians says, it is 'the kingdom of his beloved Son' (1.13).

2. The Sending of the Son

For the synoptic gospels the messianic call of Jesus begins with his baptism in the Spirit of God. It is understandable that Paul and John – with a point of view markedly determined by Easter – should see in this call of Jesus his eternal sending by God the Father. We always encounter the 'sending' formula in conjunction with the name of the Son, for the One sent.[20] The One who sends is called God or Father. The sending formula covers more than the story of Jesus' call. It includes the whole coming, the whole appearance and activity of Jesus seen in the light of his divine origin. We are adopting Pauline theology here, because it especially stresses the soteriological significance of Jesus' sonship.

> When the time had fully come, God sent forth his Son, born of a woman, born under the law, to redeem those who were under the law, so that we might receive adoption as sons (Gal. 4.4).

The sending of the Son includes Jesus' birth and circumcision. The Son is subjected to the law so that he may redeem those who live under the law: the Jews. He redeems them for what is his own existence and relationship to God – for sonship. In so doing he fulfils Israel's true destiny. If, according to what we are told here, God sends 'his Son', then it is the Father's Son who is sent, not some 'son of God'. The idea of the Son employed by Paul is in line with the Christian tradition we described in the previous section. In the sending, the Son is wholly understood in the light of the Father, and in this sending the Father is revealed as the Father through the Son. Through the sending of the Son, that is to say, the sonship is communicated and received in faith. By sonship therefore we certainly have to understand the special relationship between Jesus and the One who sent him; but this relationship is no longer merely exclusive; it is now inclusive at the same time. It is communicated to believers in such a way that they are absorbed into it. But the difference between the sending and the receiving forbids us to reduce the sonship of Jesus to the sonship of believers or, conversely, to reduce the sonship of believers to the sonship of Jesus.

We find the other 'sending' formula in Romans 8.3f.

> For God sent his own Son in the likeness of sinful flesh . . . in order that the just requirement of the law might be fulfilled in us, who walk not according to the flesh but according to the Spirit.

Again the One who sends is the Father, for in sending 'his own Son' God reveals himself as the Father of the Son. As the sentence structure of Galatians 4.4 also shows, the sending in the form of sinful flesh serves to overcome that flesh through the transformation in the Spirit. Whereas in Galatians the goal of the sending was the communication of sonship, here it is life in the Spirit – life in the Spirit of a child of God. This is shown by Romans 8.15:

> For you did not receive the spirit of slavery to fall back into fear, but you have received the spirit of sonship, whereby we cry, Abba, Father.

When Paul inserts the semitic 'Abba' into the otherwise Greek text at this point, it is because he is talking about the prayer and proclamation of the 'historical' Jesus. The liberty of his prayer to the Father reveals the sonship. Through the 'Abba' prayer believers are taken into the fellowship of the Son with the Father. This happens through the Spirit. Luther translated the phrase which the English Bible (RSV) knows as 'the spirit of sonship' by the phrase *kindlicher Geist* – childlike spirit; but he does not mean any regression into irresponsibility. On the contrary, what he means is emancipation: the people who believe through the Son are no longer slaves under the law of a divine master. They are the beloved children of the heavenly Father. Sonship and to be the child of God therefore means liberation, the chance to come of age. As the Father's own sons and daughters, believers become 'heirs of God and joint heirs with Christ' in the fellowship of the Son. That is to say, they acquire both the rights of domicile and the rights of inheritance in the kingdom of the Father and the Son. The prayer to the Father is therefore the supreme expression of this new liberty of God's children and these new rights of the justified. In the fellowship of the Son, sons and daughters talk to God as to a Father. God does not speak like the master or lord who has to be unquestioningly obeyed; God listens to the requests and suggestions of his children like a Father. The men and women who are liberated through the Son are not supposed merely to listen and obey; they can also ask, and share decisions. In the context of the spirit of sonship, the sending of the Son shows nothing less than the opening of the fellowship of the Father to his own Son, and the opening of the fellowship of the Son to his Father, for the world.

Whereas in Paul the Father of the Son is always called 'God', in the Gospel of John we find a consistent acceptance and development of the synoptic tradition, which talked about Jesus as 'the Son'.[21] Where Jesus is called the Son, God is always termed the Father. It is always the Father of the Son and the Son of the Father. In the First Epistle of John 2.22–24, confession of faith and denial touch on both at once: 'No one who denies the Son has the Father. He who confesses the Son has the Father also.' In John's Gospel the revelatory saying of Matthew 11.27 seems to be the basic pattern of many statements: the Father loves the Son, the Son loves the Father. The Father knows the Son, the Son knows the Father.

The Father has given everything to the Son: judgment, life, inheritance, those that are his own. The statements about the sending correspond to the statements about the revelation, and in John's Gospel too show the fellowship of the Father and the Son as a fellowship open to the world in the Spirit. It is only the statements about the glorification of the Father through the Son that go beyond Matthew 11.27.

3. The Form of the Trinity

In the synoptic story of Jesus' baptism and call, as well as in Jesus' own manifestation of the Father, we come across a clearly perceptible trinitarian form. It is founded conceptually on the self-differentiation of God inherent in the Jewish idea of the divine Wisdom, which is in eternity God's beloved child and seeks a home on earth. The idea took many forms, none of them fixed in Judaism; but through the history of Jesus it became specific. The 'inward' or 'theological' history of Jesus is the history of the Son with the Father. It is not the history of a person with a god. In relation to God Jesus understood himself as 'the Son'. The 'Abba' revelation of God's nature dominated his own relation to God as well as his proclamation of God to men and women. His preaching of the kingdom and the effect he had were founded on his relationship to his Father. Consequently they cannot be interpreted monotheistically; they have to be understood in a trinitarian sense: Jesus reveals God as the Father of the Son and himself as this same Son of the Father. He takes people – weary and heavy-laden men and women – into the history between this Father and this Son. He reveals that history. The secret of the kingdom which he brings to the poor is to be found in his fellowship with the Father.

The baptism, call, proclamation and ministry of Jesus takes place through the Spirit and in the Spirit. Both the story of the baptism and the account of his earliest proclamation in Nazareth refer to this (Luke 4.18ff.). This Spirit allows the Son to say 'Abba, beloved Father'. This Spirit 'leads' Jesus to his temptations in the wilderness and up to Jerusalem, to his sufferings and death there. It accompanies Jesus' proclamation with signs and wonders. It is the Spirit who descends upon the Son from the Father. It is the Spirit of the messianic era, which is to descend on all flesh. The history of Jesus is as incomprehensible without the action of the Spirit as it would be without the God whom he called my Father, or without his activity out of the existence of 'the Son'.

The Trinity which is descernible in the sending formulas has an analogous form. The Father sends his Son. The Son is sent by his Father. Through the sending, the fellowship of the Father and the Son becomes so all-embracing that men and women are taken into it, so that in that fellowship they may participate in Jesus' sonship and call on the Father in the Spirit. What the call of Jesus reveals is not merely the sending of a prophet or the sending of the Messiah, but this sending of the Son. In the sending of the Son, God differentiates himself from himself and yields himself up. The sending of the Son therefore finds its foundation in a movement which takes place in the divine life itself: it is not merely a movement outwards. It comes from the trinitarian differentiation of the divine unity. There is no other way in which we can understand the sending of the Son through the Father.

At this stage in the history of the Son the Trinity means:

– The Father sends the Son through the Spirit.

– The Son comes from the Father in the power of the Spirit.

– The Spirit brings people into the fellowship of the Son with the Father.

§3 THE SURRENDER OF THE SON

1. *The Passion of Jesus*

The history of Jesus' passion did not only begin when he was taken prisoner and tortured by the Roman soldiers. It began at the moment when he resolved to go to Jerusalem with the men and women who were his disciples. In Jerusalem his passion for the messianic kingdom – a passion which he had expressed through proclamation, healing, and by eating and drinking with the poor, the sick and the outcasts of society – was bound to come up against the protest of the priests of his own people and the resistance of the Roman occupying power. The announcement that 'the Son of man must suffer many things, and be rejected' (Mark 8.31) hung heavy over the road to Jerusalem. Jesus' passion has its active side in his resolve to go to Jerusalem. It is no unwilling, fortuitous suffering; it is a *passio activa*.

Jesus' passion has an outward and an inward side. On the outward side are Jesus' rejection by the most prominent groups of his people as a blasphemer, and his execution by the Romans as a rebel against the Roman world order. The inward aspect is his forsakenness by the God whom he calls 'Abba, my Father', and whose fatherly kingdom he proclaimed to the poor. The pain which Jesus suffered from his God and Father is the special thing about this passion on Golgotha compared with the history of the sufferings of so many innocent and righteous people. The stories of Gethsemane and Golgotha tell the history of the passion which takes place between the Father and the Son.

In the night before his arrest, Jesus went into the garden of Gethsemane.[22] He took three disciples with him and 'began to be greatly distressed and troubled', writes Mark (14.33). 'He began to be sorrowful and fearful [troubled]' writes Matthew (26.37). 'My soul is very sorrowful, even to death' he says (Mark 14.34) and begs his friends to stay awake with him. Then he throws himself on the ground in horror and fear (Mark 14.35). Earlier too, he had often withdrawn at nights to the solitariness of some mountain in order to be united with his Father in the prayer of his heart. But in Gethsemane for the first time he does not want to be alone with his God. He is evidently afraid of him. That is why he seeks the protection of his friends. Then comes the prayer which in its original version sounds like a demand: 'Father, all things are possible to thee; remove this cup from me' (Mark 14.36) – spare me this suffering. In Matthew and Luke this prayer has a more modest sound: 'if it be possible' or 'if thou art willing' 'let this cup pass from me'.

What suffering is meant by 'the cup' – 'the cup of staggering' (Isa. 51.17,22)? Is it the plea to be kept from having to die? Is it the prayer for deliverance from death? I think it is fear of separation from the Father, horror in the face of 'the death of God'. God, Jesus' Father, does not hear his prayer. He rejects it. Elsewhere the gospel tells us 'I and the Father are one'. But here the Father withdraws from the Son, leaving him alone. That is why the disciples fall into a deep sleep, out of grief. It is only by contradicting his very self that Jesus clings to fellowship with the God who as Father withdraws from him: 'Not what I will, but what thou wilt.'

This *unanswered prayer* is the beginning of Jesus' real passion – his agony at his forsakenness by the Father. Of course there is also quite simply fear of the horribly slow death ahead of him. It would be ridiculous to say – as Augustine did – that, as the Son of God, Jesus could not have experienced the fear of death, because his soul lived in unbroken enjoyment of divine bliss and power; and that he only suffered in the body. But it would be equally foolish to see him as an especially sensitive person who was overcome by self-pity at the prospect of the torments of death awaiting him. In the fear that laid hold of him and lacerated his soul, what he suffered from was God. Abandonment by God is the 'cup' which does not pass from him. The appalling silence of the Father in response to the Son's prayer in Gethsemane is more than the silence of death. Martin Buber called it the eclipse of God. It is echoed in 'the dark night of the soul' experienced by the mystics. The Father withdraws. God is silent. This is the experience of hell and judgment.

Luther related the church's doctrine about Christ's descent into hell to this agony of his from Gethsemane to Golgotha.[23] The experience of being forsaken by God is the nadir of Christ's humiliation: '*Derelinqui enim a deo hoc est a vita et salute ire in regionem longinquam mortis et inferni*' – 'Not only in the eyes of the world and his disciples, nay, in his own eyes too did Christ see himself as lost, as forsaken by God, felt in his conscience that he was cursed by God, suffered the torments of the damned, who feel God's eternal wrath, shrink back from it and flee.'[24] This was how he interpreted the passion of the assailed and tempted Christ – the Christ who was assailed and tempted by God. That is why for Luther Christ was not the most perfect of men; he was the most tempted and therefore the most miserable of all 'the damned of this earth'. And he was not merely assailed by fear and suffering in his human nature, as scholastic tradition would have it. He was assailed in his person, his very essence, in his relationship to the Father – in his divine sonship. The much later Epistle to the Hebrews also links Jesus' sufferings in Gethsemane with the relationship between the Son and the Father:

> In the days of his flesh, Jesus offered up prayers and supplications, with loud cries and tears, to him who was able to save him from death, and he was heard for his godly fear. Although he was the Son, he learned obedience through what he suffered (Heb. 5.7–8).[25]

At the end of Christ's passion there is another prayer: the de-

spairing cry to God with which Christ dies: 'My God, why hast
thou forsaken me?' (Mark 15.34). He hung nailed to the cross for
three hours, evidently in an agony which reduced him to silence,
waiting for death. Then he died with a loud cry which is an
expression of the most profound rejection by the God whom he
called 'Abba', whose messianic kingdom had been his whole passion, and whose Son he knew himself to be.

This must surely be the very kernel of the Golgotha story, historically speaking; for the notion that the Saviour's last words to
God his Father could possibly have been this cry of despair could
never have taken root in the Christian faith if it had never been
uttered, or if the despair had not been at least perceptible in Christ's
death cry.

People cannot get used to the idea that this cry of the God-
forsaken Son stands at the centre of the Christian faith. The history
of the tradition shows that the horror and dismay that emanates
from it was later softened down, and the saying was replaced by
more pious parting words – the words of the evening prayer in
Psalm 31.5 which we find in Luke, for example: 'Into thy hands
I commit my spirit' (23.46); or John's 'It is finished'. It is only the
Epistle to the Hebrews (5.7) which reminds us again of the great
cry with which Jesus dies.

This cry is not made any more acceptable to us because it echoes
the opening words of Psalm 22 and – according to Jewish custom
– stands for the whole psalm. For one thing, the psalm ends with
a glorious prayer of thanksgiving for deliverance from death – and
there was no deliverance on Golgotha. For another, after a short
time the crucified Jesus was no longer capable of saying anything
at all. Early manuscripts of Mark's Gospel express the cry of
dereliction even more drastically: 'Why hast thou exposed me to
shame?' and 'Why hast thou cursed me?'[26] And the Epistle to the
Hebrews holds fast to this remembrance of the assailed Christ
when it says that ' χωρὶς θεοῦ' – far from God or, perhaps better,
without God 'he tasted death for us all' (Heb. 2.9).[27] It is not by
chance, either, that this cry is the only time that Christ does not
call God familiarly 'my Father', but addresses him as if from a long
way off and quite officially and formally as 'my God'.

What he was afraid of, what he struggled with in Gethsemane
and implored the Father to save him from, did not pass from him.
It happened on the cross. The Father forsook him and delivered

him up to the fear of hell. The One who knew himself to be the Son is forsaken, rejected and cursed. And God is silent. Paul was therefore interpreting this rightly when he took it to mean that from Gethsemane to Golgotha Christ suffered God's judgment, in which everyone is alone and against which no one can stand: 'For our sake he made him to be sin' (II Cor. 5.21), 'he became a curse for us' (Gal. 3.13).

Where, after Easter, were these remembrances of Jesus' death kept alive and present in the church? It was in the celebration of the Lord's supper; for Paul already cites, as the early tradition of the primitive church: 'for as often as you eat this bread and drink this cup, you proclaim the Lord's death until he comes' (I Cor. 11.26). Psalm 22 as a whole can be shown to have had an influence on the structure of the eucharistic celebrations of the early church, because it talks about the forsakenness of the righteous man, and about his salvation and the feast of thanksgiving.[28] When the gospels give us Jesus' death cry in the words of the first verse of Psalm 22, it is true that they are really thinking of the whole psalm, because they are thinking of Easter and are speaking at the Lord's table. So there can be no question of their having meant by their interpretation of Jesus' death cry that Jesus prayed the whole psalm on the cross, as a lament. In this case the quotation from the opening of the psalm certainly does not mean that the whole psalm was quoted.

> The curious supposition that when he uttered the first verse of the psalm he was already thinking of the final verses (in which the innocent and righteous sufferer who has for a time been forsaken by God, once more partakes of divine grace) . . . finds no justification in the Gospel accounts.[29]

The Fathers were wrong when, in order to preserve Christ's divinity, they declared that Jesus was praying for us, not for himself (Cyril's view); or that he only made himself out to be weak in order to deceive Satan and so to vanquish him all the more completely (Athanasius). And modern theologians are just as wrong when they try to preserve Jesus' inward faith against all the appearances of despair. By doing so they only make Jesus a pattern for faith in the sense of the motto 'despairing yet consoled'; and they obscure Jesus as the sacrament of salvation, who through his own forsakenness overcomes ours.

Finally, it is important to notice that it is only here on the cross that, for the first and only time in his life, the Son addresses God, not as Father but as God (Hebrew *Eloheni*, Aramaic *Eloi*). The prayer in Gethsemane was still addressed to 'the Father'. But the Father did not hear the prayer. On the cross the Father forsook the Son and hid his face from him, as the sun was hidden in deepest darkness on Golgotha. According to Amos 8.9–10, this darkness is grief over the loss of 'the only son'. It is precisely this that is the cross in Jesus' crucifixion; the being forsaken by the God whom he called 'my Father', and whose Son he knew himself to be. Here, in the relationship between the Father and the Son, a death was experienced which has been rightly described as 'eternal death', 'the death of God'. Here 'God' is forsaken by 'God'. If we take the relinquishment of the Father's name in Jesus' death cry seriously, then this is even the breakdown of the relationship that constitutes the very life of the Trinity: if the Father forsakes the Son, the Son does not merely lose his sonship. The Father loses his fatherhood as well. The love that binds the one to the other is transformed into a dividing curse. It is only as the One who is forsaken and cursed that the Son is still the Son. It is only as the One who forsakes, who surrenders the other, that the Father is still present. Communicating love and responding love are alike transformed into infinite pain and into the suffering and endurance of death.

2. The Surrender of the Son

Paul comes closest to the mystery of Golgotha with his theology of surrender, of giving up.[30] In the gospels, which depict the death of Jesus in the light of his life and his message, παραδιδόναι has an unequivocally negative sense. It means to deliver up, to betray, to make over, to cast out; this is clear from the story of the betrayer Judas. To say that Jesus was forsaken by the Father on the cross means that the Father cast him off and cursed him. Paul too uses the expression 'given up' in Romans 1.18ff. for the divine wrath and judgment over the sin of men and women. People who abandon the invisible God and worship created things will be abandoned by God and given up to their own cravings.

Paul expresses a radical reversal of what is meant by 'surrender' or 'giving up' when he stops looking at Jesus' abandonment by God in the light of his life, and views it in the light of his resurrection. The God who has raised Jesus from the dead is the same God who has 'given him up' to death on the cross. In the forsakenness of the cross itself – the forsakenness out of which Jesus cries 'Why?' – Paul already sees the answer to the cry: 'He who did not spare his own Son but gave him up for us all, will he not also give us all things with him?' (Rom. 8. 32). According to this the Father has forsaken, abandoned his own Son, as Paul especially stresses here, and given him up to death. He puts it even more strongly: 'For our sake he made him to be sin' (II Cor. 5.21) and 'he became a curse for us' (Gal. 3.13). The Father forsakes the Son 'for us' – that is to say, in order to become the God and Father of the foresaken. The Father 'delivers up' the Son in order through him to become the Father of those who have been delivered up (Rom. 1.18ff.). The Son is given over to his death in order that he may become the brother and saviour of the condemned and the cursed.

The Son suffers death in this forsakenness. The Father suffers the death of the Son. So the pain of the Father corresponds to the death of the Son. And when in this descent into hell the Son loses the Father, then in this judgment the Father also loses the Son. Here the innermost life of the Trinity is at stake. Here the communicating love of the Father turns into infinite pain over the sacrifice of the Son. Here the responding love of the Son becomes infinite suffering over his repulsion and rejection by the Father. What happens on Golgotha reaches into the innermost depths of the Godhead, putting its impress on the trinitarian life in eternity.

But according to Galatians 2.20, the Son was not only given up by the Father. He also 'gave himself for me'. In the event of surrender there is not merely an object; there is a subject too. His suffering and death was active, a *passio activa*, a path of suffering that he entered upon quite deliberately, a dying that he consciously affirmed. According to the hymn which Paul took up in Philippians 2, the self-giving of the Son consists in his emptying himself of his divine form, in his taking on himself the form of a servant, in his lowering of himself, and in his obedience 'unto death, even the death of the cross' (AV). For the Epistle to the Hebrews (5.8) 'he learned obedience through what he suffered'. He suffered from the prayer which went unanswered, from his forsakenness by the Father. It was from *this* that he 'learned' obedience and self-giving. This is in accordance with the synoptic account of the passion.

Theologically this means an inner conformity between the will of the surrendered Son and the surrendering will of the Father. That is what the Gethsemane story is about too. But this profound community of will arises at precisely the point when the Son is furthest divided from the Father, and the Father from the Son,[31] in the accursed death on the cross, in 'the dark night' of that death. On the cross the Father and the Son are so deeply separated that their relationship breaks off. Jesus died 'without God' – godlessly. Yet on the cross the Father and the Son are at the same time so much one that they represent a single surrendering movement. 'He who has seen the Son has seen the Father.' The Epistle to the Hebrews expresses this by saying that Christ offered himself to God 'through the eternal Spirit' ($\delta\iota\grave{\alpha}\ \pi\nu\varepsilon\acute{\upsilon}\mu\alpha\tau o\varsigma\ \alpha\grave{\iota}\omega\nu\acute{\iota}o\upsilon$) (9.14). The surrender through the Father and the offering of the Son take place 'through the Spirit'. The Holy Spirit is therefore the link in the separation. He is the link joining the bond between the Father and the Son, with their separation.

Paul interpreted the event of God-forsakenness on the cross as the giving up of the Son, and interpreted the giving up of the Son as the love of God. What the love of God is – the love 'from which nothing can separate us' (Rom. 8.39) – becomes event on the cross and is experienced under the cross. The Father who sends his Son through all the abysses and hells of God-forsakenness, of the divine curse and final judgment is, in his Son, everywhere with those who are his own; he has become universally present. In giving up the Son he gives 'everything' and 'nothing' can separate us from him. This is the beginning of the language of the kingdom of God, in which 'God will be all in all'. Anyone who perceives God's presence and love in the God-forsakenness of the crucified Son, sees God in all things, just as, once having faced the experience of death, a person feels the living character of everything in a hitherto un-dreamed of way.

The Gospel of John sums up this giving up of the Son in the key sentence: 'God so loved the world that he gave his only Son, that whoever believes in him should not perish but have eternal life' (3.16). 'So' means 'in this way', the way of forsakenness in the death on the cross which he suffered 'for us'. And the First Epistle of John (4.16) defines God by saying 'God is love'. It is not just that God loves, in the same way that he is sometimes angry. He *is* love. His very existence is love. He constitutes himself as love. That is what happens on the cross. This definition only acquires its full force when we continually make the way that leads to the definition clear to ourselves: Jesus' forsakenness on the cross, the surrender of the Son by the Father and the love which does everything – gives everything – suffers everything – for lost men and women. God is love. That means God is self-giving. It means he exists for us: on the cross. To put it in trinitarian terms – the Father lets his Son sacrifice himself through the Spirit.[32] 'The Father is crucifying love, the Son is crucified love, and the Holy Spirit is the unvanquishable power of the cross.'[33] The cross is at the centre of the Trinity. This is brought out by tradition, when it takes up the Book of Revelation's image of 'the Lamb who was slain from the foundation of the world' (Rev. 5.12). Before the world was, the sacrifice was already in God. No Trinity is conceivable without the Lamb, without the sacrifice of love, without the crucified Son.[34] For he is the slaughtered Lamb glorified in eternity.

What happens in Jesus' passion is the giving up of the Son through the Father. In giving up his own Son, God cuts himself off from himself and sacrifices his own self. The giving up of the Son reveals a pain in God which can only be understood in trinitarian terms, or not at all.

The form of the Trinity which is revealed in the giving up of the Son appears as follows:
– The Father gives up his own Son to death in its most absolute sense, for us.
– The Son gives himself up, for us.
– The common sacrifice of the Father and the Son comes about through the Holy Spirit, who joins and unites the Son in his forsakenness with the Father.

§4 THE EXALTATION OF THE SON

Now that we have looked at the history of Jesus the Son from its historical and its theological viewpoints let us turn to its eschatological future. His resurrection from the dead and his future in glory have to be understood from the aspects of the manifestation of the Son and his homecoming to the Father. And here we shall show that a trinitarian structure also underlies the eschatological proclamation of the risen Christ and the Christ who is to come. In what follows we shall be concentrating on this trinitarian structure.

1. The Raising of Jesus from the Dead

Without at this point developing a detailed theology of the resurrection,[35] we must none the less show the eschatological character
of the Easter appearances and the trinitarian form of the Christ
perceived in them. We shall take our bearings here from those
passages in the Easter kerygma which talk about Jesus as 'the Son
of God'.

Jesus was crucified publicly. But the risen Christ encountered
only the women and the disciples who had gone up to Jerusalem
with him. Many people saw his death in weakness on Golgotha.
But only a few were aware of his appearance in power and glory.
What did the Easter witnesses see? In what living form did they
see the crucified Jesus? How did they recognize him?

'Seeing' is always the reason which is given for the Easter proclamation and the Easter faith.[36] The Greek ὤφθη has a whole
series of meanings here. It can mean 'Christ was seen'; or 'Christ
appeared'; or 'Christ let himself be seen'; or 'God revealed him'.
In all these possible interpretations, what is intended is a *revelation
formula*. It is the seeing of something which someone is permitted
to see in a particular way. The activity issues from the one who
appears. The person affected is passive; he 'suffers' this appearance.
Consequently what is meant is not the recognition of something
which is always present and which everyone can see, if he only
takes the trouble to look carefully enough. A 'seeing' of this ex-
ceptional kind is usually called a vision. The Easter visions of the
women and the disciples are not open to proof, for they are not
repeatable; whereas every proof rests on the repeatability of the
experience, or on the ability to reproduce the experiment. The texts
never talk at any point about a possible repetition of the Easter
'seeing' of the risen Jesus. But then how are we to interpret it?
How did the people affected understand it themselves? Even if
these visions are not general, in the sense that they are repeatable,
they can none the less embody a universal claim.

As the language through which it is described shows, the structure of the Easter 'seeing' takes the form of the messianic pre-
reflection of what is in the future, and of the apocalyptic anticipation of what is to come.[37] In the Last Days the God of the
promises to the patriarchs will appear in his glory and fulfil
throughout the whole world the hopes which he has awakened.

The whole world will then be full of his glory (Isa. 60). In the calling of the patriarchs, in the people of the covenant, and in the prophets, this coming glory already enters history, pointing the way towards its own consummation. When the crucified Jesus 'appears' in glory to the women and the disciples after his death, this then means the pre-reflection of his future in the coming glory of God.[38] Christ appears to the people concerned in the light of the future which cannot otherwise be perceived in the world as yet. One day he will appear to the whole world as he now appears to the Easter witnesses. That is to say, his Easter appearances have to be understood as the pre-reflection of his future; and what the disciples see at Easter is, correspondingly, the form taken by anticipating perception. Anyone who sees the risen Christ is looking in advance into the coming glory of God. He perceives something which is not otherwise perceptible, but which will one day be perceived by everyone.

On the foundation of this eschatological structure of Jesus' appearances and on the basis of what they themselves saw, the disciples then took up an apocalyptic symbol of hope, in order to explain what happened to the dead Jesus – which, after all, none of them actually saw. They called this event *the resurrection from the dead*. It is of course true that the apocalyptic expectation was directed towards the unique and universal raising of the dead in the Last Days (Dan. 12.2). In talking about a resurrection of Jesus *from the dead*, the Christians have altered the old apocalyptic hope in a quite decisive way. In making this alteration, what they are saying is: in this one person, ahead of all others, the End-time process of the raising of the dead has already begun. With Jesus' resurrection from the dead, history's last day is beginning: 'The night is far gone the day is at hand' (Rom. 13.12). That is why they proclaim him as 'the first fruits of those who have fallen asleep' (I Cor. 15.20), 'the first-born from the dead' (Col. 1.18), 'the pioneer of salvation'.

The idea of the raising of the dead is a metaphor taken over from the process of sleeping and waking up in the morning, which is now transferred to death and the promised life in God's own day. But as a symbol of the apocalyptic hope this idea was uniquely suited to represent the contradictory experiences of the disciples: crucified in shame – seen in glory. For the symbol of resurrection from *the dead* allows us to take Jesus' death seriously. It excludes every notion that Jesus revived after death, or that his soul went on living. On the other hand, the symbol of raising, of being wakened, allows the Easter appearance and seeing of Jesus to stand in its full dignity and significance; for it excludes all notions of a projection.

2. *The Revelation of the Son*

The Easter witnesses saw the crucified Jesus in the pre-reflection of God's coming glory on earth. On the other hand, they recognized the one appearing in this glory as Jesus, from the marks of the cross's nails, and in the breaking of bread. In what form did Jesus appear to them, according to what they say themselves? Whom did they see?

According to II Corinthians 4.6, they saw 'the glory of God in the face of Jesus Christ'. Jesus appeared to them as 'the likeness of God' (II Cor. 4.4), as 'the brightness of his glory and the express image of his person' (Heb. 1.3 AV). In the 'likeness' (*eikon*) and 'reflection' (*epaugasma*) they talk about, the glory of God himself takes form.[39] It is not reflected back from something else, but reflects itself. Although Jesus' title 'the image of God' is bound to make us think of the general vocation which man was destined for at creation (Gen. 1.26), this reference is not enough: the eternal Wisdom, God's beloved before time began, is also called 'the image of his goodness' and the 'effulgence from everlasting light' (Wisd. 7.26). The glory of God is reflected on the unveiled face of Christ, not merely as a pattern for believers, but in eternity too, for God himself. God himself finds in Christ his eternal counterpart. Yet the closeness of all men to being the image of God and the nearness of believers to that unveiled face must not be dimmed by these references.

In Galatians 1.15 Paul described his own vision of the risen Christ: 'But when he who had set me apart before I was born, and had called me through his grace, was pleased *to reveal his Son* to me, in order that I might preach him among the Gentiles . . .' The revelation which Paul experiences in the vision where he received his call has a subject and an object: God reveals his Son. He reveals the Son so that Paul may proclaim him among the Gentiles. God does not reveal 'himself'. He reveals 'his Son'. The Son is not identical with God's self. He is a subject of his own. The One who was raised from the dead and who appears in the reflection of God's coming glory is perceived by Paul as *the Son*. That is why Paul also said that Jesus, or the Son, or God's Son, was the real content of his gospel (Rom. 1.9; II Cor. 1.19). He calls his apostolic message God's gospel of his Son. He proclaims the lordship of the Son. He preaches the liberty of the sons of God. He establishes brotherhood with Jesus, the first-born among many brethren (Rom. 8.29). In this brotherhood people become like to the image of the Son, and are thereby made glorious.

For this 'gospel of the Son' Paul appeals to an early Christian confession of faith, which he takes up in Romans 1.3f., claiming to be set apart to preach

> The gospel concerning his Son, Jesus Christ our Lord, (AV) who was descended from David according to the flesh and designated Son of God in power according to the Spirit of holiness by his resurrection from the dead.

Without going into this early two-stage christology in detail, we can notice that through the resurrection from the dead God has 'enthroned' Jesus to be the Son of God in power. This has taken place through 'the sanctifying Spirit' (RSV 'the Spirit of holiness'). Who Jesus is for us is expressed by the title 'Lord'. The expression 'Son of God' is used as title here too. The royal ritual in Psalm 2.7 is being recalled here, as it was at Jesus' baptism. But the context shows that Paul has related the adoptionist formula Son of God used in Psalm 2.7 to the special Christian title 'his Son'. The enthronement as Son of God through the resurrection certainly marks a particular point in Jesus' history as men and women perceive it. Paul did not see this as being in any way a contradiction of the statement that Jesus is God's own Son in eternity. The temporally marked beginning of Jesus' ministry as 'the Son of God in power' and the statements about the pre-existence of the Son (Phil. 2.6; Col. 1.15) stand side by side, without any attempt to reconcile them. Apparently different statements are possible and necessary, in view of Jesus' different relationships and functions.

The theological formulations about the sending, the delivering up and the resurrection show that for Paul Jesus is God's own Son. He is the Son of the eternal Father. 'God's own Son' is the Son of the eternal Father. 'God's own Son' can hardly be viewed as christological title, or as a title of sovereignty. Nor is it the name for 'a calling'. Like the word Father, in this context 'Son' must be understood as a name, not as a title.

If this is true, then Jesus' sonship puts its impress on his whole ministry and activity as representative, as liberator, as redeemer, and as lord. As God's own Son he is the Lord. Consequently it is his sonship which stamps his lordship, not his lordship which gives its character to his sonship. The kingdom of the Son is the kingdom of brothers and sisters, not a kingdom of the lord and his servants.

If, finally, we ask by what means the Father raised the Son from the death to which he delivered him up, then we come face to face with the activity of the Holy Spirit: He was raised through the creative *Spirit* (Rom. 1.4; 8.11; I Peter 3.18; I Tim. 3.16). He was raised through *the glory of the Father* (Rom. 6.4). He was raised through *the power of God* (I Cor. 6.14). God's power, God's glory and the divine Spirit are used synonymously here. They are the name for something which is not the Father, and not the Son either, but which is a third divine subject in the history of Jesus, the Son.

We ought not to interpret Jesus' resurrection in merely eschatological terms. In its innermost process it is trinitarian too. This makes the express use of the Son's name necessary in these contexts. Which form of the Trinity can be perceived at this stage in the history of the Son?
− The Father raises the Son through the Spirit;
− the Father reveals the Son through the Spirit;
− the Son is enthroned as Lord of God's kingdom through the Spirit.

3. The Sending of the Creative Spirit through the Son

Where was Jesus raised *to*? The answer emerges from our insight into the means by which he was raised from the dead − the means which we have already considered. Jesus was raised into the coming glory of the Father. That is the eschatological dimension. That is why he 'sitteth at the right hand of God the Father'. That is the category of heaven as the space in which God dwells. Jesus is risen into the coming kingdom of God. Jesus is risen into the innermost being of God himself. He has been exalted into the divine origin of the Holy Spirit. That is the trinitarian centre. That is why God's glory is manifested through him in this world. That is why in this present history he is the Lord of the divine kingdom. That is why in this present time he is the 'life-giving spirit' (I Cor. 15.45), sending the Spirit upon the disciples, and the energies of the Spirit upon the church, and through the church 'on all flesh'.

Here our interest is concentrated particularly on the relationship of the risen Son to the quickening Spirit. Whereas in the sending, in the surrender and in the resurrection, the Spirit acts on Christ, and Christ lives from the works of the creative Spirit, now the relationship is reversed: the risen Christ sends the Spirit; he is himself present in the life-giving Spirit; and through the Spirit's energies – the charismata – he acts on men and women. The Spirit witnesses to Christ, and whoever confesses Christ as his Lord does so in the power of the Spirit who creates life from the dead. That is why after Easter the Spirit is called 'the Spirit of sonship' (Rom. 8.15), 'the Spirit of faith' (II Cor. 4.13), or the 'Spirit of Christ': 'Where the Spirit of the Lord is, there is freedom' (II Cor. 3.17). The Spirit proceeds from the Father and is now 'sent' by the Son (John 15.26). Through his resurrection the Son is evidently so near to the Father, and so much in the Father, that he participates in the sending of the Spirit out of its divine origin. Whereas the sending, the surrender and the resurrection of Christ were the works of the life-giving Spirit, so now the sending and outpouring of the Spirit who makes all things new becomes a work of the Son.

Here it cannot be forgotten that in the whole of the New Testament the Spirit is understood eschatologically. He is the power of the new creation. He is the power of the resurrection. He is the earnest and pledge of glory. His present efficacy is the rebirth of men and women. His future goal is the raising up of the kingdom of glory. His activity is experienced inwardly, in the heart; but it points ahead into what is outward and public. He lays hold on the soul, but will only find rest when he 'gives life to mortal bodies' (Rom. 8.11).

Which form of the Trinity do we encounter here?

— The Father raises the dead Son through the life-giving Spirit;

— the Father enthrones the Son, as the Lord of his kingdom;

— the risen Son sends the creative Spirit from the Father, to renew heaven and earth.

Whereas until his resurrection we were able to perceive in the history of Jesus the sequence: *Father – Spirit – Son*, we now encounter the sequence *Father – Son – Spirit*. What does this mean?

It means that in the sending of the Spirit the Trinity is an open

Trinity.[40] Through the sending of the creative Spirit, the trinitarian history of God becomes a history that is open to the world, open to men and women, and open to the future. Through the experience of the life-giving Spirit in faith, in baptism, and in the fellowship of believers, people are integrated into the history of the Trinity. Through the Spirit of Christ they not only become participators in the eschatological history of the new creation. Through the Spirit of the Son they also become at the same time participants in the trinitarian history of God himself. That is the profounder reason why acknowledgment of the Trinity was developed in the context of baptism first of all.[41]

The explicitly 'triadical' formulations in the New Testament are without exception baptismal formulations (Matt. 28.19). Didache 7.1 stipulates baptism in the name of the Father, the Son and the Spirit. All the acknowledgments of the Trinity that follow are baptismal ones. That is to say, Trinitarian theology is baptismal theology. It has to be, because the history of the Son and the creative Spirit of God which the New Testament relates is not a completed history. It is an inviting, eschatological history that is open in a forward-looking direction. Through baptism people are absorbed into it. The doctrine of the Trinity has baptism as its original *Sitz im Leben* – its situation in life.

Which form of the Trinity do we encounter in baptism?

— In baptism we encounter the divine Trinity as the eschatological history of God which is open in a forward-looking direction.

— The *unity* of the Father, the Son and the Spirit is hence an *open* unity, not a closed one.

— It is open for *unification* with believers, with mankind, and with the whole creation.

§5 THE FUTURE OF THE SON

The eschatological hope is also directed towards a trinitarian event in the New Testament. Let us first of all pursue exegetically the other uses of the name of Son which is given to Jesus in the New Testament.[42]

In I Thessalonians 1.9–10 Paul demands that people turn away from the service of idols and turn to the 'living and true God'. This new direction comes about in the power of the expectation of 'his

Son from heaven, whom he raised from the dead, Jesus, who delivers us from the wrath to come'.

The hope of the church is directed towards the parousia of Jesus, whom God has raised from the dead. He will come as 'the Son of God'. Here expectation of the parousia is expectation of the Son. The Son is expected as the saviour of his brothers and sisters. He will not come as the unknown judge. He will come as the familiar brother. We may hope for his judgment. We do not have to be afraid of it.

The way that Paul conceived of the eschatological future (I Cor. 15.22–28 and Phil. 2. 9–11) is no different from this, but it is a little more precise; for he presents *the eschatological future* as *an event within the Trinity*.

The subject of I Corinthians 15.22ff. is the future of world history and the consummation of the divine rule.

For as in Adam all die,
  so also in Christ shall all be made alive.
But each in his own order:
Christ the first fruits,
  then at his coming those who belong to Christ.
Then comes the end,
  when he delivers the kingdom to God the Father
  after destroying every rule and every authority and power.
For he must reign until he has put all his enemies under his feet.
The last enemy to be destroyed is death.
  . . .
When all things are subjected to him,
  then the Son himself will also be subjected
to him who put all things under him,
that God may be everything to every one (AV: that God may be
  all in all).

First of all the resurrection process will be brought to an end: first Christ; then Christians in Christ's parousia; and after that death will be destroyed, and all men and women will be liberated from his power. If God exalts Christ alone to be Lord, then he 'must' reign over everything and everyone; otherwise God would not be God. That is why all other rulers have to be destroyed. The sole lordship of Christ is universal. And because he is 'Lord both of the dead and of the living' (Rom. 14.9) he cannot rest until death too has been destroyed. But if death is no more, then Christ with his life-giving Spirit has made all the dead live. Then his rule is consummated. Then his goal is achieved. Then all promises and hopes are fulfilled.

But Christ himself is not then as yet complete. That is why Paul now talks about an inner-trinitarian process: the Son to whom the Father has subjected everything will then subject himself to the Father and will give the kingdom (*basileia*) over to him. In verse 28 Paul calls Christ explicitly *the Son*. His aim in doing so is to make it clear that it is only in the eschatological transfer of the divine rule to the Father that the Son completes his obedience and his sonship.[43]

The divine rule was given by the Father to the Son through Christ's resurrection. In the final consummation it will be transferred from the Son to the Father. 'The kingdom of the Son' will then become 'the kingdom of glory' of the triune God in which 'God will be all in all'. The rule of Christ is therefore eschatologically limited. It begins in hiddenness with his sending and in open manifestation with his resurrection. It extends to 'the dead and the living'. It will be consummated in the parousia, in which Christ will make the dead live and will destroy death itself.[44] But the rule of Christ, for its part, serves the greater purpose of making room for the kingdom of glory and of preparing for God's indwelling in the new creation, 'so that God will be all in all'. The lordship of Christ, the risen One, as well as the kingdom of the One who is to come, is in an eschatological sense *provisional*. It is only completed when the universal kingdom is transferred to the Father by the Son. With this transfer the lordship of the Son ends. But it means the consummation of his sonship. It follows from this that all Jesus' titles of sovereignty – Christ, kyrios, prophet, priest, king, and so forth – are *provisional* titles, which express Jesus' significance for salvation in time. But the name of Son remains to all eternity. According to Paul, the whole Christian eschatology ends in this inner-trinitarian process, through which the kingdom passes from the Son to the Father. Eschatology accordingly is not simply what takes place in the Last Days in heaven and on earth; it is what takes place in God's essential nature.

Here we must particularly note the mutual workings of the

Father and the Son: the Father subjects everything to the Son, the Son subjects himself to the Father. Through 'the power of the resurrection' the Son destroys all other powers and death itself, then transferring the consummated kingdom of life and the love that is free of violence, to the Father. The kingdom of God is therefore transferred from one divine subject to the other; and its form is changed in the process. *So God's triunity precedes the divine lordship.* The divine lordship is exercised within the divine trinity. It follows from this:

1. It is not the doctrine of the Trinity which interprets the rule of God; it is the very converse that is true: the rule of God in the form of the rule of the Son and in the form of the lordship of the Father interprets the eternal life of the divine Trinity.

2. God's rule is not merely an *opus trinitatis ad extra*; it is at the same time an *opus trinitatis ad intra*. At this point the Augustinian distinction is not correct.

Finally, we again ask: what form of the Trinity can we perceive in these eschatological processes?

— The Father subjects everything to the Son;
— the Son transfers the consummated kingdom to the Father;
— the Son subjects himself to the Father.

This corresponds precisely to the close of the famous hymn in Philippians 2.9–11:

> Therefore God has highly exalted him
> and bestowed on him the name which is above every name,
> that at the name of Jesus every knee should bow,
> in heaven and on earth and under the earth,
> and every tongue confess
> that Jesus Christ is Lord,
> to the glory of God the Father.

God assigns the universe to Jesus, his Son. All confess and enjoy the lordship of Jesus 'to the glory of God the Father'. So ultimately Christ's whole lordship serves the purpose of glorifying the Father.

It is the Son who is the real actor in this consummation of salvation and in this glorification of God; and the Father is really the one who receives. In eschatology all activity proceeds from the Son and the Spirit; the Father is the receiver of the kingdom, the power and the glory, for ever and ever.

What trinitarian order can we perceive in the eschatological consummation?

In the sending, delivering up and resurrection of Christ we find this sequence:

Father – Spirit – Son.

In the lordship of Christ and the sending of the Spirit the sequence is:

Father – Son – Spirit.

But when we are considering the eschatological consummation and glorification, the sequence has to be:

Spirit – Son – Father.

§6 TRANSFORMATIONS OF THE OPEN TRINITY

1. The rule of Christ is the rule of the Son. It displays a trinitarian structure in both history and eschatology, for it springs from the co-workings of three divine subjects: Father, Son and creative Spirit.

2. Father, Son and Spirit do not only combine or work together according to a single pattern. In the sending, in the surrender and in the resurrection, the Father is the actor, the Son the receiver, and the Spirit the means through which the Father acts on his Son and the Son receives the Father.

In the lordship of the Son and the diffusion of the creative Spirit, the Son together with the Father are the actors. The Spirit takes his sending from the Son, just as he takes his issue from the Father.

In eschatology, finally, the Son is the actor: he transfers the kingdom to the Father; he subjects himself to the Father. But in eschatology the Holy Spirit is the actor equally: he glorifies the Father through the praise of all created beings who have been liberated by Christ's rule. The Father is the One who receives. He receives his kingdom from the Son; he receives his glory from the Spirit.

3. A theological doctrine of the Trinity can only be biblically justified if the history of God to which the Bible testifies, itself displays trinitarian forms. It then has to follow these trinitarian forms. In the historical and eschatological testimony of the New

Testament, we do not merely find one, single form of the Trinity. We find a trinitarian co-working of Father, Son and Spirit, but with changing patterns.

We find the order Father – Spirit – Son; the order Father – Son – Spirit; and finally the order Spirit – Son – Father. Up to now, however, dogmatic tradition has only worked with a single pattern. And in the West this pattern has always been Father – Son – Spirit.

4. There is no doubt that the common denominator of the changing trinitarian patterns is the rule of God. The scarlet thread that runs through the biblical testimonies might be called the history of the kingdom of God. But what this history of the kingdom of God is about, is really the trinitarian history of the kingdom. It does not merely run its course on earth – which is to say outside God himself – as dogmatic tradition ever since Augustine has maintained. On the contrary, it takes place in its earthly mode within the Trinity itself, as the history of the kingdom of the Father, the Son and the Spirit.

5. The trinitarian history of the kingdom of God is an eschatologically open history *now*. Baptism is the practice of the doctrine of the Trinity, because it is through faith and baptism that the trinitarian history of God's kingdom takes possession of men and women. The concept of the Trinity is formulated first of all in a person's confession of faith in baptism, in prayer and in praise.

6. If the history of the kingdom is this history of God which is open and inviting in a trinitarian sense, how can we talk about *God's unity*? If the three divine subjects are co-active in this history, as we have shown they are, then the unity of the Trinity cannot be a monadic unity. The unity of the divine tri-unity lies in the *union* of the Father, the Son and the Spirit, not in their numerical unity. It lies in their *fellowship*, not in the identity of a single subject. That is quite clear from the Gospel of John. Jesus says according to John 10.30: 'I and the Father are one' (ἕν). He does not say 'I and the Father are one and the same' (εἷς). The unity of Jesus the Son with the Father is a unity which preserves their separate character, indeed actually conditions it. Moreover it is not a closed unity; it is an open union. That is why we can read in the High Priestly prayer (John 17.21): 'that they may all be one; *even as* thou, Father, art in me, and I in thee, that they also *may be in us* ...'. The fellowship of the disciples with one another has to resemble the union of the Son with the Father. But not only does it have

to resemble that trinitarian union; in addition it has to be a union within this union. It is a *fellowship with God* and, beyond that, a *fellowship in God*. But that presupposes that the triunity is open in such a way that the whole creation can be united with it and can be one within it. The union of the divine Trinity is open for the uniting of the whole creation with itself and in itself. So the unity of the Trinity is not merely a theological term; at heart it is a soteriological one as well.

IV

The World of the Trinity

Whereas up to now we have derived our knowledge of the Trinity from the history of Jesus the Son, we must now see the figure of the Son against the comprehensive horizon of the history of the triune God with the world. For the universal significance of the history of the Son could not otherwise be understood. As far as the order of perception is concerned, the doctrine of the Trinity we have expounded has *christology* as its premise; for it is only christology that makes the knowledge and concept of the triune God necessary. But the christology it presupposes is an *open* christology: open for perception of the creation of the world through the Father of Jesus Christ, and open for perception of the transfiguration of the world through the Holy Spirit, who proceeds from the Father of Jesus, the Son. The Apostles' Creed already shows how special, historical christology is fitted into the all-embracing divine Trinity of God; for the creed groups acknowledgment of God the Creator and his works, and acknowledgment of God the Holy Spirit and his work, as first and third articles, round the second article, which treats of God the Son and the events of his life. And most Christian dogmatics follow the structure of the Apostles' Creed.

Starting from the christology of the Son as we have developed it, we must now enquire about its consequences for belief in the creation of the world and for the hope of its transfiguration. 'The works of the Trinity' are traditionally ascribed in each case to one person of the Trinity in particular (although this does not mean the exclusion of the others). Consequently creation is seen as 'the work' of the Father, atonement as 'the work' of the Son, and sanctification as 'the work' of the Spirit. We shall adhere to this disposition, but we shall change the names given to the divine works, considering 'the creation of the Father', 'the incarnation of the Son' and 'the transfiguration of the Spirit'. Our purpose here is not to describe these trinitarian works themselves. That is the function of the doctrine of creation, christology, and eschatology.

Here – in order to deepen and extend the insights acquired in the previous chapter – we shall be asking what we know about the Trinity from these divine 'works'. Although we have here initially taken up the traditional Augustinian concept of the *opera trinitatis*[1], we shall not follow the traditional epistemological method, deducing the actor from the act and the master from the work. These ethical and pre-eminently masculine analogies between actor and acts, master and works, have only a very limited value for a perception of the relationship between God and his world. They obscure more than they illuminate.

We shall start from the assumption that the relationship between God and the world has a *reciprocal* character, because this relationship must be seen as a living one. Every living and life-promoting determination of someone else has its origin in self-determination, and it reverberates on that self-determination. A purely one-sided relationship is not a living relationship at all. If the relationships that make up life are reciprocal, then even God cannot be thought of simply in his significance for the world and for human history. The world and human history must also be perceived in their significance for God. What God means for the world was expressed in the doctrine of the *opera trinitatis ad extra*. But this doctrine was incapable of expressing what the world means for God. We shall be enquiring about the reciprocal effects. That is to say, in our consideration of all the *opera trinitatis ad extra* – the creation of the world, the incarnation, and the world's transfiguration – we shall also be asking about the *opera trinitatis ad intra* which are bound up with them, meaning by that the love of the Father for the Son, the love of the Son for the Father, and the glorification of the Father and the Son through the Spirit. But in actual fact it is not a question of the 'works' of the Trinity 'outwards' and 'inwardly' at all; it is a matter of the 'sufferings' which correspond reciprocally to the works. Outward acts correspond to inward suffering, and outward suffering corresponds to inward acts. This means that God's outward and inward aspects are intertwined in a totally different way from the picture suggested by the spatial metaphors, outward/inward. The creation is a work of divine humility. The suffering of love is God's supreme work on God himself.

We can already show these reciprocal workings of *actio* and *passio* in the concept of decision as well. 'God decides in favour of the world.' His decision affects himself first of all and then, through his self-determination, it affects the world. This two-sided structure of decision has been depicted first of all as the *opera dei ad extra interna* and then, secondly, as the *opera dei ad extra externa*.[2] But this fails to bring out the divinely determined self of God which suffers the decision. The definition does not comprehend the passion of God which is the foundation of his action. Nor is the world's retroactive effect on God comprehended either, as long as God can be thought of merely as the One who is eternally efficacious.

If we ask the reverse question: what does the creation of the world and its history mean for God himself? then we are presupposing that the world is not a matter of indifference for God himself, but that it represents an object, a counterpart, for his passionate interest. His world in heaven and on earth is the object of his will towards good; it is the counterpart of his love for freedom; and in both these things it is the fulfilment of his hope for a free response to his own goodness and love. Just as God goes out of himself through what he does, giving his world his own impress, so his world puts its impress on God too, through its reactions, its aberrations and its own initiatives. It certainly does not do so in the same way; but that it does so in its *own* way there can be no doubt at all. If God is love, then he does not merely emanate, flow out of himself; he also expects and needs love: his world is intended to be his home. He desires to dwell in it.

§1 THE EVENT OF SALVATION AND BELIEF IN CREATION

Both the Old and the New Testaments make it plain that the biblical belief in creation is determined by experience of the event of salvation and by hope for that salvation's completion. Both Israel and the Christian faith, each in its own way, has 'a soteriological understanding of the work of creation',[3] and an eschatological understanding of the event of salvation.[4] This is so because the experience of salvation is not merely the experience of 'my' or 'our' salvation; what is experienced is salvation for everything and everyone. A universal significance is always inherent in the particular experience of salvation. Otherwise it could not be the experience of salvation at all.

The *universal presupposition* of the particular experiences out of which Israel and the church emerged is expressed by the fact that belief in the God who liberates and redeems them is belief in the Creator of all people and things. The *universal goal* of the special experiences of God shared by Israel and the church can be summed up by saying that the God who liberates and redeems them is hoped for as the One who will complete and fulfil the history of all people and all things. Through belief in creation and hope for salvation, the salvation that is experienced in a particular and individual way is understood in its universal dimensions. This process has of course its other side too. If salvation is understood in a universal sense, then, conversely, the universe too is viewed in the redeeming light of its salvation.

1. The Exodus Experience and the Messianic Hope

The biblical belief in creation grew up in its initial form out of Israel's historical experience of God in exodus, covenant, and the occupation of the promised land. It took its particular character from these experiences: the God who led Israel out of Egypt is the Creator who leads the world out of chaos and makes its orders the orders of his covenant. In both the Yahwist and the Priestly Writing, 'creation in the beginning' does not mean a primordial paradisal state. It means the history that precedes salvation history.[5] That is why creation is grasped as being the work of God's grace. The orders of creation are narrated in the form of a 'history'. It is creation that opens up the prospect of history.[6] God's history with his world therefore begins with creation, not just with the Fall. The creation of the world is open for the history of the world. For it is with the creation of the world that time begins. Because time is only perceived through change – change in things and conditions – the world of creation is a changeable world. Stamped by the saving experience of the exodus from slavery into freedom, the world with its orders is understood as a creation of God's, formed from the primal waters and from chaos. It is a creation open to time, open to the future, and open to change. It is an 'open system', full of every potentiality.[7] Consequently it also has to be understood as a threatened world: it is surrounded by chaos. The powers of corruption reach into the midst of it, in night and the sea.

The writings of Israel which we find in the Old Testament do not merely testify to the exodus experience and to faith in creation. In prophecy, they also witness to *the messianic hope* for the new, final exodus into eternal freedom; and this is associated with an eschatological hope for the final salvation out of chaos, and its eternal transfiguration in the presence of God. In thinking about the new, Babylonian captivity of the people, Deutero-Isaiah especially proclaims a new exodus, a new Servant of God and a new saving event. This also means a change in the view of the world as this God's creation: it is going to become the scene of his coming glory.[8]

The messianic vision of the new exodus picks up the remembrance of the first exodus but goes beyond it, by virtue of hope. Those that go out will neither hunger nor thirst (Isa. 48.21). Their path is easy, because all hindrances will be cleared away (Isa. 49.11). The people will not leave 'in haste', but will move as if they were taking part in a festive procession, led by God himself (Isa. 52.12). Nature will participate in the joy of the final liberation of God's people. The mountains will break out into rejoicing and the trees will clap their hands (Isa. 49.13; 55.12). 'Waters shall break forth in the wilderness, and streams in the desert' (Isa. 35.6). All nations will see it. Their idols shall be as nothing and will perish in their impotence (Isa. 41.11; 42.17; 45.24). They will know the God of Israel as their salvation and their strength (Isa. 45.14f.).

We need only add to this the visions of the future in the First and Third Isaiahs to see how this prophetic hope for salvation became the source for a new understanding of creation. In the vision in which he received his call (Isa. 6.3), the prophet looks into the future: 'The whole earth full of his glory.' What does this mean?

The whole land will be 'full of the knowledge of the Lord' (Isa. 11.9). 'The wolf shall dwell with the lamb, and the leopard shall lie down with the kid . . . The cow and the bear shall feed; their young shall lie down together; and the lion shall eat straw

like the ox. The sucking child shall play over the hole of the asp
... (11.6ff.). The peace of this creation goes beyond the creation
story told by the Yahwist or the Priestly Writing. The vision of
the great banquet of the nations on Mount Zion (Isa. 25.6ff.)
also goes further than the creation accounts: 'He will swallow
up death for ever.' Trito-Isaiah sums up the whole wealth of the
images in the terse promise: 'Behold, I create new heavens and
a new earth; and the former things shall not be remembered or
come into mind. But be glad and rejoice for ever in that which
I create' (65.17f.).

The messianic future of creation completes and fulfils the initial
creation. The exodus out of chaos and the viable order existing
within the threat of chaos will be followed by the transfiguration
of creation in the eternally unveiled presence of God; by the enduring righteousness of the world and its eternal pacification. God
himself will dwell in 'his world'.

2. Faith in Christ and Experience of the Spirit

The Christian understanding of creation is coloured by the new
experience of salvation in Christ. The first accounts of creation
were determined by Israel's experience of exodus and covenant;
the prophets' hopes for salvation evoked the visions of the new
creation; and in the same way Christian experiences of salvation
and hopes for redemption also determine the Christian belief in
creation. In the New Testament too belief in creation is intended
to demonstrate the universal significance of the experience of salvation, presented as the salvation of the universe. If Christ is the
foundation for the salvation of the whole creation, then he is also
the foundation of creation's very existence. If, being the foundation
of salvation, he is all creation's goal, then he has been its foundation from eternity. This idea lies behind the statements about Christ
as the mediator of creation.[9]

The first approaches to statements of this kind are to be found
in Paul. Here they are merely thoughts, drawn into service to help
justify the universality of Christ's rule and in order to show the
world-wide liberty of believers. In the dispute which arose in Cor-
inth about whether to buy the meat that had been offered to idols
or whether to abstain from it, the apostle declares: 'For us there

is *one* God, the Father from whom are all things and for whom we exist, and *one* Lord, Jesus Christ, through whom are all things and through whom we exist' (I Cor. 8.6). Consequently the Christian's acts are free in every situation. The world belongs to his Lord.

In the deutero-Pauline Epistle to the Ephesians (1.9ff.) this idea is expressed as 'the uniting of all things' (ἀνακεφαλαίωσις) in Christ. It is only in the Epistle to the Colossians (1.15–17) and in Hebrews 1.2 that it is explicitly stated for the first time that God created the world 'through him'.

This 'mediator of creation' is called 'the image of the invisible God', 'the first-born of all creation', 'the brightness of his glory' (AV) and 'the express image of his person' (AV). These are all images which were used to describe God's eternal Wisdom in the Wisdom literature of the Old Testament.[10] Wisdom is one with God and yet confronts him independently. It is not merely understood as one of God's attributes, although it is probably not yet viewed as a person *in* God either. Through Wisdom God creates the world, through Wisdom he orders the world, and through Wisdom he will one day glorify the world. The mediation of glory and the mediation of creation are one and the same in the Wisdom tradition. Job 28, Proverbs 8 and Ecclesiasticus describe the Wisdom that mediates between God and his world in a more and more personal way. The New Testament perception of Christ as mediator of creation has a clear *Sophia* christology as its premise. The *Logos* christology of the Gospel of John goes back to this when it is stated that 'All things were made through him (the Word, the Logos), and without him was not anything made that was made' (John 1.3).[11]

On the one hand, through Christ's creative mediation, the salvation experienced and revealed through him is related, not merely to believers, and not merely to men and women, but to the whole of reality. Christ came 'to his own home' (John 1.11), not into a strange land. That is why even though Christians are 'strangers and sojourners' in this perverted world, they too are at home in God's real creation as its true citizens. The experience of salvation makes the extension of the experience of salvation to the whole of existence and to 'all things' necessary. Salvation is liberating because it includes everything, accepting all things into an all-embracing hope.

On the other hand, it is only through the understanding of Christ as the mediator of creation that an explicitly Christian doctrine of creation comes into being. It represents an interpretation of God's world which is quite individual, compared with the Old Testament creation accounts, and with the prophetic creation hopes as well. If Christ is the mediator of creation, then creation can only be conceived of in trinitarian terms, if it is to be understood in Christian terms at all.

The New Testament writings do not only witness to the experience of salvation in Christ, and to faith in Christ as the mediator of creation; they also testify to the experience of the Holy Spirit, and the hope that through him *the world will be transfigured*, transformed into God's world, which means into God's own home.[12] This hope is expressed in continually new visions of *the indwelling of God* in this new world. The experience of the Spirit is expressed in words quite distinct from those describing creation and God's 'works' in history. The words used for the Spirit are 'outpouring', 'flowing', and so forth. The Spirit is 'poured out' on all flesh in the Last Days (Joel 2.28ff.; Acts 2.16ff.), and then old and young, men and women, all alike, will have dreams and visions. Through the Holy Spirit the love of God is 'poured out' into our hearts, Paul says when he is talking about believers (Rom. 5.5). People are 'born' anew of the Spirit (John 3.3, 5f.). The charismata, the gifts and energies of the Spirit in the new fellowship, will not be 'created'; as fruits of *charis*, the gift of the Spirit itself, they will be 'effected' (I Cor. 12). These are the divine energies which already quicken life now, in the present, because they are the energies of the new creation of all things.

A new *divine presence* is experienced in the experience of the Spirit. God does not simply confront his creation as creator. He is not merely, as the incarnate One, the representative and advocate for men and women. In the Spirit God dwells in man himself. The experience of the Spirit is therefore the experience of the Shekinah, the divine indwelling. The Shekinah is a divine presence which was otherwise only experienced in the Temple, in worship on the Lord's day. But now men and women themselves, in their own bodies, already become the temple of the Holy Spirit (I Cor. 6.13–20). In the end, however, the new heaven and the new earth will become the 'temple' of God's indwelling. The whole world will become God's home. Through the indwelling of the Spirit, people and churches are already glorified *in the body*, now, in the present. But then the whole creation will be transfigured through the indwelling of God's glory. Consequently the hope which is kindled by the experience of the indwelling Spirit gathers in the future, with panentheistic visions. Everything ends with God's being 'all in all' (I. Cor. 15.28 AV). *God in the world* and *the world in God* – that is what is meant by the glorifying of the world through the Spirit. That is *the home of the Trinity*. If the world is transformed and glorified into this through the Holy Spirit, then creation can only be conceived of in trinitarian terms, if it is to be understood in Christian terms at all.

§2 THE CREATION OF THE FATHER

In order to avoid anticipating a detailed doctrine of creation, here we shall only consider the questions about the creation of the world that affect God himself, presenting the doctrine of creation as a doctrine of God.

1. Contingentia mundi

One of the first and most important questions about the doctrine of creation is the question of the *contingentia mundi*. Is the creation of the world necessary for God himself, or is it merely fortuitous? Does it proceed from God's nature, or from his will? Is it eternal, or temporal?

Christian theism has always been anxious to depict creation as solely the work of *God's free will*;[13] as a work depending entirely on God, without any significance for God himself. In order to stress the free nature of the act of creation and its character as a pure act of grace, this tradition ascribed to God absolute liberty, in the sense of unlimited power of disposal: God need not have created the world. There are no inner reasons and no outward compulsions for his action. God is self-sufficient. His bliss is self-complete. He is perfect and needs neither his own creative expression of himself, nor a creation. But it was his good pleasure to create a world with which he could be 'well pleased'. That is why he created a reality corresponding to himself.

Christian theism, in ascribing creation solely to the decree of God's free will, therefore has to fall back on *God's essential nature* in order to avoid the impression of divine arbitrariness: even if

God can create what he wants, he only actually creates what is in accord with himself.[14] If his nature is perfect goodness, then he cannot create evil. In the biblical concept of 'what is well pleasing to him', the liberty of the divine will and correspondence with the divine nature are reconciled in the best possible way. Reconciling chance and necessity, and excluding arbitrariness and compulsion, God's world must then be understood as 'a play of his divine good pleasure'.[15] But all the same, the fictitious suggestion of arbitrariness in God leaves behind it a residue of despotism in the concept of God: the relationship of love which God had in view when he created free men and women is not in accord with the absolutism of pure power; for power is replaced by mutual friendship.[16]

Christian panentheism, on the other hand, started from the divine essence:[17] Creation is a fruit of God's longing for 'his Other' and for that Other's free response to the divine love. That is why the idea of the world is inherent in the nature of God himself from eternity. For it is impossible to conceive of a God who is not a creative God. A non-creative God would be imperfect compared with the God who is eternally creative. And if God's eternal being is love, then the divine love is also more blessed in giving than in receiving. God cannot find bliss in eternal self-love if selflessness is part of love's very nature. God is in all eternity self-communicating love. The Father loves the Son eternally, and the Son also eternally returns the Father's love. But this inner-trinitarian love is the love of like for like, not love of the other. It is blissful love in the continual response from the being like in nature to itself. But it is not yet creative love, which communicates itself by overcoming its opposite, which 'gives life to the dead and calls into existence the things that do not exist' (Rom. 4.17). It is not yet the love that responds out of the being that is other. Is this not the reason why the divine love presses even beyond the Trinity? Does it not seek its 'image', which is to say its response, and therefore its bliss, in men and women?

The speculative theology of the nineteenth century picked up mystical ideas and maintained that it was God's nature to reveal and communicate himself. For as eternal love God was also his own self-communication, indeed his own self-giving. And that meant that the world and the image to which God wanted to communicate himself (man) was already envisaged from eternity in God himself. God emptied himself by virtue of his love, out of the necessity of his being, going out to 'his Other', the world, and only came fully to himself by virtue of that Other's response to his love. But this is to identify the idea of the world with the Son of God.[18] The process of creating the world is then identified with the inner-trinitarian life of God, and vice versa: the world process is the eternal life of God himself. God's love for his Other is then in actual fact nothing else than the extended love of God for the one like himself. The deification of the world and humanity is the necessary conclusion: anyone who knows that he is eternally loved by God becomes God's eternal Son. So God is as dependent on him as he is on God.[19] The elements of truth in this view are turned into their opposite once the capacity to distinguish is suppressed by the will towards synthesis. What is Other in confrontation with God is not identical with the otherness of God. It is true that the love of God the Father for the world is the same love as the love for his only begotten Son, but that does not turn the world into the Son, or make the Son the world. It is true that those who are loved by God and those who return his love become 'sons of God' (Rom. 8.14). But they do not become 'the only begotten Son'. They become 'God's sons' because God's only begotten Son is as such predestined to be 'the first-born among many brethren'. In order to understand the history of mankind as a history *in* God, the distinction between the world process and the inner-trinitarian process must be maintained and emphasized.

One way of reconciling the elements of truth in Christian theism and Christian pantheism emerges when we cease to interpret God's liberty as arbitrariness, and the nature of God as a divine natural law. The naturalistic images of an eternally productive divine substance (*natura naturans*) are just as inappropriate as the images of the absolutist monarch in heaven. If God's nature is goodness, then the freedom of his will lies in his will to goodness. That is why we have to say: 'The world is a goodly purpose, in accord with God's love, not a fortuitous one.'[20] If we lift the concept of necessity out of the context of compulsive necessity and determination by something external, then in God *necessity* and *freedom* coincide; they are what is for him axiomatic, self-evident. For God it is axiomatic to love, for he cannot deny himself. For God it is axiomatic to love freely, for he is God. There is consequently no reason why we should not understand God as being from eternity self-communi-

cating love. This does not make him 'his own prisoner'. It means
that he remains true to himself.

From eternity God has desired not only himself but the world
too, for he did not merely want to communicate himself to himself;
he wanted to communicate himself to the one who is other than
himself as well. That is why the idea of the world is already
inherent in the Father's love for the Son. The eternal Son of God
is closely related to God's idea of the world. The *Logos* through
whom the Father has created everything, and without whom
nothing has been made that was made is only *the other side of the
Son*. The Son is *the Logos* in relation to the world. The Logos is
the Son in relation to the Father. The Father utters the eternal
Word in the Spirit and breathes out the Spirit in the eternal utterance of the Word. Through the eternal Son/Logos the Father creates
the world. He is the mediator of creation. It is for his incarnation
that God preserves the world. He is creation's liberator. It is in
looking towards his kingdom of freedom that God loves those
whom he has created. He is the crown of creation.

2. God's Self-Limitation

There is one question which has barely been considered at all in
Christian theology, although it is a much discussed point in the
Jewish kabbalistic tradition. That is the idea of creation *outwards*
or *inwards*.

Christian theology – following the pattern of the creation account in the Priestly Document – has consistently distinguished
between an act of God inwards and an act of God outwards. God
has an inner, self-sufficing life. Creation is an act of the triune God
in his unity, directed outwards. We therefore have to distinguish
between the inner life of God and an act of God outwards, in
creation, incarnation and redemption. The inner life of God only
has significance for his outward acts in that it provides their reason
and justification. For it is only as *causa sui* that God can be *causa
mundi*. Augustine's formulation became definitive for the Western
church's doctrine of God: 'Opera trinitatis ad extra indivisa esse,
tribus personis communia, salvo tamen earum ordine et
discrimine.'[21]

The simple counter-question is: can the omnipotent and omnipresent God have an 'outward' aspect at all? Is there, in fact, an

extra Deum for these *opera ad extra*? If we start from the assumption that there is, then we must assume, not only God's self-constitution in eternity, but an equally eternal non-divine or counter-divine entity, which would be 'outside'. But would this not be to contradict God's divinity, which means his omnipresence?

And if (because of creation out of chaos and *creatio ex nihilo*) we have to say that there is a 'within' and a 'without' for God – and that he therefore goes creatively 'out of himself', communicating himself creatively the one who is Other than himself – then we must after all assume a *self-limitation* of the infinite, omnipresent God, preceding his creation. In order to create something 'outside' himself, the infinite God must have made room for this finitude beforehand, 'in himself'. But does not creation as *opera ad extra* then presuppose an inversion of God which releases that *extra* in the first place?

It is only God's withdrawal into himself which gives that *nihil* the space in which God then becomes creatively active. But is creation then really a being and an other existing 'outside' God? Must we not say that this 'creation outside God' exists simultaneously *in God*, in the space which God has made for it in his omnipresence? Has God not therefore created the world 'in himself', giving it time *in* his eternity, finitude *in* his infinity, space *in* his omnipresence and freedom *in* his selfless love?

The trinitarian relationship of the Father, the Son and the Holy Spirit is so wide that the whole creation can find space, time and freedom in it. Creation as God's act in Nothingness and as God's order in chaos is a male, an engendering notion. Creation as God's act in God and out of God must rather be called a feminine concept, a bringing forth: God creates the world by letting his world become and be in *himself*: Let it be!

Isaac Luria developed this idea in his doctrine of *zimsum*.[22] *Zimsum* really means 'concentration' or 'contraction', a withdrawal into the self. Luria transformed the ancient doctrine about God's concentration at the single point of his Shekinah in the Temple, into the doctrine of God's concentrated inversion for the purpose of creating the world. The 'existence of the universe was made possible through a shrinkage process in God'. That is his answer to the question: since God is 'all in all', how can anything else that is not God exist at this specific point? How can God create out of 'nothing' when there cannot be such a thing as nothing, since his essence is everything and interpenetrates everything? Luria's answer is that God has released a certain sector of his being, from which he has withdrawn – 'a kind of primal, mystical space'; and into this, accordingly, he can issue from himself in his creation and his revelation. The very first act of the infinite Being was therefore not a step 'outwards' but a step 'inwards', a 'self-withdrawal of God from himself into himself', as Gershom Scholem puts it; that is to say, it was a *passio Dei*, not an *actio*. The very first act of all is therefore an act that veils, not one that reveals; a limitation on God's part, not a de-limitation. It is only in Act II that God issues from himself as creator into that primal space which he had previously released in Act I.

The world process is therefore to be understood as a two-sided one. Every stage in the creation process contains within itself the tension between the light flooding back into God and the light that breaks forth from him. In other words, every act outwards is preceded by an act inwards which makes the 'outwards' possible. God, that is to say, continually creates inwards and outwards simultaneously. He creates by withdrawing himself, and because he withdraws himself. Creation in chaos and out of nothing, which is an act of power, is also a self-humiliation on God's part, a lowering of himself into his own impotence. Creation is a work of God's humility and his withdrawal into himself. God acts on himself when he acts creatively. His inward and his outward aspects therefore correspond to one another and mirror one another. His action is grounded in his passion. Jakob Emden is no doubt right when he says that the doctrine of *zimzum* is the only serious attempt ever made to think through the idea of 'creation out of nothing' in a truly theological way.[23] Even if we do not follow the speculations in natural philosophy which developed out of it, the basic idea of this doctrine gives us the chance to think of *the world in God* without falling victims to pantheism, and to see the history of the divine self-humiliation and the history of human freedom in a continual relationship of reciprocity.

Luria's doctrine of *zimzum* is part of his doctrine of God's Shekinah. Christian theology talks about 'God's indwelling' in the doctrine of the Holy Spirit. The outpouring of the Holy Spirit 'into our hearts' (Rom. 5.3) and 'on all flesh' (Joel 2.28–32; Acts 2.17) is the beginning of the new, eschatological creation. It will be completed when God is 'all in all' (I Cor. 15.28 AV). *God will dwell in* this perfected creation and, on the other hand, creation itself will live *from God.*

If Christian faith looks back to 'creation in the beginning', it will already discover the presence of the Holy Spirit there, as the creative Spirit. Faith cannot develop any view of creation that excludes the Spirit. Creation only exists in the power of the divine Spirit, which has entered into it. It would perish if God withdrew his Spirit from it (Ps. 104.29f.). That is why the whole creation also sighs and longs for the revealing of the liberty of the children of God. It is the divine Spirit who cries out for redeeming freedom in enslaved creation (Rom. 8.9ff.). The existence of creation in the Spirit shows itself in the torment, the striving and the tension of all matter, and in the hunger of all living things for freedom.[24]

If we think about this external state of affairs, transferring it by a process of reflection to the inner relationship of the Trinity, then it means that the Father, through an alteration of his love for the Son (that is to say through a contraction of the Spirit), and the Son, through an alteration in his response to the Father's love (that is, through an inversion of the Spirit) have opened up the space, the time and the freedom for that 'outwards' into which the Father utters himself creatively through the Son. For God himself this utterance means an emptying of himself – a self-determination for the purpose of a self-limitation. Time is an interval in eternity, finitude is a space in infinity, and freedom is a concession of the eternal love. God withdraws himself in order to go out of himself. Eternity breathes itself in, so as to breathe out the Spirit of life.

The federal theological tradition has termed this God's trinitarian decision to create the world, interpreting it as God's innertrinitarian covenant.[25] But it has never developed the implications. For it is in this eternal covenant of the Trinity, a covenant made for creation and glorification, that the self-determination of the Father, the Son and the Spirit takes place; and this self-determination, as self-limitation, means making room for creation and making possible the liberty of the non-divine image of God in God.

3. Trinitarian Creation

What inner-trinitarian form can be perceived in the creation of the world out of God in God?

It is in his love for the Son that the Father determines to be the

Creator of the world. It is because he loves the Son that he becomes the Creator. His self-communicating love for the one like himself opens itself to the Other and becomes creative, which means anticipating every possible response. Because he creates the world by virtue of his eternal love for the Son, the world is, through his eternal will, destined for good, and is nothing other than an expression of his love. The world is good, just as God is himself goodness. That is why God has pleasure in it. That is why he can expect his image, man, to respond to his creative love, so that he may not only enjoy bliss with his Son, in eternity, but may also find bliss in man, in time. If we were to understand creation merely as an *opus trinitatis indivisum ad extra*, then we could only proceed from a *decision of will* on the part of the *one* God, and would not be in a position to define the act of creation any more precisely than that. But if we proceed from the inner-trinitarian relationships of the Persons in the Trinity, then it becomes clear that the Father creates the one who is his Other by virtue of his love for the Son. So creation does not only correspond to God's will; it corresponds to his eternal love as well. Contrary to the Augustinian tradition, it is not that the work of creation is only '*appropriated*' to the Father, though being actually the work of the whole Trinity. On the contrary, creation is actually a product of the Father's love and is ascribed to the whole Trinity.

If the Father creates the world in his love for *the Son*, then he also creates the world *through him*. In his eternal Son he sees the world. It is for fellowship with the Son that he destines men and women. Everything that is made, is made to point in the direction of the free kingdom of the Son. So it is from eternity that the Son has been destined to be the Logos, the mediator of creation. If he is destined to be the mediator of creation, then he is also destined to be the 'centre' for free mankind – destined, that is, for incarnation, and to be the leader and Lord of the kingdom of liberty. The idea of the Son's mediating function in creation (which is necessary for the trinitarian concept) stands in correlation both to the idea of the incarnation of God's Son, and to the idea of the lordship of the Son of Man.

Can we say that, since the Son is destined to be the Logos, he is the divinely immanent archetype of the idea of the world? This can be said in the sense of eternal love, since the Son is in eternity the complete response to the self-communicating love of the Father, so that in the Son the Father arrives at blissful love. If the Father creates the world by virtue of his love for the Son, then by virtue of the Son's answering love the world becomes the bliss of God the Father and the Son. That is what is meant by the ancient statement according to which the 'purpose' of creation was 'to glorify God'. The purpose of creation, and God's desire for self-communication, is fulfilled in the free joy of existence, in the happiness of gratitude and the eternal praise of created beings. It is in fellowship and in the correspondence to the Son's responding, self-giving love for the Father that creation arrives at its truth and God's image on earth achieves freedom. So it is through the Son that the Father creates the world.

He creates through the operation of *the Holy Spirit*. He does not only create out of chaos, through his word of command, as the formulations in the Priestly Writing would have us suppose. Nor, as Ecclesiasticus later writes, does he simply create *ex nihilo*. True though that is, he creates out of the powers and energies of his own Spirit. It is the powers and energies of the Holy Spirit that bridge the difference between Creator and creature, the actor and the act, the master and the work – a difference which otherwise seems to be unbridged by any relation at all. This certainly does not make creation divine, but it is nevertheless brought into the sphere of the Spirit's power, and acquires a share in the inner life of the Trinity itself. A trinitarian doctrine of creation is able to absorb the elements of truth in the idea of creation as God's 'work' and in the notion of creation as a divine overflowing or 'emanation'. The Holy Spirit is 'poured out'. The metaphor of emanation belongs to the language of pneumatology. It is therefore wrong to polemize continually against the neo-Platonic doctrine of emanation in considering the Christian doctrine of creation. Creation in the Spirit has a closer relationship to the Creator than the act has to the actor or the work to the master. All the same, the world is not 'begotten' by God, as is the Son, who is one in essence with the Father. This intermediate situation, between creation and en-gendering, is expressed by the 'pouring out' of the energies of the creative Spirit. This Spirit is the divine breath of life which fills everything with *its own life*. For the creation from God in God, the trinitarian order is this:

The Father creates the world out of his eternal love through *the Son*, for the purpose of finding a response to his love in time, in the power of *the Holy Spirit*, which binds together what is in itself different.

In creation all activity proceeds from the Father. But because the Son, as Logos, and the Spirit, as energy, are both involved – each in its own way and yet equally – creation must be ascribed to the unity of the triune God. In his creative love God is united with creation, which is his Other, giving it space, time and liberty in his own infinite life.

§3 THE INCARNATION OF THE SON

Again, without anticipating a detailed christology, let us here only consider the questions arising from the doctrine of the incarnation as they affect the concept of God.

1. *Cur Deus homo?*

In christology too it is a fundamental question whether for God the incarnation is *fortuitous* or *necessary*. Is it based on God's will or on his nature?

Dogmatic tradition is familiar with two answers:

(*a*) The incarnation of the Son of God was made necessary by man's sin; it was necessary for his reconciliation.[26]

(*b*) God intended the incarnation of the Son of God from eternity. His intention was formed together with the idea of the world, though taking precedence over it; so that creation represents the external framework and preparation for the Son's incarnation.[27]

In the first case the incarnation is merely an 'emergency measure' on God's part, taken in order to counter the emergency of sin in the world. In the second case the incarnation belongs to the eternally self-communicating love of God itself.

In the first case the incarnation is only thought of as the functional presupposition for the atoning sacrifice on the cross. It has no significance of its own. Consequently the bond between God and man in Christ will be dissolved once reconciliation has been completed and sin, with its consequences, has been eliminated. In the second case it is only the incarnation of the Son which completes creation-in-the-beginning through the new bond between God and man manifested in Christ the Son, and through the brotherhood into which he receives believers. The incarnation of the Son then becomes the foundation of the new creation.[28] The fundamental theological decision about this question has often been talked out on the basis of the speculative question: would the Son of God have become man if the human race had remained free of sin?[29]

If the incarnation of the Son is viewed merely as the functional presupposition for the atoning sacrifice made necessary by sin, then it is an expression of the saving will of God *outwards*. It only affects God's relationship to the world, not his understanding of himself. God can save sinners by sending his Son; but he does not have to do so. His own nature remains untouched by the sending of the Reconciler. He did not suffer through human sin and does not gain anything – anything additional to himself – through the reconciliation of the world. Once the incarnate Son of God has achieved the reconciliation of the world with God, he himself becomes superfluous. His mediation between the gracious God and sinful men and women is bound to come to an end when he himself ceases to have a function. This is already inherent in the concept of the mediator; otherwise the mediator would stand in the way of what he mediates. Once creation has been redeemed, purified from sin and liberated from death, the God-Man no longer has any place in it. Any functional and merely soteriological christology is manifestly on the wrong track, simply because it abolishes itself in this way.[30] This applies to the patristic definition according to which God becomes man so that we men may become as gods; and it is equally true of modern 'representative' christologies. The incarnation of the Son is more than merely a means to an end. Christology is more than the presupposition for soteriology.

Even if we make the 'emergency' of human sin the starting point, so as to grasp the necessity of divine reconciliation, and in order to expect the coming of the divine Reconciler, we must go beyond the measure of human need if we are to understand grace as *God's* grace.

It is true that love is brought to its act of mercy through the need of the beloved; but as love it precedes this form of mercy – precedes even the pitiable state of the beloved. The beloved's need is only the occasion (*occasio*) for the love, not its reason (*causa*). The necessity moulds the specific form which the love has to assume if it is to save; but love's inward passion and its manifest interest come first. That is why love cannot stop loving once the acute need of the beloved is at an end. Ultimately, love cannot be content simply to overcome sin. It only arrives at its goal when it has also overcome the conditions that make sin possible. Love does not merely want to vanquish the death of the beloved; it wants to overcome the beloved's mortality too, so that he may be eternally beside the beloved and so that the beloved may be eternally beside himself.

Applied to christology, this means that the incarnation of the Son is the perfected self-communication of the triune God to his world. But the fact that, from the manger to the cross, the incarnate Son has to take upon him the form of a servant, in order to heal through his sufferings and save through his death, is determined by sin and death, which pervert God's world and enslave men and women.

According to Paul Christ was not merely 'delivered for our offences' but was also 'raised again for our justification' (Rom. 4.25 AV). Reconciling sinners with God through his cross, he brings about the new righteousness, the new life, the new creature through his resurrection. The justification of the sinner is more than merely the forgiveness of sins. It leads to new life: 'Where sin increased, grace abounded all the more' (Rom. 5.20). This is the way Paul expresses the imbalance between sin and grace, and the *added value* of grace. This surplus of grace over and above the forgiveness of sins and the reconciliation of sinners, represents the power of the new creation which consummates creation-in-the-beginning.[31] It follows from this that the Son of God did not become man simply because of the sin of men and women, but rather for the sake of perfecting creation. So 'the Son of God would have become man even if the human race had remained without sin'. That is how we should have to answer the question, if we wanted to embark on empty speculation.

But how are the creation of the world and the incarnation connected? The creation of the world culminates in the making of human beings 'to be the image of God' (Gen. 1.26f.; Ps. 8).[32] This statement about man has to be interpreted as both destiny *and* promise. If Christ is called the incarnation of the Son, and if in his manifested form he is called the One who has become man, then in him we have the fulfilment of the promise made to man that he will be 'the image of the invisible God'. Christ is the 'true man' in this perverted and inhumane world.[33] It is therefore in fellowship with him that believers discover the truth of human existence. And this means that the incarnation of the Son has a significance of its own.

This brings us to a further definition in the trinitarian concept of creation: *the Son* is *the Logos* through whom the Father creates his world. The Son is that *image* of God for which God destines human beings. In relation to them the Son is God's true 'ikon'. That is why the initial creation is open: it waits for the appearance 'of man', of true man, the person corresponding to God, God's image. These dimensions are inherent in the New Testament christ-ological titles 'ikon', 'image', 'reflection of God'. It is only because in relation to human beings the Son is God's *primordial image* that he can become 'the first-born among many brethren' (Rom. 8.29). Anyone who is 'made like unto the Son of God' enters into the truth of his human destiny and fulfils his divine promise.

But if God's world is designed for men and women, and if the incarnation of the Son fulfils this design of creation, then in inten-tion the incarnation precedes the creation of the world. The fact that the eternal Son of the Father becomes God's created ikon then belongs to his eternal destiny. This is in accordance with the Son as Logos, which he becomes for the sake of creation. The creation of the world and the incarnation therefore intervene deeply in the inner-trinitarian relationships of God. Again, we can make the meaning of this event clear to ourselves from the life of love.

The incarnation of the Son is neither a matter of indifference for God nor is it necessary for his divinity. If God is love, then – as we have already said – it is part of his loving self-communication and a matter of course for him to communicate himself, not only to his 'like' but also to his 'other'. It is only in and through its Other that love becomes *creative love*. *Self-communicating love*, however, only becomes fulfilled, blissful love when its love is returned. That is why the Father finds bliss in the eternal response to his love through the Son. If he communicates his love for the Son creatively through him to the one who is other than himself, then he also desires to find bliss through this other's responsive love. But this responsive love is a free response. If the Son becomes 'man' that is to say, the image of God – then he communicates his responsive love to those who are destined for manhood and womanhood – destined, that is, to be the image of God; he gathers them into his relationship of sonship to the Father and communicates to them his own liberty, which is above the world. In this way the incarnate Son glorifies the Father in his world and perfects humanity's creation, which destines men and women to be the image of God. This of course presupposes the forgiveness of sins and the reconciliation of sinners through his death, as well as the liberation of men and women in his universal kingdom. But reconciliation and liberation through Christ are directed towards man's destined 'likeness' to 'the image of God'. That is to say, what is at stake is the fulfilment of the promise given with creation.

2. The Kenosis of God

We must again ask whether the incarnation of the Son is really a divine act directed outwards, or whether it corresponds to an inner-trinitarian process. If, as we have shown, the significance of the Son's incarnation is his true humanity, then the incarnation reveals the true humanity of God.[34] That is not an anthropomorphic way of speaking, which is therefore not in accordance with God's divinity; it is the quintessence of his divinity itself.

The self-humiliation of God, which we already talked about in connection with the doctrine of the creation of the world, is fulfilled in the incarnation of the Son. God permits an existence different from his own by limiting himself. He withdraws his omnipotence in order to set his image, men and women, free. He allows his world to exist *in* his eternity. The divine kenosis which begins with the creation of the world reaches its perfected and completed form in the incarnation of the Son.

But we also talked about God's humiliation of himself in connection with the *indwelling* of the Spirit and the divine Wisdom *in history*. For through his Shekinah God participates in man's destiny, making the sufferings of his people his own. Conversely, through his indwelling, people participate in his life and in his will; they love with his love and suffer with his suffering.[35] The God who in his indwellings confronts himself, becomes recognizable in the incarnate Son who confronts the Father in the world.

In the incarnation of the Son the triune God enters into the limited, finite situation. Not only does he enter into this state of being man; he accepts and adopts it himself, making it part of his own, eternal life. He becomes *the human God*.

If this is the meaning which is inherent in the incarnation of the

Son as such, then God's self-humiliation is completed and perfected in the passion and death of Jesus the Son. Here too an indwelling significance is perceptible: God does not merely enter into the finitude of men and women; he enters into the situation of their sin and God-forsakenness as well. He does not merely enter into this situation; he also accepts and adopts it himself, making it part of his own eternal life. The kenosis is realized on the cross. Of course it serves the reconciliation and redemption of men and women, but it also contains in itself this other significance: God becomes the God who identifies himself with men and women to the point of death, and beyond. The incarnation of the Son is not something transitional. It is and remains to all eternity. There is no God other than the incarnate, human God who is one with men and women.

The *outward incarnation* presupposes *inward self-humiliation*. That is why the incarnation intervenes in the inner relations of the Trinity.

Again we can make this clear from the image of love. Love that communicates itself requires response if it is to find bliss. But from his image in the world the Father can only expect the love that is a free response; and in order to make this free response possible, love must concede freedom and offer freedom to the beloved. In order to experience the free response it desires, love must wait patiently. It cannot compel a response by violence. For the sake of freedom, and the love responded to in freedom, God limits and empties himself. He withdraws his omnipotence because he has confidence in the free response of men and women.

God does not encounter men and women 'as God'; he encounters them in human form, in the incarnate and crucified Son. With respect to God's omnipotence this means a limitation. But with respect to God's goodness it is a de-limitation. His strength is made perfect in weakness. The traditional doctrine about God's kenosis has always looked at just the one aspect of God's self-limitation, self-emptying and self-humiliation. It has overlooked the other side: God's limitations inwardly are de-limitations outwards. God is nowhere greater than in his humiliation. God is nowhere more glorious than in his impotence. God is nowhere more divine than when he becomes man.

3. *The Only Begotten Son, the First-Born of Many Brethren*

The twofold meaning of the sonship of Jesus, inwards and outwards, for God and for man, can be perceived best from the change
from 'only begotten Son' (μονογενής) to 'the first-born of many
brethren' (πρωτότοκος).[36]

The 'only begotten Son' is the Father's only, own, eternal Son.
We are told that the Father sends him into the world, that he
delivers him up to death on the cross 'for us all', that he raises and
exalts him. The idea of the 'only begotten' Son invokes the category
of exclusiveness. It is in this category that he exists; it is in this
that he is delivered up and exalted: he and he alone, the one for
the many.

'The first-born among many brethren', on the other hand, means
the first among many successors, one brother among other brothers
and sisters. What the only begotten Son does and suffers is *unique*;
it happens *only once*. What the first-born brother does and suffers
is *for the first time*, in an open fellowship.

What the dogmatic doctrine of the two natures termed 'Christ's
divinity' really means Jesus as 'only begotten Son' in his exclusiveness and uniqueness. What it called 'Christ's humanity' really has
to do with Jesus as 'the first-born among many brethren'. For the
one person of Jesus Christ is not a matter of two metaphysically
different 'natures'. It is an expression of his exclusive relationship
to the Father, by reason of his origin, and his inclusive relationship
of fellowship to his many brothers and sisters. His relationship to
God is the relation of God's own Son to his Father. His relationship
to the world is the relationship of the eldest to his brethren
(Rom. 8.29) and of the first-born of all creation to other created
beings (Col. 1.15). There is no brotherhood of Christ without his
sonship. But his sonship is never without his brotherhood.[37]

What do the words 'first born' mean? The link with the term
eikon, image, suggests that the only begotten Son of the Father is
at the same time *the prototype* for the brothers and sisters who
find their way to the Father in fellowship with him, and who with
him become the heirs of the coming kingdom. But what is meant
too (as the connection with the phrase 'of like form' shows) is that
the only begotten Son of the Father is at the same time the *leader*
of salvation and liberty for the brothers and sisters who follow
him. It is not only the *being* of Jesus Christ, but also his *way* into

passion and glory which is meant by 'being of like form'. Believers enter into the fellowship of Christ's sufferings and take the impress of the cross – become cruciform. They hope to become of like form with the transfigured body of Christ in glory (Phil. 3.21). That is why we can talk about both 'our crucified Brother' and 'our risen Brother'. What is meant is the whole form of existence which is lived by Jesus Christ and which takes its stamp from him.

There is no fellowship with Jesus the Son except what we find in fellowship with Jesus the brother. Fellowship with Jesus the brother is participation in his mission and his fate. Fellowship with Jesus the brother means ultimately participation in the liberation of the whole enslaved creation, which longs for the 'revealing of the liberty of the Sons of God' (Rom. 8.19,21) and for the experience of the 'redemption of the body' (Rom. 8.23).

4. Trinitarian Incarnation

In the incarnation of the Son the triune God communicates himself wholly and utterly. In the incarnation of the Son God himself fulfils the promise made to mankind in creation – the promise that man should be 'the image of God'. In the incarnation of the Son God humiliates himself, accepting and adopting threatened and perverted human nature in its entirety, making it part of his eternal life. In the incarnation the only begotten Son becomes the first-born of many brothers and sisters, who find the Father through his brotherhood, so becoming free to deliver enslaved creation.

Through the incarnation of the Son *the Father* acquires a twofold counterpart for his love: his Son and his image. In this he experiences a twofold response to his love: the response of the Son, which is self-evident – a matter of course – and the free response of the image; the unique response of the Son, and the multifarious response of the Son's brothers and sisters. This means an increase of his riches and his bliss.

In his character as ikon, *the Son* becomes the first-born among many brethren. Through this he throws open to his brothers and sisters his relationship of sonship to the Father, gathering them into his divine liberty and into his rule over God's world. In fellowship with the only begotten Son, people become co-opted sons and daughters of the Father.

In the incarnation of the Son *the Trinity* throws itself open, as it were. The Father of the Son becomes the Father of the new, free and united human race. Through the brotherhood of the Son God's children enter into the trinitarian relations of the Son, the Father and the Spirit. As people in the world, they simultaneously exist 'in God' and 'God in them'.

§4 THE TRANSFIGURATION OF THE SPIRIT

In this section too we shall only be dealing with those pneumato-logical questions that touch on the concept of God. But for this some basic concepts which have a bearing on the understanding of the Holy Spirit and his activity have to be clarified.

1. The Resurrection and the Outpouring of the Spirit

According to the gospels, before Easter the activity of the Spirit was apparently confined exclusively to Jesus.[38] He preaches and acts in the power of the Spirit, but the Spirit is not transferred to the disciples. They only receive the divine Spirit after Easter, and because of Easter. That is why John 7.39 says: 'For as yet the Spirit had not been given, because Jesus was not yet glorified.' This is also reflected in the history of baptism. Up to Easter Jesus was the only one in the whole circle of the disciples who had been baptized. But after Easter the disciples baptized all believers. Baptism takes place in the divine Spirit. It presupposes his presence: in the case of Jesus, in his own person; after his resurrection, in the community of believers.

The resurrection of the crucified Jesus precedes the general out-pouring of the Spirit. On this date the eschatological era begins. According to Luke, the pentecostal event (Acts 2) fulfils the Joel promise in salvation history. Paul expounded this in a detailed christological interpretation. Jesus was raised 'through the Spirit' (Rom. 8.11). The Spirit is the divine power that gives life to the dead (I Cor. 6.14). He is the divine energy of the new creation. If Jesus is raised through the Spirit, then he is obviously raised *in* the Spirit. As the second Adam, the risen One becomes the life-giving Spirit (I Cor. 15.45). This makes the identifying formula possible: 'The Lord is the Spirit' (II Cor. 3.17). This identification provides the justification for the phrase according to which Jesus, from being an object of the Spirit's activity, becomes the subject of the sending of the Spirit on to the church. In sending the disciples out into the world with the mission of his Father, the risen Christ gives them the Holy Spirit (John 20.21f.). It is through the risen Christ that God pours out the Holy Spirit (Titus 3.5f.).

It is on the strength of this that the New Testament calls the Spirit *the Spirit of God* (Rom. 8.9,11,14; I Cor. 2.11,14). He 'proceeds from the Father', 'comes from the Father', 'is sent by the Father' (John 15.26; 14.26; I John 4.1).[39] But he is also called '*the Spirit of Christ*', '*the Spirit of the Lord*', or '*the Spirit of his Son*' (Phil. 1.19; II Cor. 3.17; Gal. 4.6). In considering the eschatological event of Christ's resurrection and the experience of the Spirit we therefore have to talk about the Holy Spirit in trinitarian terms. In this context, however, this does not as yet say anything about the character of the Spirit. If he is linked with the Father as subject, or with the Son as subject, then this can also mean the strength, the power, the energy which proceeds from God or from Christ.

If the resurrection of Christ from the dead is the Spirit's first eschatological 'work', how then are we to understand Christ's *resurrection*? Christ is raised from the dead into God's eternal life. That is what is meant by the word resurrection. But it also means at the same time the *transfiguration* of the humiliated and crucified Jesus into the glory of God.[40] Transfiguration means both a glorifying and a transformation.

The story of the transfiguration in the synoptic gospels (Mark 9.2–9; Matt. 17.1–9; Luke 9.28–36) describes what is meant by the word. The story of what happened on the mountain is to be understood as something that anticipates the disciples' Easter experience. The glorification of Jesus in the eternal presence of God is told in the form of a theophany. His form begins to shine in a supernatural light.

Paul tells us what is meant by transformation in Philippians 3.21, when he says that 'our lowly body will be like his (Christ's) glorious body'. What is meant is a change in the body's *form*: a change from the form of humility, marked by sin and death, to the form of glory, liberated from sin and death, marked by the inexhaustible, creative livingness of God. Resurrection is therefore either to be understood as Christ's bodily metamorphosis, or it is not understandable at all. The Old Testament idea of the resurrection of the dead already resists every form of spiritualizing reinterpretation. The eschatological 'work' of the Holy Spirit is physical resurrection, physical transfiguration, and transformation of the physical form of existence. It is from the transfigured humanity of the risen Christ that the Holy Spirit proceeds. It is through this that the Spirit is mediated. The One who is physically transfigured, transfigures physically, as the first-born, his brothers and sisters, who are made in the same form as himself.

The expression *glorification* is also used for Christ's resurrection, by John especially: the raising of Jesus from the dead is his glorification in a twofold way. He is exalted to be Lord of the dawning *kingdom* of God; and he is transfigured into the Lord of the coming *glory* of God (I Cor. 2.8). The coming glory of God therefore already shines on the face of Christ, lighting up the hearts of men and women, as the light shone in darkness on the first day of creation (II Cor. 4.6). God the Father glorifies Christ the Son through his resurrection, while the Son glorifies the Father through his obedience and his self-surrender. The event of their mutual glorification is the work of the Holy Spirit.

2. The Beginning of Glory

With Jesus' resurrection, transfiguration, transformation and glorification, the general *outpouring of the Holy Spirit* 'on all flesh' begins. This experience was, and is, interpreted eschatologically by Christians. The Spirit is merely the special 'first fruits' (Rom. 8.23) and the assuring 'earnest' or 'guarantee' (II Cor. 1.22) of the coming glory which fills the universe. In the Spirit people already experience now what is still to come. In the Spirit is anticipated what will be in the future. With the Spirit the End-time begins. *The messianic era* commences where the forces and energies of the divine Spirit descend on all flesh, making it alive for evermore. In the activity of the Spirit, consequently, the renewal of life, the new obedience and the new fellowship of men and women is experienced. The marks of the eschatological experience of the Spirit are boundless freedom, exhuberant joy and inexhaustible love. In the Spirit the 'new song' is sung.

The experience of the Spirit does not separate those affected by it from 'the rest of the world'.[41] On the contrary, their experience brings them into open solidarity with it. For what they experience is – *pars pro toto* – the beginning of the world's future. The experience of the Spirit is the presence of the Spirit in full and complete form. But this presence of the Spirit is the presence of future glory, which fulfils the times; it is not the presence of eternity, which obliterates time altogether. That is why this experience does not snatch people out of time but makes them open for time's future.

Finally, the experience of the *Holy* Spirit, as distinct from human forms of spiritualization and sublimation, is always a physical experience. This experience is the beginning of 'the resurrection of the body' (Rom. 8.23), which is the direct opposite of the body's repression or exploitation.[42] The experience of the Spirit sets the person who is touched by it in a beginning event which is open for the coming liberty of the whole creation, and is therefore still incomplete. The experience of the Spirit begins the completion and perfecting of the creation of human beings and all things, which makes them the home of the triune God. In *the indwelling of the Spirit*, whether it be in the heart, in the community of believers, or in the new creation, God always comes to be at home in his own world.

3. The Spirit as Subject

Is the Holy Spirit to be understood as an energy of God the Father and the Son (which means dynamistically), or as a divine person, like the Father and the Son?

It is possible to establish exegetically that 'in Paul every approach to a personalization of the Spirit is lacking', whereas in the Johannine writings the ground is slowly being prepared for the notion of the Holy Spirit as a person.[43] But whether we ought to interpret the Holy Spirit in a dynamistic or a personalistic sense is not a question of ideas about his nature which have already been formed, or still have to be formed. It is a question of what necessarily has to be said about his activity. Whether it is termed *the Spirit of God* or *the Spirit of Christ*, what is meant is an energy or power whose subject is God or Christ. Are there also statements which suggest that we ought to assume that the Holy Spirit is the independent subject of his own acts? Is the Holy Spirit the subject of acts affecting the Son and the Father? For it is only in this sense that it would be justifiable to call the Holy Spirit a divine person.

What we have just described as being the eschatological work of the Holy Spirit has not merely this aspect of liberating and perfecting the world so that it may become God's home. It has another aspect too: Jesus' glorification as Lord, and the glorification of the Father through him (Phil. 2.10–11). By renewing men and women, by bringing about their new solidarity and fellowship, and by delivering the body from death, the Holy Spirit glorifies the risen Lord and, through him, the Father.[44] This glorification of the Father through the Son in the Spirit is the consummation of creation. It expresses its perfect joy in eternal rejoicing – 'to him be glory for ever and ever' (Rev. 1.6). This is *the eternal feast* of heaven and earth with God, which makes creation's joy complete. The Holy Spirit glorifies Jesus the Son and through him God the Father. It does so through the people and things which it lays hold of, transforms and transfigures. People and things are therefore gathered into the trinitarian glorification of the Son and the Father through the Spirit. In this way they are also united with God and in God himself.

If the glorification of the Son and the Father proceeds actively from the Spirit, then *the union of God* also proceeds from him. This means the union of the Son with the Father, and of the Father with the Son. But it also means the union of men and women with God and their union in God (John 17.21).

The Spirit is *the glorifying God*. The Spirit is *the unifying God*. In this respect the Spirit is not an energy proceeding from the Father or from the Son; it is a subject from whose activity the Son and the Father receive their glory and their union, as well as their glorification through the whole creation, and their world as their eternal home. If the Holy Spirit means *the subject* who glorifies the Father and the Son, and unites the Father and the Son, then the 'exegetical question' should be capable of solution as well; for in this respect Paul too in fact understands the Holy Spirit as the centre of the act, which is to say as 'person'.

4. Trinitarian Glorification

What form of the Trinity is manifested in the activity of the Holy Spirit? A twofold trinitarian order is perceptible here:

(a) In the outpouring of the Spirit upon men and women, the Spirit comes *from the Father through the Son*. Consequently he is called *the Spirit of God* and *the Spirit of Christ, the Spirit of the Father* and *the Spirit of his Son*. The Spirit proceeds from the

Father. The Father sends him. The Son begs for the sending of the Spirit. He mediates the Spirit. He moulds it into the Spirit of sonship. At this point we do not as yet need to go into the dogmatic problem about 'Son and Spirit'. It is sufficient to perceive the trinitarian structures in the biblical testimony, in which the coming and efficacy of the Holy Spirit is understood and witnessed to. The difference between the Father and the Son, and the fellowship between them, also shapes the interpretation of the Spirit's activity.

(*b*) In *glorification* through the Spirit, however, we find the order of the Trinity reversed. In the wake of glorification, the song of praise and the unity proceed *from the Spirit through the Son to the Father*. Here all the activity proceeds from the Spirit. He is the maker of the new creation. He achieves the glorification of God through the new creation's praise and testimony. He creates for the Father in heaven that joy on earth which finally gives him bliss. It is through the Spirit that the Father receives his honour and his glory, and his union with the world. We have 'access to the Father' (Eph. 2.18) through Christ in the Spirit.[45]

If we want to describe in pictorial terms the two orders of the Trinity which are to be found in the biblical testimony, we can say: In *the first order* the divine Trinity throws itself open in the sending of the Spirit. It is open for the world, open for time, open for the renewal and unification of the whole creation. In *the second order* the movement is reversed: in the transfiguration of the world through the Spirit all men turn to God and, moved by the Spirit, come to the Father through Christ the Son. In the glorification of the Spirit, world and times, people and things are gathered to the Father in order to become *his world*.

The trinitarian movement of the sending of the Spirit from the Father through the Son may still be viewed as a 'work outwards' although it too is preceded by inner changes in the divine Trinity – changes from which this movement arises.[46] But the trinitarian movement of the gathering of the Spirit through the Son to the Father is a work 'inwards', a movement of the Trinity; by virtue of the opening of the Trinity in the sending of the Spirit, however, it is a movement into which the whole creation is gathered. All things are assembled under the head, Christ, and all tongues will confess him Lord – to the glory of the Father. All people and things then partake of the 'inner-trinitarian life' of God. They join in the responding love of the Son and will thereby become the joy of the

V

The Mystery of the Trinity

§1 A CRITICISM OF CHRISTIAN MONOTHEISM

1. *Monotheism and Monarchy*

The patristic doctrine of the Trinity does not originate in an absorption of the philosophical doctrine of the Logos, and of neo-Platonic triadologies, as has often been maintained. Its source is to be found in the New Testament witness to the trinitarian history of the Son, and in the church's practice of baptism in the name of the triune God.

The early church's doctrine of the Trinity took on form during its resistance against dangerous heresies, in which the unity of Christ with God was called in question, either on God's behalf or on Christ's. It was only in these controversies that trinitarian dogma grew up; and with the dogma grew its formulation, as philosphical terminology was given a new theological mould.

The necessary resistance against Arianism on the one hand, and the laborious surmounting of Sabellianism on the other, led to the development of an explicit doctrine of the Trinity. Both heresies are christological in nature. Consequently the dogma of the Trinity was evolved out of christology. It is designed to preserve faith in Christ, the Son of God, and to direct the Christian hope towards full salvation in the divine fellowship. The doctrine of the Trinity cannot therefore be termed 'a speculation'. On the contrary, it is the theological premise for christology and soteriology.

The heresies which forced the church to formulate the doctrine of the Trinity in its early centuries, are by no means historically fortuitous and a thing of the past. They are permanent dangers to

Christian theology.[1] The deviations which are called by the names
of Arius and Sabellius are continually among us theologically.
Consequently it is useful to repeat the fundamental decisions of the
early creeds, in spite of all the hermeneutical differences which we
today, rightly, feel and perceive. These heresies have to be treated
typologically and systematically, not merely historically.[2]

The Second Epistle of Clement (1.1) already puts its finger on
the fundamental problem when it demands that Christians think
about Jesus 'as they do about God' (ὡς περὶ θεοῦ). The reason
it gives is a soteriological one: 'For if we think any less of him than
this, then we expect but little of him.' Even externally, the adoration of Christ as God must be clearly recognizable. Pliny the
Younger reported to Rome in the first century that the Christians
in Bithynia praised Christ in their worship as if he were God (*quasi
Deo*). Ignatius of Antioch called Christ God without any differentiation at all, even though he generally added 'my' God or 'our'
God, which permits the distinction compared with 'God *per se*'. It
is here that the theological problem arises.

What is the relationship between Christ and God, and how is
the divine revelation in Christ related to God himself? How is the
differentiable relationship of Christ to God the Father related to
the unity of God himself? And how is the adoration of Christ as
God reconcilable with God's unity?

These questions became all the more important because, from
the time of the Christian apologists onwards, Christians won over
the educated in the Roman Empire by proclaiming the One God:
'ΕΙΣ ΘΕΟΣ'. It was the acceptance of philosphical monotheism
and the idea of the universal monarchy of the one God that made
Christianity a 'world religion', and that got over Christianity's
appearance of being a Jewish messianic sect, or a private religion.
But monotheism and monarchianism are only the names for two
sides of the same thing: the One is the principle and point of
integration for the Many. The One is the measure of the Many.
The One God has always been appealed to and comprehended in
the context of the unity of the world.

The expression μοναρχία is a curious hellenistic word-forma-
tion, deriving from μόνας and μία ἀρχή. It was most probably
in Alexandria that the divine *monas* – a pythagorean numerical
term – was linked together with ἀρχή to make up the word
μοναρχία. Erik Peterson has shown that it was the doctrine of the

universal monarchy of the One God which moulded Philo's hellenistic re-formation of Jewish belief: 'The God of the Jews was fused
with the monarchical concept of Greek philosophy.'[4] Among the
Christian apologists Justin, Tatian and the church Father Tertullian, this concept therefore replaces the biblical term βασιλεία and
is used for the lordship of God (Justin), the monarchical constitution of the universe (Tatian), or the singular and unique divine rule
or empire (Tertullian).[5]

Let me point out at once here that this monotheistic monarchianism was, and is, an uncommonly seductive religious-political
ideology. It is the fundamental notion behind the universal and
uniform religion: One God – one Logos – one humanity; and in
the Roman empire it was bound to seem a persuasive solution for
many problems of a multi-national and multi-religious society. The
universal ruler in Rome had only to be the image and correspondence of the universal ruler in heaven.

Both the acceptance of the fundamental monotheistic monarchical idea and its conquest through the doctrine of the Trinity must
be counted among the great theological achievements of the early
church; and this is true, not merely in the sphere of the doctrine
of faith, but in the realm of political theology as well. For monotheism was, and is, always a 'political problem' too.[6]

Strict monotheism has to be theocratically conceived and implemented, as Islam proves. But once it is introduced into the doctrine
and worship of the Christian church, faith in Christ is threatened:
Christ must either recede into the series of the prophets, giving
way to the One God, or he must disappear into the One God as
one of his manifestations. The strict notion of the One God really
makes theological christology impossible, for the One can neither
be parted nor imparted. It is ineffable.[7] The Christian church was
therefore right to see monotheism as the severest inner danger,
even though it tried on the other hand to take over the monarchical
notion of the divine lordship.

Strict monotheism obliges us to think of God without Christ,
and consequently to think of Christ without God as well. The
questions whether God exists and how one can be a Christian then
become two unrelated questions. But if on the other hand trinitarian dogma maintains the unity of essence between Christ and God,
then not only is Christ understood in divine terms; God is also
understood in Christian ones. The intention and consequence of

the doctrine of the Trinity is not only the deification of Christ; it is even more the Christianization of the concept of God. God cannot be comprehended without Christ, and Christ cannot be understood without God. If we are to perceive this, we not only have to reject the Arian heresy; the Sabellian heresy must be dismissed with equal emphasis.

2. Monotheistic Christianity: Arius

The first possible way of abandoning Christ's divinity in favour of the One God can be found in what is known as *subordinationism.* The doctrine of Jesus' divinity grew up out of the biblical testimony to Jesus' sonship, and out of the Johannine doctrine of the Logos. The alternative, on the other hand, has its roots in early Christian *Spirit christology.*[8] According to this pneumatological christology, it was not the eternal Son of the Father who in Jesus became man; it was the divine Spirit, who took up his dwelling in him. That is to say, Jesus taught and ministered as a man imbued with the Spirit. His power was the power of the divine Spirit. Through the power of the Spirit he led a perfect life which provides an authoritative model for all believers. This can be termed dynamistic subordinationism. It sets Jesus among the prophets, even if as the last and most perfect of them. Spirit christology dominates *adoptionist subordinationism* as well. According to this, Jesus was adopted as Son of God through the Spirit, so that he might become the first-born among many brethren. The strength of these christologies lies in the fact that they bring out the force of the Spirit as subject in Jesus' life and ministry. Their weakness is that, for the sake of the One God, they are unable to bring Jesus into any essential unity with the Father. This means that although they can find in him the foundation for a new morality, they cannot arouse any hope for full fellowship with God through him. The confession of faith in Christ does not burst apart the concept of the One God. Consequently Christ has to be subordinated to this One God.

Paul of Samosata went a step further. He took up the doctrine of the Logos, which had meanwhile become prevalent, but interpreted the divine Logos as an attribute of the One God. God is one and has only one visage. Consequently Jesus cannot be God himself, but only the manifestation of one of God's attributes, an attribute which is called Wisdom, Spirit or Logos. This is the inner power in which Jesus led a sinless and hence exemplary life. Jesus was essentially perfect and a model for us, precisely because he subordinated himself to the one God.[9]

Arius, a pupil of Lucian of Antioch, then became the advocate of subordinationism in its fullest form. He too starts from the idea of the One God. He thinks of God as the simple, supreme substance which, by virtue of its indivisible unity, also represents the ground of all being. The One is the cause of the many and their measure, but it is not caused itself. The One God is therefore the causeless Cause of all things. But because the One is indivisible, it is also ineffable. The One God is by definition 'incommunicable'.[10] Consequently, for the fellowship of God and all things, there has to be a mediation through intermediaries. Arius called the mediating intermediary between the One God and the manifold world 'Son' (in terms of Christian tradition) and (in philosophical terminology) 'Logos'. He is the creation of the One God, but the first, and hence the created being who is prototypical for all others. If he occupies this first mediating position, then he must himself, like all created beings, be alterable, mutable and temporal. If he were not, he could neither form the world nor rule over it. Arius can only see 'the Son' as 'the first-born of creation', not as the only begotten Son of the Father, because he feels compelled to adhere to the unity of the One God.

This first-born of all creation, God's Wisdom and Reason, has appeared in Jesus. Consequently Jesus can be called the first-born Son, but not the only begotten Son. Arianism's greatness lay in the way it brought Jesus and the divinity manifested in him as close as possible to the One God, yet without destroying God's undivided unity. Its monarchianism took the form: One God – one Logos – one world – one world monarchy. Its christology of the first-born Son permitted only this graduated succession of being and authority.

Arianism is monotheistic Christianity in its purest form. Its mediator christology admittedly moves Christ into the sphere of mythical intermediaries. At the same time, it is impossible to talk about a 'created' or 'semi-divine' God, which was what Harnack complained of.[11] It is rather a question of a universal 'prototype christology'. A christology of this kind cannot provide any foundation for the redemption that makes full fellowship with God possible;

it can only offer the basis for a new morality, for which Jesus' life provides the pattern and standard.

It was with difficulty, and only with the help of Constantine's imperial authority, that the Council of Nicaea was able to comdemn Arianism in 325, and that it was able to win acceptance for (and establish as dogma) the complete unity of nature between Jesus Christ 'the only begotten Son', and the Father. 'The only-begotten Son of God' (μονογενής) is 'God of God, light of light, very God of very God, begotten not made, being of one substance with the Father'. But this thesis of the *homousios* cast up a whole series of new problems.

What is the relation between the only begotten Son of the Father and the first-born of creation?

If Jesus, the only begotten Son, is 'of one substance' with God the Father, how are we to understand God's unity?

If the Father is 'of one substance' with the only begotten Son, how are we to interpret the sovereignty of God?

If the *homousios* does not merely identify Christ with God, but identifies God with Christ as well, then the divine unity can no longer be interpreted monadically. It has to be understood in trinitarian terms. But that leads to fundamental changes in the doctrine of God, in christology and in politics. Christian faith can then no longer be called 'monotheistic' in the sense of the One God. God's sovereignty can then no longer be understood as the 'universal monarchy' to which everything is subjected. It has to be interpreted and presented as the redeeming history of freedom.

3. Christian Monotheism: Sabellius

The other form of Christian monotheism is to be found in *modalism*.[12] It is often viewed as the other extreme from subordination-ism and its precise opposite; but in fact it is only the reverse side of the same thing. For modalism too is dominated by the basic idea of the One God and of the universal monarchy, which can be exercised only by this one subject. Of course the method of safe-guarding this undivided unity of God's is a different one: Christ is no longer subordinated to the one God; he is dissolved, dissipated in that one God.

'We must think about Jesus Christ as we do about God', the Second Epistle of Clement demands. This is modalism's starting point: Jesus Christ is God, he is our God. This was undoubtedly the belief of the early Christian community. But theologically it gives rise to a problem: if Christ is our God, then the Father and the Son must be, not merely *one* but in fact *one and the same*. The One God is then called Father, inasmuch as he makes himself the subject of his revelation. He is then called 'Son' and 'Holy Spirit', inasmuch as he becomes the object and power of his own revelation.

An early form of maintaining God's simple unity in this way can be found in Syrian patripassianism: 'The Father himself appeared in the flesh by making himself the Son; he himself suffered; he himself died; he himself raised himself.'[13] According to this thesis, the history of Christ can have only *one* subject. It is the One God who appears to us *as* Father, *as* Son and *as* Spirit. The *trias* only comes into being in the revelation of the *monas*.

In the Christian community modalistic piety was, and is, often supported by bishops who think that they are standing on the sure ground of the church when they declare that Christ is God. In Rome this was apparently the church's official teaching in the second century. It was only the theological polemic of Hippolytus against Noetus, and Tertullian's struggle against Praxeas, which showed the dangers inherent in this view and which made it obvious that it was in fact a heresy.[14]

It was Sabellius who gave modalism its theological formulation, and it was he who later gave his name to this whole trend.[15] The basic ideas are not at all complicated. In the history of his revelation and his communication of salvation, the One God takes on three forms: in the form of the Father he appears to us as the *creator* and law-giver; in the form of the Son he appears as the *redeemer*; in the form of the Holy Spirit he appears as the *giver of life*. Father, Son and Spirit are the three manifestations or modes of appearance of the One God. But this One God himself is as unknowable, unnamable and ineffable as the 'One' itself.

Sabellius called the three modes of appearance of the One God not merely manifestations, but also ἰδία/περιγραφή, that is to say, 'something in God, something indwelling in him'. The One God therefore does not merely appear to us in a threefold manner: in salvation history he *is* actually threefold to a certain degree, in so far as he is 'the indweller' of his own manifestations and, through them, dwells in the world. Sabellius distinguishes between the One God and his indwellings. The One God himself is without distinction, incommunicable and hence unknowable. But he allows himself to be known in history in the indwellings which are known by the three names. Sabellius even succeeds in thinking of God's monadic unity, not rigidly but (with the help of Stoic terms) as containing movement. It can expand itself and contract, develop and gather together.[16] Of course, as Marcellus of Ancyra critically added, this does not mean expanding the divine being; it means expansion of the divine will and activity. This already indicates that the One God is not merely to be thought of as monadic substance but at the same time as identical subject as well.[17]

Sabellius and Marcellus reduced the one God and the Christian Trinity to a common denominator in what seems at first sight to be a quite convincing way. The One God is the eternal, uncompounded, undivided light whose rays are refracted in different ways, according to receptivity, in the world of men and women. But if the One God only appears *as* Father, *as* Son and *as* Spirit, then this phraseology already indicates the 'unreal' nature of the manifestations. Who or what the One God himself is cannot be perceived, because it cannot be communicated. Consequently the recognition of the manifestations of God *as* . . . cannot communicate any fellowship with *God himself* either.

This modalism is only seemingly a theology of Christ's divinity. In actual fact it leads to the dissolution of Christ's divinity in the ineffable and incommunicable Oneness of the Godhead *per se*. The statement that 'Christ is God' ultimately makes Christ disappear in the One God. Conversely, the manifestation of the One God as Christ is condemned to unreality. In this way too the intellectual compulsions of monotheistic thinking prevail. Monotheism is common to both Sabellianism and Arianism. But whereas throughout the history of the church Arianism was always tainted with 'liberalism' and heresy, Sabellian modalism was at times established church doctrine; and whether it has really been overcome even now is the question which the Eastern church still puts to the whole trinitarian doctrine of the churches of the West.

In modern times, the theology of Friedrich Schleiermacher shows how closely these two extremes converge.[18] His christology of the productive prototype or model certainly absorbed Arian elements, as his concept of the first-born Son shows. But his doctrine of God displays Sabellian features, as can be seen from the pamphlet in which he pays tribute to the Sabellian doctrine of the Trinity compared with the Athanasian one. For 'the father of modern Protestantism', Jesus counted as being God's Son because he was the first-born, prototypical and pattern man of God. In the wake of his rehabilitation of the elements of truth in Sabellianism, Schleiermacher arrived at the recognition 'that the highest Being, as He really is, apart from this Trinity – *the monas* – would also be entirely contained within himself and totally unknown to all others; but that this could only be so provided there were nothing outside Him.'[19] Even in Schleiermacher the compulsion inherent in the concept of the One God prevails: subordinationism in his christology and modalism in his trinitarian doctrine are the results.

4. The Foundation of the Doctrine of the Trinity: Tertullian

With his treatise against Praxeas (*c.* 215) Tertullian counts as being the initiator of a trinitarian solution of the problems in the Christian doctrine of God which were thrown up by subordinationism and modalism. The Fathers learnt from Tertullian, even if they did not mention his name. He perceived the problems more clearly than anyone before him, and the brilliance of his language and his skill in definition made new answers possible. Through him the theological discussion moved on to a new level. Admittedly new questions cropped up on this level too.[20]

For Tertullian, God is from all eternity One, but not alone. His Reason (*logis, ratio*) or Wisdom (*sophia, sermo*) must be called equally eternal. The One God is in reality not a numerical or monadic One, but a unity which is differentiated in itself. The Logos proceeds from God through the act of eternal *generatio*, thereby becoming 'the Son'. Tertullian interprets this process as *prolatio*, in order to be able to say that the Son and the Father are *distincti* but not *divisi*, *discreti* but not *separati*. They are distinguished in their divine unity and are hence in their distinction one. The third to issue forth is the Holy Spirit. The Father sends him through the Son, and he is bound to the Father and the Son through the unity of the divine substance. In order to make this differentiated unity clear, Tertullian draws on gnostic and neo-Platonic images such as sun – ray – reflection; or source – brook – river. The images are used to describe distinguishable individualities of the same matter. The monarchy of God is not abolished through this trinitarian differentiation, for the Son and the Spirit are subordinated to the Father. The Father is at the same time the whole divine substance. As *portiones totius* the Son and the Spirit have their being from him, and they carry out his will. When the work of the world's redemption and perfecting has been fulfilled, they will give back their authority to the Father.

The remarkable features of this initial outline are:

1. The trinitarian differentiation of the divine *monas: una substantia – tres personae;*

2. The distinctions in the unity: *distincti, non divisi; discreti, non separati;*

3. The new verbal coinage *trinitas*, which now takes the place of the divine *monas*.

But Tertullian was only able to develop these trinitarian differentiations in God because he replaced the $\theta\varepsilon\grave{o}\varsigma\ \dot{\varepsilon}\sigma\tau\grave{\iota}\nu\ \varepsilon\check{\iota}\varsigma$ by $\theta\varepsilon\grave{o}\varsigma\ \dot{\varepsilon}\sigma\tau\grave{\iota}\nu\ \check{\varepsilon}\nu$. Yet if God is *one*, and not one-and-the-same, who exercises the monarchy? The Father: for the Father is at the same time the total substance; the Son is a derivation and the Spirit is a part of him. But are the trinitarian differentiations then not after all merely modes of manifestation of the One God in the work of redemption? Tertullian tried to fend off this conclusion by distinguishing between monarchy and economy. The monarchy of the Father belongs within the divine Trinity itself, and it must be distinguished from the dispensation of salvation (economy) in creation. The Son is begotten, the world is created. The Holy Spirit goes forth, the world is redeemed.

Yet the line which Tertullian draws between the immanent and the economic Trinity is a fluid one, for if the Son and the Spirit proceed from the Father for the purpose of creating the world and for the work of redemption, then they must also return into the Oneness of the Father when these purposes are fulfilled, so that 'God may be all in all'.

The original One would then only differentiate itself in a trinitarian sense, in order to complete and perfect itself into the All-One. But that would mean that God is only to be thought of in trinitarian terms where his creative and redemptive self-communication is concerned, and not for his own sake. In these ideas the category of unity after all prevails over the triunity once more. This proves that it is not merely the concept of the *monas* which is the basic problem of the Christian concept of God. It is the concept of *monarchia* too. If these terms are not differentiated and altered, a Christian doctrine of God is not really possible.

5. Trinitarian Monarchy: Karl Barth

As we said in Chapter I, under the conditions of modern European times God is no longer thought of as supreme substance. He now counts as absolute subject. Consequently, ever since German Idealism the divine *monas* has been interpreted as the absolute, *identical subject*. God is the subject of his own being and his own revelation. The concept of God's 'self-revelation' pushes out earlier ideas about mediations that reveal God; and the notion of God's 'self-communication' now becomes the quintessence of the Christian doctrine of salvation.

The primordial image of the 'absolute subject' in heaven corresponds to the modern perception of human subjectivity as regards nature and history; and the personal God in eternity corresponds to the bourgeois culture of personality. It is the absolute personality of God that makes man a person. Out of the eternal divine Thou, man receives his personal ego and becomes the subject who is superior to the world. For these historical reasons it is quite understandable that the early church's trinitarian formula: *una substantia – tres personae* should now be replaced by the formula: one divine subject in three different modes of being.[21] The modern bourgeois concept of personality and subject seems to make traditional talk about the three Persons of the Trinity impossible. But if the subjectivity of acting and receiving is transferred from the three divine Persons to the one divine subject, then the three Persons are bound to be degraded to modes of being, or modes of subsistence, of the one identical subject. But viewed theologically this is a late triumph for the Sabellian modalism which the early church condemned. The result would be to transfer the subjectivity of action to a deity concealed 'behind' the three Persons. And the consequences of this would be a monotheism only fortuitously connected with Christianity in any way, a general transcendentality and a vague human religiosity which would simply swallow up the particular identity of the Christian faith. These are certainly only dangers if these ideas are taken to their ultimate conclusion. But the germs are already present whenever idealistic modalism penetrates the Christian doctrine of the Trinity, threatening to disperse the three distinct persons and subjects of 'the history of the Son' in favour of 'the One God'. Consequently we must be alive to these tendencies in even the best contemporary theologies.

It is of decisive importance for the doctrine of God whether we start from the Trinity in order to understand the sovereignty of God as the sovereignty of the Father, the Son and the Spirit, or whether we think in the reverse direction, proceeding from the sovereignty of God in order to secure this as being the sovereignty of the One God by means of the doctrine of the Trinity. If we start from the sovereignty of God, then our premise is God as the identical subject of his rule. The doctrine of the Trinity can then only be presented as 'Christian monotheism'.[22] It is nothing other than a development of the recognition that God is Lord. This was the starting point Karl Barth chose, both in *Christlichen Dogmatik im Entwurf* (1927), §9 and in *Church Dogmatics* (1932; ET 1936), §8. A comparison of the two indicates the original problems of Barth's trinitarian doctrine.

In 1927 Barth developed the doctrine of the Trinity out of the logic of the concept of God's self-revelation. Consequently his guiding principle is: 'God's word is God in his revelation. God reveals himself as the Lord. He alone is the revealer. He is wholly revelation. He himself is what is revealed.'[23] With this answer to the logical questions about the subject, predicate and object of the statement 'God has spoken, Deus dixit' Barth believed that he was entering upon 'the whole field of the doctrine of the Trinity'.[24] 'God's revelation is God's word without any foundation in an Other. It is God's speech grounded in itself.'[25] God's revelation is 'the revelation of his rule . . . *over against* men, *in* men, *over* men, *for* men.'[26] In order to justify the absolute sovereignty of revelation and lordship as God's self-revelations and his own lordship, Barth employs the doctrine of the Trinity. It is to this, therefore, that man's 'absolute dependency' corresponds. The idea of self-revelation secures the 'autousia' the 'subjectivity of God'.[27] Consequently, according to Barth the doctrine of the Trinity has to be the 'assertion and emphasizing of the notion of the strict and absolute unity of God.' What unity is meant? 'The one divine I or subject, which reveals in revelation the triuneness of his Godhead, his rule, his divine I-ness or subjectivity.'[28] As this string of interchangeable terms shows, according to Barth the lordship of God precedes the Trinity, logically speaking. He defines God's essence as being God's sovereignty. The revelation of God's sovereignty is nothing other than the assertion of his divine subjectivity or 'I-ness', i.e., God's 'personality'. 'The *Deus unus trius*, the one personal God who is the threefold personal God who can never become an object to the thought directed towards him.'[29] This last sentence shows Barth's particular interest in the doctrine of the Trinity especially clearly. He is interested in it for the sake of securing the sovereignty of God – and in order to ward off the danger of the objectification of God by human beings.

In 1932 as well, in §8 of the *Church Dogmatics*, Barth clings to this 'The Root of the Doctrine of the Trinity' in the concept of revelation and sovereignty.[30] But where earlier he thought he could develop the Trinity out of the logic of the concept of revelation, and therefore began with God the revealer, he now begins with 'the concrete form of (biblical) revelation', with God the Son, the Godhead Jesus Christ.[31] Consequently he arrives at the curious sequence 'unveiling, veiling and impartation' in the biblical testimony of revelation: Easter, Good Friday, Pentecost, or the figure of the Son, the Father and the Spirit.[32]

Barth equates the sovereignty of God with the concept of God's nature, and makes the latter the equivalent of God's divinity. This equation then also includes 'what we to-day call the "personality" of God'.[33] But if all these terms are used for the sovereign subject of the divine lordship and revelation, then it is impossible to go on talking about 'three Persons', to whom subjectivity and 'I-ness' would have to be ascribed in relation to the other persons. The only remaining possibility is to talk about 'three modes of being' in God. Barth quotes the neo-scholastic Diekamp approvingly: 'In God as there is one nature so there is . . . one self-consciousness'.[34] In this case 'God is one in three ways of being' means: God is 'the one personal God' in the mode of the Father, in the mode of the Son, in the mode of the Holy Spirit.[35]

Barth holds that the Trinity is a *repetitio aeternitatis in aeternitate*, and believes that he can reconstruct this by means of a shift of emphasis in the statement: '*God* reveals *himself* as the *Lord*.' But to understand God's threefold nature as eternal repetition or as holy tautology does not yet mean thinking in trinitarian terms. The doctrine of the Trinity cannot be a matter of establishing the same thing three times. To view the three Persons merely as a triple repetition of one and the same God would be somewhat empty and futile.[36]

Barth's Idealist heritage finally betrays itself in the use of the reflection structure to secure God's subjectivity, sovereignty, selfhood and personality. Thus Fichte talked about 'being', about 'the existence of being' and about 'the bond of love' or of reflection, which permits the two to be one.[37] If instead of thinking of God deistically as substance, we think of him theistically as subject, then this triadic process of reflection is intellectually necessary. It is through self-distinction and self-recollection that God shows himself to be the absolute subject. That is the reflection structure of absolute subjectivity. A reflection of subjectivity like this has not necessarily anything whatsoever to do with the biblical testimony to the history of God. The notion of God's reflexively differentiated subjectivity and self-revelation can be conceived even without any biblical reference at all.[38] Consequently Barth's new approach in the *Church Dogmatics* in 1932 is understandable. It was necessary. Christian belief must begin, not with the God who reveals himself, the Father, but with the concrete and specific revelation, the Son, the Godhead Jesus Christ. But this idea of the revelation of the God who reveals himself was developed out of that reflection logic. Consequently in the *Church Dogmatics* the same problems crop up again. They are the problems of pneumatology.

The God who reveals himself in three modes of being can no longer display subjectivity in his state-of-revelation, the Holy Spirit. The Spirit is merely the common bond of love linking the Father with the Son. He is 'the power that joins the Father and the Son'.[39] But this bond is already given with the relationship of the Father to his beloved Son and vice versa. The Father and the Son are already one in their relationship to one another, the relationship of eternal generation and eternal self-giving. In order to think of their mutual relationship as love, there is no need for a third Person in the Trinity. If the Spirit is only termed the unity of what is separated, then he loses every centre of activity. He is then an energy but not a Person. He is then a relationship but not a subject. Basically, the reflection Trinity of the absolute subject is a duality.[40] It is only when the Holy Spirit is understood as the unity of the difference, and the unity of the Father and the Son, that a personal and active function in the trinitarian relationship can be ascribed to him. Barth then only formally secures the divine person of the

Holy Spirit through the common 'proskynesis' of the Spirit with the Father and the Son.[41] He is not alone in this. Ever since Augustine, whenever the Spirit is merely termed the *vinculum amoris* between the Father and the Son, it is enough to assume a 'duality' in God. The third 'mode of being' does not add anything special and individual to the Revealer and his Revelation. 'That the Father and the Son are the one God is the reason why they are not just united but are united in the Spirit in love; it is the reason, then, why God is love, and love is God.'[42] According to this statement of Barth's, the Spirit is a duplication of the love in which the Father eternally generates the Son and the Son eternally obeys the Father. He is this love itself. But both ideas contradict tradition, which has termed the Holy Spirit the third Person of the Trinity, and not merely the correlation of the two other Persons.

If this approach provides no justification for the Holy Spirit's independent existence as Person in the Trinity, we must ask in return whether in this 'duality' God the Son can really be called Person in the full sense of the word. The principle 'God reveals himself as the Lord' means that all activity proceeds from the Father, both within the Trinity and in history. The Father must in the strict sense be termed God, subject, 'I', the one divine 'personality'. Barth's phrase about 'God in Christ' can in trinitarian terms only mean: the Father in the Son. But in the reflection logic of the absolute subject, the Son is nothing other than the self of the divine 'I', the counterpart, the other, in whom God contemplates himself, finds himself, becomes conscious of himself and manifests himself. No real independent, personal activity can be assumed in God's self in the implementation of the divine sovereignty. We must therefore either ascribe 'the one divine personality' to the Father (as Athanasius did), or, like Sabellius, we must ascribe it to a subject for whom all three trinitarian Persons are objective, even as 'modes of being'. The way of speaking about the three Persons or modes of being *in* God tempts one to the latter assumption. But who, then, should that absolute personality be *in* whom the three modes of being manifest themselves, and who constitutes himself in three modes of being?

The reason for the difficulties Barth gets into here with his acceptance of the Idealistic reflection Trinity of the divine subject, is that he puts the divine lordship before the Trinity and uses the 'doctrine of the Trinity' to secure and interpret the divine subjectivity in that lordship. That is why Barth presents the 'doctrine of the Trinity' as Christian monotheism and argues polemically against a 'tritheism' which has never existed.[43] That is why he uses a non-trinitarian concept of the unity of the one God – that is to say, the concept of the identical subject.

Barth uses the doctrine of the Trinity in order to secure the sovereignty of God in his rule. If he had stopped here, then his theology of the sovereignty of God would only really be an extension of Schleiermacher's anthropology of man's 'absolute dependency'. It is difficult to find in this a justification for human liberty. It is true that by 'lordship' Barth means nothing other than liberty: 'Lordship means freedom.' 'Godhead in the Bible means freedom.'[44] But in Barth's early works it is always only a question of God's liberty, which man has to recognize and welcome as lordship over him himself. It is only in the later volumes of *Church Dogmatics* that the biblical idea of covenant makes it possible for Barth to talk about a partnership, a mutual relationship, even about friendship between God and free man, in which God does not merely speak and decree, but also hears and receives.[45]

6. *Threefold Self-Communication: Karl Rahner*

Karl Rahner developed his doctrine of the Trinity with an astonishing similarity to Barth and almost the same presuppositions.[46] And the conclusions he arrives at are in accordance with this. On the basis of the modern, changed concept of the person, we ought no longer to talk about *una substantia – tres personae*, but about a single divine subject in three 'distinct modes of subsistence'. This thesis is certainly only given its apologetic justification on the basis of the changed consciousness of the modern world; but it leads to a profound alteration in the substance of the Christian doctrine of the Trinity. In order to avoid drawing attention to this, Rahner also conjures up the dangers of a 'vulgar tritheism', which he describes from the outset as 'a much greater danger than Sabellian modalism'.[47] But Sabellian modalism – or, to be more precise, Idealistic modalism – is what Rahner himself is in danger of, like Schleiermacher and Barth.

Rahner claims that the statement about there being three Persons in God almost inevitably evokes the misunderstanding that in God there are three different consciousnesses, spiritualities, centres of activity, and so forth. But it is tritheistic, and therefore wrong, to think of the three Persons of the Trinity as three different 'personalities with different centres of activity'. We therefore have to exclude from the concept of person everything which would mean three 'subjectivities'. Why is this open to misunderstanding and wrong? Because, Rahner maintains, in secular speech today we talk about one 'person' as distinct from another person, and then think 'that in each of these persons, simply so that they can be persons and different from one another, there is an independent, free, self-disposing centre of action in knowledge and freedom, different from others; and that the person is constituted by this very fact.'[48] But in the Christian doctrine of the Trinity a centre of activity defined in this way can only be postulated about 'the one, unique, divine essence'. 'The uniqueness of the essence means and includes the uniqueness of a single consciousness and a single freedom.'[49] In saying this Rahner is only repeating Diekamp's neo-scholastic thesis about the '*one* nature, the *one* cognition, the *one* consciousness' in God, which Barth follows too.

The critical question which has to be asked here is directed towards the modern concept of person. What Rahner calls 'our secular use of the word person' has nothing in common with modern thinking about the concept of person.[50] What he describes is actually extreme individualism: everyone is a self-possessing, self-disposing centre of action which sets itself apart from other persons. But the philosophical personalism of Hölderlin, Feuerbach, Buber, Ebner, Rosenstock and others was designed precisely to overcome this possessive individualism: the 'I' can only be understood in the light of the 'Thou' — that is to say, it is a concept of relation. Without the social relation there can be no personality. What Rahner reads into 'the secular use of the word' is the individual's freedom of disposal, which is determined by property, not the person's social liberty, which is opened up through community. And 'the individual and his property' (Stirner) is a concept that suits neither free men nor God. Ignatius Loyola's *Spiritual Exercises* may inculcate the freedom of the individual who disposes over himself, with the thesis '*anima mea in manibus mea semper*': but this is far from being the modern concept of person; it is that concept's individualistic reduction. Rahner accepts this idea, however, and then, understandably enough, finds that it is not applicable to the three Persons of the Trinity but can only be used for the unique essence and consciousness of God. And in this way he introduces this individualistic idea into the nature of God himself. The 'one unique essence' of God is 'the sameness' of the absolute subject and must hence be understood in an exclusive sense. In order to stress the subjectivity of the 'One' God, who acts towards us 'in a threefold way' Rahner prefers to use the description 'the threefold God' (*Dreifaltigkeit*) instead of the usual 'triune God', the three-in-one (*Dreieinigkeit*). The phrase of his choice is not merely modalistic but also a bad German translation of *trinitas*.

'The one God subsists in three distinct modes of subsistence.'[51] With the phrase 'distinct modes of subsistence' Rahner would like to rehabilitate the truth behind the terms 'hypostasis' and 'person' in the doctrine of the Trinity – a truth which today has become open to misunderstanding. He appeals to Aquinas's definition of person: '*subsistens distinctum in natura rationali*', in order to put aside Boethius' definition: '*Persona est naturae rationalis individua substantia.*' For Boethius *substantia* and *subsistentia* means 'existing in itself and not in another'. Rational nature acquires existence through its person, so that this nature, as predicate of this person, can be stated to be its subject.[52] Boethius's classic definition of person does in fact imply subjectivity, act-centre, 'I-ness' and consciousness. In order to avoid this impression Rahner picks up a definition of person which he ascribes to Aquinas but which Aquinas never used. It derives from the neo-scholasticism of Lonergan, whose book *De Deo Trino* Rahner used.[53]

Is then, according to Rahner, 'mode of subsistence' to be understood non-personally as a mode of actuality without subject, consciousness and will? Because the modes of subsistence within the Trinity do not represent distinct centres of consciousness and action, there cannot be any mutual 'Thou' between them either. 'The Son is the self-utterance of the Father, and must not be conceived as again "uttering", the Spirit is the "gift" which does not, in its turn, again give.'[54] Here again Rahner is citing Lonergan. But if there is no 'Thou' within the Trinity, then there is 'not really any *mutual* love between the Father and the Son within the Trinity either, since "mutual" presupposes two acts; there is a loving self-acceptance of the Father – which is the foundation of difference – and of the Son, because of the *taxis* of knowledge and love.'[55] But if, in order to avoid 'the danger of tritheism', we are not permitted to think of mutual love between the Father and the Son within the Trinity, then it is impossible to say, either, that the Holy Spirit proceeds from the love of the Father and the Son, and constitutes 'the bond of love' between the Father and the Son.

But then who is the Holy Spirit? According to Rahner he is God inasmuch as 'the salvation that deifies us has arrived in the innermost centre of the existence of an individual person'. Who then is the Son? He is 'this one and the same God in the concrete historicity of our existence, strictly present as himself for us in Jesus Christ'. And who is the Father? 'Inasmuch as this very God who comes to us in this way as Spirit and Logos is the incomprehensible ground and origin of his coming in Son and Spirit and maintains himself as such, we call the one God, the Father.' To sum up: 'The one and the same God is given for us as Father, Son-Logos and Holy Spirit, or: the Father gives us himself in absolute self-communication through the Son in the Holy Spirit.'[56] In this last formulation it becomes clear that Rahner transforms the classical doctrine of the Trinity into the reflection trinity of the absolute subject; and the way he does this is plain too. The 'self-communication' of the Absolute has that differentiated structure which seems so similar to the Christian doctrine of the Trinity. But in fact it makes the doctrine of the Trinity superfluous. The fact that God gives us himself in absolute self-communication *can* be associated with Father, Son and Spirit but it does not have to be. On the other hand what is stated biblically with the history of the Father, the Son and the Spirit is only vaguely paraphrased by the concept of God's self-communication.

For Rahner the one, single God-subject is the Father. The Son is the historical instrument, and the Holy Spirit 'in us' is the place of God's self-communication. Rahner therefore prefers to use the term Logos instead of the name of the Son. But can one then still go on talking about a self-communication and self-giving on the part of the Son? Can one then talk about a vouchsafing of the Spirit? If salvation history is reduced to the self-communication of the Father, the history of the Son is no longer identifiable at all. If the self-communication of the Father is the one and only direction of the Trinity, then a particular light is thrown on Rahner's thesis that 'The "economic" Trinity is the "immanent" Trinity and vice versa'.[57] The process of self-communication is the very essence of God, and the divine essence consists of the trinitarian process of self-communication. Rahner certainly stresses that the 'absolute self-communication of God is something totally undeserved', just as Barth stresses the free grace of God's revelation of his lordship. But if the lordship of God is God's essence, and God's essence is his own self-communication, then not only is the trinitarian differentiation in God surrendered; the distinction between God and the world is in danger of being lost too. In the Holy Spirit who is experienced in the 'innermost centre of existence of an individual person', people rise into the inexhaustible mystery of God himself.

This can no doubt be viewed as the mystical variant of the Idealistic doctrine of the 'trinitarian' reflection structure of the absolute subject. Rahner's Idealistic modalism leads back again from the doctrine of the Trinity to the Christian monotheism of 'the one unique essence, the singularity of a one, single consciousness and of a single liberty of the God' who is present in the innermost centre of existence 'of an individual person'. Here the absolute subjectivity of God becomes the archetypal image of the mystic subjectivity of the person who withdraws into himself and transcends himself, that 'self-possessing, self-disposing centre of action which is separate from others'. Rahner's reinterpretation of the doctrine of the Trinity ends in the mystic solitariness of God. It obscures the history of the Father, the Son and the Spirit to which the Bible testifies, by making this the external illustration of that inner experience. Is there really any 'greater danger' than this 'modalism'?

7. *What Divine Unity?*

Trinitarian theology grew up through the theological remoulding of philosophical terms. This can be seen very well from the history of the concept 'person'. The remoulding of the concept of God's unity necessary for an understanding of the triune God and his history, on the other hand, was evidently much more difficult. The philosophical starting point, which was the monadic interpretation of the One God, continually asserted itself in the history of the early church, even though Arianism was rejected and Sabellianism was overcome. Even where people were able to differentiate the concept of God's unity in trinitarian terms, the monadic interpretation held its ground in the concept of monarchy, whether it was understood as the monarchy of the Father within the Trinity or as the extra-trinitarian divine monarchy over the world.

The early creeds, which set the trend for tradition, remain ambivalent where the question of God's unity is concerned. The Nicene Creed, with its use of *homousios* as keyword, suggests a unity of substance between Father, Son and Spirit. But the Athanasian Creed, with the thesis '*unus Deus*', maintains the identity of the one divine subject.

So are Father, Son and Spirit *one* in their possession of the same divine substance, or *one and the same*, in being the same divine subject? Can the unity of the three distinct Persons lie in the homogeneity of the divine substance, which is common to them all, or does it have to consist in the sameness and identity of the one divine subject?

In the first case we should have to think of the unity of God as neuter, as the terms οὐσία or *substantia* suggest. In the second case we ought really only to talk about the One God, as the concept of the absolute subject demands.

In the first case the threeness of the Persons is in the foreground, while the unity of their substance is the background. In the second case the unity of the absolute subject is in the foreground, and the three Persons recede into the background. The first case is obviously open to the charge of tritheism; the second case to the reproach of modalism. In the first case the word tri-unity is used, while in the second case the threefold God (the *Dreifaltigkeit*) is the preferred term. In the first case we proceed from the three Persons and enquire about their unity; in the second case we start from the One God and ask about his trinitarian self-differentiation. If the biblical testimony is chosen as point of departure, then we shall have to start from the three Persons of the history of Christ. If philosophical logic is made the starting point, then the enquirer proceeds from the One God.

After considering all this, it seems to make more sense theologically to start from the biblical history, and therefore to make the unity of the three divine Persons the problem, rather than to take the reverse method – to start from the philosophical postulate of absolute unity, in order then to find the problem in the biblical testimony. The unity of the Father, the Son and the Spirit is then the eschatological question about the consummation of the trinitarian history of God. The unity of the three Persons of this history must consequently be understood as a *communicable* unity and as an *open, inviting unity, capable of integration*. The *homogeneity* of the divine substance is hardly conceivable as communicable and open for anything else, because then it would no longer be homogeneous. The *sameness* and the identity of the absolute subject is not communicable either, let alone open for anything else, because it would then be charged with non-identity and difference. Both these concepts of unity – like the monadic concept – are exclusive, not inclusive. If we search for a concept of unity corresponding to the biblical testimony of the triune God, the God who unites others with himself, then we must dispense with both the concept of the one substance and the concept of the identical subject. All that remains is: the unitedness, the at-oneness of the three Persons with one another, or: the unitedness, the at-oneness of the triune God. For only the concept of unitedness is the concept of a unity that can be communicated and is open. The one God is a God *at one* with himself. That presupposes the personal self-differentiation of God, and not merely a modal differentiation, for only persons can be at one with one another, not modes of being or modes of subjectivity. The at-oneness of the three divine Persons is neither presupposed by these Persons as their single substance nor is it brought about as the sameness or identity of the divine lordship or self-communication. The unitedness, the at-oneness, of the triunity is already given with the fellowship of the Father, the Son and the Spirit. It therefore does not need to be additionally secured by a particular doctrine about the unity of the divine substance, or by the special doctrine of the one divine lordship.

The Father, the Son and the Spirit are by no means merely *distinguished* from one another by their character as Persons; they are just as much united with one another and in one another, since personal character and social character are only two aspects of the same thing. The concept of person must therefore in itself contain the concept of unitedness or at-oneness, just as, conversely, the concept of God's at-oneness must in itself contain the concept of the three Persons. This means that the concept of God's unity cannot in the trinitarian sense be fitted into the homogeneity of the one divine substance, or into the identity of the absolute subject either; and least of all into one of the three Persons of the Trinity. It must be perceived in the *perichoresis* of the divine Persons. If the unity of God is not perceived in the at-oneness of the triune God, and therefore as a *perichoretic* unity, then Arianism and Sabellianism remain inescapable threats to Christian theology.

§2 THE DOXOLOGICAL TRINITY

1. *The Economy and Doxology of Salvation*

Ever since the repulse of modalism through Tertullian, it has been usual to distinguish between the economic and the immanent Trinity. The economic Trinity designates the triune God in his dispensation of salvation, in which he is revealed. The economic Trinity is therefore also called the revelatory Trinity. The immanent Trinity is the name given to the triune God as he is in himself. The immanent Trinity is also called the substantial Trinity. This distinction cannot mean that there are two different Trinities. It is rather a matter of the same triune God as he is in his saving revelation and as he is in himself.

Is the distinction between *God for us* and *God in himself* a speculative one? And if it is speculative, is it necessary? This distinction is usually substantiated by the freedom of the divine decision and by human salvation's character of grace. God is perfect; he is self-sufficient; he is not bound to reveal himself. We experience our salvation by his grace, undeservedly and beyond our deserts. The distinction between an immanent Trinity and an economic Trinity secures God's liberty and his grace. It is the logically necessary presupposition for the correct understanding of God's saving revelation.

This distinction between immanent and economic Trinity would be necessary if, in the concept of God, there were really only the alternative between liberty and necessity. But if God *is* love, then his liberty cannot consist of loving or of not loving. On the contrary, his love is his liberty and his liberty is his love. He is not compelled to love by any outward or inward necessity. Love is self-evident for God.[58] So we have to say that the triune God loves the world with the very same love that he himself *is*. The notion of an immanent Trinity in which God is simply by himself, without the love which communicates salvation, brings an arbitrary element into the concept of God which means a break-up of the Christian concept. Consequently this idea safeguards neither God's liberty nor the grace of salvation. It introduces a contradiction into the relationship between the immanent and the economic Trinity: the God who loves the world does not correspond to the God who suffices for himself. Before the unchangeable God, everything is equal and equally indifferent. For the loving God, nothing is a matter of indifference. Before an equivocal, an undecided God, nothing is significant. For the God who in his love is free, everything is infinitely important. But the immanent and the economic Trinity cannot be distinguished in such a way that the first nullifies what the second says. The two rather form a continuity and merge into one another.

The other and specific starting point for distinguishing between the economic and the immanent Trinity is to be found in *doxology*. The assertions of the immanent Trinity about eternal life and the eternal relationships of the triune God in himself have their *Sitz im Leben*, their situation in life, in the praise and worship of the church:

Glory be to the Father and to the Son and to the Holy Ghost!

Real theology, which means the knowledge of God, finds expression in thanks, praise and adoration. And it is what finds expression in doxology that is the real theology. There is no experience of salvation without the expression of that experience in thanks, praise and joy. An experience which does not find expression in this way is not a liberating experience. Only doxology releases the experience of salvation for a full experience of that salvation. In grateful, wondering and adoring perception, the triune God is not made man's object; he is not appropriated and taken possession of. It is rather that the perceiving person participates in what he perceives, being transformed into the thing perceived through his wondering perception. Here we know only in so far as we love. Here we know in order to participate. Then to know God means to participate in the fullness of the divine life. That is why in the early church the doxological knowledge of God is called *theologia* in the real sense, being distinguished from the doctrine of salvation, the *oeconomia Dei*. The 'economic Trinity' is the object of kerygmatic and practical theology; the 'immanent Trinity' the content of doxological theology.

If we start from this distinction, then it becomes clear that doxological theology is *responsive* theology. Its praise and its knowledge of God are a response to the salvation that has been experienced. If the immanent Trinity is the counterpart of praise, then knowledge of the economic Trinity (as the embodiment of the history and experience of salvation) precedes knowledge of the immanent Trinity. In the order of being it succeeds it.

But how and why do we arrive at the one perception from the other? In doxology the thanks of the receiver return from the goodly gift to the giver. But the giver is not thanked merely for the sake of his good gift; he is also extolled because he himself is good. So God is not loved, worshipped and perceived merely because of the salvation that has been experienced, but for his own sake. That is to say, praise goes beyond thanksgiving. God is recognized, not only in his goodly works but in his goodness itself. And adoration, finally, goes beyond both thanksgiving and praise. It is totally absorbed into its counterpart, in the way that we are totally absorbed by astonishment and boundless wonder. God is ultimately worshipped and loved for himself, not merely for salvation's sake. Of course all the terms of doxology crystallize out of the experience of salvation. But they grow up out of the conclusion drawn from this experience about the transcendent conditions which make the experience possible. And in this way they necessarily go beyond any individual experience and arrive at that experience's transcendent ground. In this way doxological terms remain inescapably bound to the experience of salvation and do not go speculatively beyond it. They remain related to the experience of salvation precisely because they are directed towards the God himself whose salvation and love has been experienced.

It follows from this interlacing of the doctrine of salvation with doxology that we may not assume anything as existing in God himself which contradicts the history of salvation; and, conversely, may not assume anything in the experience of salvation which does not have its foundation in God. The principle that the doctrine of salvation and doxology do not contradict one another is founded on the fact that there are not two different Trinities. There is only one, single, divine Trinity and one, single divine history of salvation. The triune God can only appear in history as he is in himself, and in no other way. He is in himself as he appears in salvation history, for it is he himself who is manifested, and he is just what he is manifested as being. Is this a law which infringes God's liberty? No, it is the quintessence of God's truth. God can do anything, but 'he cannot deny himself' (II Tim. 2.13): 'God is faithful.' Consequently we cannot find any trinitarian relationships in salvation history which do not have their foundation in the nature of the triune God, corresponding to him himself. It is impossible to say, for example, that in history the Holy Spirit proceeds from the Father 'and from the Son', but that within the Trinity he proceeds 'from the Father alone'. God's truth is his faithfulness. Consequently we can rely on his promises and on himself. A God who contradicted himself would be an unreliable God. He would have to be called a demon, not God. The true God is the God of truth, whose nature is eternal faithfulness and reliability. That is why the principle behind the Christian doctrine of the Trinity is:

Statements about the immanent Trinity must not contradict statements about the economic Trinity. Statements about the economic Trinity must correspond to doxological statements about the immanent Trinity.

2. The Historical Experience of Salvation

Where is the empirical starting point of the experience of salvation, if we want to draw inferences from it about the immanent Trinity?

A starting point often chosen in the nineteenth century is the fact that man is made in God's image. This point of departure is already at the root of the psychological doctrine of the Trinity, which originated with Augustine and became widespread in the West. God's image, man, leads us to draw certain inferences about man's divine prototype. Of course this does not mean starting from the ambiguity of man as he actually exists. What is meant is rather man as he had been renewed through the experience of salvation and faith, so that he may become God's image. In the bourgeois world of the nineteenth century, this was what was understood by *personality*:

> Nations, ruler, slave subjected,
> All on this one point agree:
> Joy of earthlings is perfected
> In the personality.[59]

If the destiny and the goal of God's image on earth is to be found in the development of the personality, then the divine prototype must also be the model for this personality. Richard Rothe was the first to declare that God is 'absolute personality', and out of the metaphysics of personality he derives a curious doctrine of the Trinity. God can only become personal by means of an eternal process which is trinitarian in kind. Defined as he is by self-consciousness and self-activity, God becomes absolute personality in an eternal process of self-objectification and self-subjectification.[60] In later editions of his 'Theological Ethics', Rothe gave up this metaphysical construction. But, instead, I. A. Dorner picked up the idea again, letting 'absolute personality' proceed from the trinitarian process of the divine life and spirit, as its result.[61] Martin Kähler followed him with the thesis: 'The Trinity is the unique form of the divine personality.' He meant by this 'that the divine nature consummates its life in three hypostases (persons) by means of a threefold personal relationship which reverts back to itself. The fact that the Trinity is the unique form of the divine personality therefore only emerges from knowledge of the biblical Christ.'[62] Kähler called the distinction between Father and Son 'God's self-differentiation', holding the 'threefold personality' to be the unique and incomparable definition of God. Yet this reduces the three Persons of the Christian doctrine of the Trinity to modalities of the one absolute personality. The process of self-differentiation and self-identification of the absolute subject has little to do with the Christian doctrine of God, even if Martin Kähler was able to believe that the idea of the 'threefold personality' emerged from knowledge of the biblical Christ. But in fact the idea of the threefold, absolute personality is just as speculative as the neo-Platonic triadologies, which patristic theology drew upon to illustrate the doctrine of the Trinity.

But if God is absolute personality, differentiated in a threefold way, then the fully developed human personality of the bourgeois world is this personality's *image*. The modalistic reduction of the Trinity to absolute personality leads anthropologically to a theological reason and religious justification for the modern bourgeois world's cultivation of the individual: every individual must be able to develop himself into a many-sided personality. He only has to observe the equal rights of every other person to life, liberty and happiness. The other person is the only thing that limits the development of one's own personality and the realization of one's own self. But as individuals are we already God's image in our relationship to ourselves? Is it possible to become a personality solely in our self-relationship and its development? A person is only God's image in fellowship with other people: 'In the image of God he created him; male and female he created them' (Gen. 1.27).

That is the reason why men and women can only become persons in relation to other men and women. It is not the completed and fulfilled individual personality that can already be called the image of God on earth; it is only the completed community of persons. But this does not point to an 'absolute personality' in heaven. It points to the tri*unity* of the Father, the Son and the Spirit.

The empirical starting point Karl Barth chose for knowledge of the Trinity was the sovereignty or *lordship of God*. He decided that the proclamation and the belief that 'God is the Lord' was the root of the doctrine of the Trinity. God's subjectivity is perceived in his lordship and is expressed and preserved through the doctrine of the Trinity. Here the lordship of God takes over the position which 'absolute personality' enjoyed in I. A. Dorner. And, as in Dorner, the reduction of the trinitarian Persons to divine modes of being follows. But because, in contrast to Dorner, Barth links the idea of God's lordship indissolubly with the idea of his self-revelation in Christ, Christ alone is the image and correspondence of God on earth.

Karl Rahner certainly defined the 'threefold God as transcendent primal ground of salvation history', as the title of his treatise indicates; but the treatise's content is not in accordance with its title. In reality Rahner talks about the threefold God as the transcendent primal ground of his own 'self-communication'. For Barth, God's self-revelation could only be consummated by a single identical subject; and for Rahner the same is true of God's self-communication. It is inescapably obvious that, for the sake of the identity of the self-communicating divine subject, Rahner has to surrender the interpersonal relations of the triune God. And with this, of course, the prototypical character of the triune God for the personal fellowship of men and women in the church and in society collapses too. The person who corresponds to the God who communicates himself under a threefold aspect, is the person who makes himself available, who transcends himself, but who is none the less turned inwards and solitary.

In Chapter III we interpreted salvation history as 'the history of the Son' of God, Jesus Christ. We understood this history as the trinitarian history of God in the concurrent and joint workings of the three subjects, Father, Son and Spirit; and we interpreted it as the history of God's trinitarian relationships of fellowship. The history of the Son is not implemented by a single subject. Consequently even the divine life itself cannot be implemented by a single subject either. So we have to comprehend the triune God as the 'transcendent primal ground' of this trinitarian history of God if we are to praise him, to magnify him, and to know him as the one who he himself is. In contrast to the psychological doctrine of the Trinity, we are therefore developing a social doctrine of the Trinity, and one based on salvation history.

The reduction of the Trinity to a single identical subject (even if the subject is a threefold one) does not do justice to the trinitarian history of God. The reduction of the three Persons to three modes of subsistence of the one God cannot illuminate salvation history in the fullness of God's open trinitarian relationships of fellowship. We have understood the unity of the divine trinitarian history as the open, unifying at-oneness of the three divine Persons in their relationships to one another. If this uniting at-oneness of the triune God is the quintessence of salvation, then its 'transcendent primal ground' cannot be seen to lie in the one, single, homogeneous divine essence (*substantia*), or in the one identical, absolute subject. It then lies in the eternal perichoresis of the Father, the Son and the Spirit. The history of God's trinitarian relationships of fellowship corresponds to the eternal perichoresis of the Trinity. For this trinitarian history is nothing other than the eternal perichoresis of Father, Son and Holy Spirit in their dispensation of salvation, which is to say in their opening of themselves for the reception and unification of the whole creation.

The history of salvation is the history of the eternally living, triune God who draws us into and includes us in his eternal triune life with all the fullness of its relationships. It is the love story of the God whose very life is the eternal process of engendering, responding and blissful love. God loves the world with the very same love which he is in himself. If, on the basis of salvation history and the experience of salvation, we have to recognize the unity of the triune God in the perichoretic at-oneness of the Father, the Son and the Holy Spirit, then this does not correspond to the solitary human subject in his relationship to himself; nor does it correspond, either, to a human subject in his claim to lordship over the world. It only corresponds to a human fellowship of people without privileges and without subordinances. The perichoretic at-oneness of the triune God corresponds to the experience of the community of Christ, the community which the Spirit unites through respect, affection and love. The more open-mindedly people live with one another, for one another and in one another in the fellowship of the Spirit, the more they will become one with the Son and the Father, and one in the Son and the Father (John 17.21).

God as almighty power and lordship – this notion of God is mediated and enforced from 'above to below'. But God as love is experienced in the community of brothers and sisters through mutual acceptance and participation. That applies too to any human order of society which deserves the name of 'human' in the Christian sense: the further the acceptance of the other goes, the deeper the participation in the life of the other is the more united people who have been divided by the perversions of rule will become. In the community of Christ it is *love* that corresponds to the perichoretic unity of the triune God as it is manifested and experienced in the history of salvation; in human society it is solidarity that provides this correspondence. We shall be taking up and developing this idea in Chapter VI.

3. The Relationship between the Immanent and the Economic Trinity

The patristic tradition liked to distinguish and relate the Trinity's immanence and its economy as the Platonists distinguished and related the Idea and its appearance. To talk Idealistically about the substantial and the revealed Trinity presupposes a similar distinction. It is this distinction which the modern differentiation between 'God in himself' and 'God for us' is following. People would like to distinguish God and the world from one another, so as to be able to say that the world is dependent on God, but that God is not dependent on the world. A distinction of this kind between God and the world is generally a metaphysical one: the world is evanescent, God is non-evanescent; the world is temporal, God is eternal; the world is passible, God is impassible; the world is dependent, God is independent. It is obvious that these distinctions in the metaphysical doctrine of the two natures are derived from experience of the world, not from experience of God. This judgment, which distinguishes God in the world from the world itself, is then used in the doctrine of the Trinity to distinguish between God's immanence and his economy. But the distinction between

God and the world cannot be sufficient to distinguish God from God. It imposes limitations on the triune God which are laid down, not by him, but by human experience of the world. This results in insolluble problems such as whether the impassible Son of the eternal Father can have suffered on the cross, whether the immutable Father can love his creation, and whether the eternal Spirit can liberate a world that is essentially dependent. The general metaphysical distinctions between God and the world become false if they are applied to the history of the Son. So in the doctrine of the Trinity we have to set about things in the reverse way: God distinguishes himself from the world through his own self. The distinction between the Trinity's immanence and its economy must lie in the Trinity itself and must be implemented by it itself. It must not be imposed on it from outside.

In his distinction between the immanent and the economic Trinity, Barth first of all adhered to the Platonic notion of correspondence: what God revealed himself as being in Jesus Christ, he is in eternity, 'beforehand in himself'. For this is the truth of God in time and eternity: 'God corresponds to himself'. It is only in his account of Christ's death on the cross that Barth breaks through the unilinear view of correspondence, which thinks of it from above to below, from within to without. Christ's death on the cross acts from below upwards, from without inwards, out of time back into the divine eternity 'He is the Lamb slain, and the Lamb slain from the foundation of the world. For this reason, the *crucified* Jesus is the "image of the invisible God".'[63] The meaning of the cross of the Son on Golgotha reaches right into the heart of the immanent Trinity. From the very beginning, no immanant Trinity and no divine glory is conceivable without 'the Lamb who was slain'. So in Christian art too there are hardly any representations of the Trinity in heaven without the cross and the One crucified. If we start from the assumption that the perceptions and conceptions about the immanent Trinity in doxology are built up on the basis of the experience of salvation, then this immediately becomes comprehensible: anyone who owes his salvation to the delivering up of the Son to death on the cross can never think of God in the abstract, apart from the cross of Christ. For him, God is from eternity to eternity 'the crucified God'. Only 'the Lamb that was slain is worthy to receive power, and riches, and wisdom, and strength, and honour, and glory and blessing' (Rev. 5.12).

I myself have tried to think through the theology of the cross in trinitarian terms and to understand the doctrine of the Trinity in the light of the theology of the cross.[64] In order to grasp the death of the Son in its significance for God himself, I found myself bound to surrender the traditional distinction between the immanent and the economic Trinity, according to which the cross comes to stand only in the economy of salvation, but not within the immanent Trinity. That is why I have affirmed and taken up Rahner's thesis that 'the economic Trinity *is* the immanent Trinity, and vice versa'.[65] If the central foundation of our knowledge of the Trinity is the cross, on which the Father delivered up the Son for us through the Spirit, then it is impossible to conceive of any Trinity of substance in the transcendent primal ground of this event, in which cross and self-giving are not present. Even the New Testament statement 'God *is* love' is the summing up of the surrender of the Son through the Father for us. It cannot be separated from the event on Golgotha without becoming false. The thesis about the fundamental *identity* of the immanent and the economic Trinity of course remains open to misunderstanding as long as we cling to the distinction at all, because it then sounds like the dissolution of the one in the other.[66] What this thesis is actually trying to bring out is the interaction between the substance and the revelation, the 'inwardness' and the 'outwardness' of the triune God. The economic Trinity not only reveals the immanent Trinity; it also has a retroactive effect on it. The Augustinian distinction between the *opera trinitatis ad extra*, which are undivided (*indivisa*) and the *opera trinitatis ad intra*, which are divided (*divisa*) is insufficient.[67] It ascribes unity to God outwards and 'threeness' inwardly. But the event of the cross (which is an 'outward' event) can only be understood in trinitarian terms – i.e., terms that are 'divided' (*divisa*) and differentiated. Conversely, the surrender of the Son for us on the cross has a retroactive effect on the Father and causes infinite pain. On the cross God *creates* salvation outwardly for his whole creation and at the same time *suffers* this disaster of the whole world inwardly in himself. From the foundation of the world, the *opera trinitatis ad extra* correspond to the *passiones trinitatis ad intra*. God as love would otherwise not be comprehensible at all.

The relationship of the triune God to himself and the relationship of the triune God to his world is not to be understood as a one-way relationship – the relation of image to reflection, idea to appearance, essence to manifestation – but as a mutual one. The concept 'mutual relationship' does not equate God's relationship to the world with his relationship to himself. But it says that God's relationship to the world has a retroactive effect on his relationship to himself – even though the divine relationship to the world is primarily determined by that inner relationship. The growth of knowledge of the immanent Trinity from the saving experience of the cross of Christ makes this necessary. The pain of the cross determines the inner life of the triune God from eternity to eternity. If that is true, then the joy of responsive love in glorification through the Spirit determines the inner life of the triune God from eternity to eternity too. Just as the cross of the Son puts its impress on the inner life of the triune God, so the history of the Spirit moulds the inner life of the triune God through the joy of liberated creation when it is united with God. That is why Christian doxology always ends with the eschatological prospect, looking for 'the perfecting of thy kingdom in glory, when we shall praise and adore thee, Father, Son and Holy Spirit, for ever and ever'.[68]

If it is the quintessence of doxology, then the doctrine of the immanent Trinity is part of eschatology as well. The economic Trinity completes and perfects itself to immanent Trinity when the history and experience of salvation are completed and perfected. When everything is 'in God' and 'God is all in all', then the economic Trinity is raised into and transcended in the immanent Trinity. What remains is the eternal praise of the triune God in his glory.

§3 THE IMMANENT TRINITY

We have seen that the knowledge and the representation of the immanent Trinity is to be found in the sphere of doxology, which responds to the experience of salvation and anticipates the kingdom of glory. In this eschatological sense the Trinity is a mystery (*mysterion*) which is only manifested to us here in the experience of salvation. To talk about 'the mystery of the Trinity' does not mean pointing to some impenetrable obscurity or insoluble riddle. It means with unveiled face already recognizing here and now, in the obscurity of history, the glory of the triune God and praising him in the hope of one day seeing him face to face.

The ideas and concepts with which we know God and conceive

him for ourselves all derive from this impaired life of ours. They have the imprint of a history of Godlessness and Godforsakenness. It is only in a fragmentary way that they are suited to bring to expression the doxology of liberated life in fellowship with God. By the phrase 'in a fragmentary way' we mean here that these ideas and concepts have to suffer *a transformation of meaning* if they are to be applied to the mystery of the Trinity. All theological work on the doctrine of the Trinity is devoted to this transformation of meaning. The concepts and terms must correspond to and be suited to the thing that has to be conceived and comprehended. This theological effort of understanding is itself already a part of doxology.

In the following pages we are going to discuss some basic concepts in the doctrine of the Trinity in this light, though I have no intention of covering the ground with the completeness of a handbook.[69] We shall begin with the constitution of the Trinity itself and shall then go on to think about some trinitarian concepts.

1. The Constitution of the Trinity

The Father, the Son and the Spirit are worshipped and extolled together and in one breath.

(a) Who is the Father?

In the Apostles' Creed God is called 'Father' twice: firstly at creation – 'I believe in God the Father Almighty, maker of heaven and earth'; secondly after Christ's ascension – 'He sitteth at the right hand of God, the Father Almighty'. This double mention has led to an ambiguity in the understanding of God the Father. Are we to call God the Father because he is almighty and – by virtue of his almighty power – is the creator of heaven and earth? Or is he the almighty Father of the Son, who sits at his right hand?

If God is the almighty Father because he is the origin and lord of all things, then he will be feared and worshipped, as Zeus already was, because he is the father of the universe:

> When the primordial holy Father
> with tranquil hand
> sends blessed lightnings
> from rolling clouds

over the earth,
I kiss the hem of his garment,
childlike in awe, faithful in heart.[70]

As father of the universe he is the universe's highest authority. All other authorities take their powers from him, so that patriarchal hierarchies grow up on this pattern: God the Father – the father of the church – the father of his country – the father of the family. This patriarchal religion is quite obviously not trinitarian; it is purely monotheistic. It is understandable that the European movement for freedom should have been sparked off, both religiously and politically, by this patriarchal, father religion. European atheism means nothing other than the liberation of human beings from this super-ego in the soul and in heaven, which does not really deserve the name of Father at all.

If we think in trinitarian terms on the other hand, we begin with the second definition in the Apostles' Creed: God the Father is the Father of his only begotten Son Jesus Christ, who became our elder brother. It is in respect of this Son that God must be called 'Father'. His fatherhood is defined by the relationship to this Son, and by the relationship of this Son Jesus Christ to him. Consequently, in the Christian understanding of God the Father, what is meant is not 'the Father of the universe', but simply and exclusively 'the Father of the Son' Jesus Christ. It is solely the Father of Jesus Christ whom we believe and acknowledge created the world. It is in the trinitarian sense that God is understood as Father – or he cannot be understood as Father at all. But anyone who wants to understand the trinitarian God as Father must forget the ideas behind this patriarchal Father religion – the super-ego, the father of the family, the father of his country, even 'the fatherly providence'. He must gaze solely at the life and message of his brother Jesus: for in fellowship with the only begotten Son he will recognize that the Father of Jesus Christ is his Father too, and he will understand what the divine fatherhood really means. The name of Father is therefore a theological term – which is to say a trinitarian one; it is not a cosmological idea or a religious-political notion. If God is the Father of this Son Jesus Christ, and if he is only 'our Father' for his Son's sake, then we can also only call him 'Abba', beloved Father, in the spirit of free sonship. It is freedom that distinguishes him from the universal patriarch of father religions.

The ambiguity of the Father of the universe and the Father of Jesus Christ ceases if we distinguish clearly between the creation of the world and the generation of the Son. God is Father solely in respect of the only begotten Son. No fatherliness in the literal sense can be detected from the creation of the universe, or from providence. When the Creator is called 'Father', what is meant in Christian terms is that creation proceeds from the Father of the Son – that is to say, from the first Person of the Trinity: the Father creates heaven and earth through the Son in the power of the Holy Spirit. Factually, the trinitarian definition of the Father precedes the cosmological one. Consequently the creation process is manifestly a work of the Trinity. The Lord's prayer is in fact directed towards the first Person of the Trinity, not the whole Trinity, as Augustine thought. It is in fellowship with the first-born Son that Jesus' brothers and sisters pray to his Father, calling him 'our Father'. Through the doctrine of the Trinity, therefore, God's name of Father is indissolubly linked with Jesus the Son, and is in that way Christianized.

It is only this Father who can be said to have 'generated' his only begotten Son in eternity. Here, significantly enough, the statements of Trinitarian doctrine vary between the 'generation' and the 'birth' of the Son from the Father. The German creed, for example, talks, not about the *only begotten* Son, but about the only Son *born* to the Father. Both statements are intended to make it clear that the Son was not 'created' by the Father, as the world was, but that he proceeded from the substance of the Father and is hence of the same substance as the Father, which cannot be said of any created being, not even men and women.

But if the Son proceeded from the Father alone, then this has to be conceived of both as a begetting and as a birth. And this means a radical transformation of the Father image; a father who both begets and bears his son is not merely a father in the male sense. He is a motherly father too. He is no longer defined in unisexual, patriarchal terms but – if we allow for the metaphor of language – bisexually or transexually. He has to be understood as the motherly Father of the only Son he has brought forth, and at the same time as the fatherly Mother of his only begotten Son. It was the Orthodox dogmatic tradition especially which took the Trinity seriously, defending it against any danger of monotheism; and it was just this tradition which made the boldest statements at this point. According to the Council of Toledo in 675 'it must be held that the Son was created, neither out of nothingness nor yet out of any substance, but that He was begotten or born out of the Father's womb (*de utero Patris*), that is, out of his very essence'.[71] Whatever may be said about God's gynaecology according to this explanation, the point of these bi-sexual statements about the trinitarian Father is the radical rejection of monotheism, which is always patriarchal.

Monotheism was and is the religion of patriarchy, just as pantheism is probably the religion of earlier matriarchy. It is only the doctrine of the Trinity, with the bold statements we have quoted, which makes a first approach towards overcoming sexist language in the concept of God. It leads to a fellowship of men and women without privilege and subjection, for in fellowship with the first-born brother, there is no longer male or female, but all are one in Christ, and joint heirs according to the promise (Gal. 3.28f.).

In the eternal begetting and birth of the Son, God proves himself Father and is Father indeed. The Son and the Spirit proceed eternally from the Father, but the Father proceeds from no other divine person. Hence – or so the doctrine of the trinitarian processions states – he cannot himself be constituted out of a relation to anything else. The Father must be constituted through himself. That is the reason why he – the origin of the Son and the Spirit – is called the one who is 'utterly and absolutely without origin or beginning', *principium sine principio*. He, being himself without origin, is the origin of the divine Persons of the Son and the Spirit. If one does not want God to disappear into Sabellian obscurity, then one must see the eternal origin of the Trinity in the Father. But this means that God the Father must be doubly defined: first of all, being himself without origin, he is the origin of the Godhead; secondly, he is the Father of the Son and the One who brings forth the Spirit. The Father is therefore defined through himself and through his relations to the Son and to the Spirit. The Son and the Spirit, on the other hand, are defined through the Father and through their own relations. But this inner-trinitarian 'monarchy of the Father' only defines the inner-trinitarian constitution of God, not the world monarchy of a universal Father.

Metaphysical thinking in terms of origin has been employed in the doctrine of the inner-trinitarian processions from earliest times. The Trinity, which is the origin of the world, is in its turn traced back to an eternal 'origin of the Godhead' in the Father. This thinking in terms of origin derives from cosmology and can therefore only be haltingly applied to the mystery of the Trinity, that is to say, in realization of its inappropriateness. It can only be used appropriately if the logical compulsion to monarchial reduction and the non-trinitarian notion of the single origin (both of which are inherent in it) are overcome. In spite of the 'origin' of the Son and the Spirit in the Father, we have to adhere to the equally primordial character of the trinitarian Persons (if we want to go on thinking in these terms at all) because otherwise the Trinity threatens to dissolve in monotheism. But if we talk about an order of origin within the Trinity, we must underline its uniqueness and its incomparability when contrasted with any order of origin which is thought of cosmologically. If we keep these differences in mind, then the concept of origin (ἀρχή) can certainly be used as an aid to thinking; and we shall be employing it in this way in what follows.

(b) Who is the Son?

The statements about the second Person of the Trinity are not so problematical. The Son is the 'only', the 'only begotten', eternal Son of the Father. He is not created *ex nihilo* but – as the metaphors of generation and birth suggest – proceeds from the substance of the Father. Consequently he is one in substance or essence with the Father and has everything in common with him, except his 'Personal' characteristics. The statements about the 'eternal generation' or 'begetting' of the Son make the name of Son an exclusively theological term, that is to say, a trinitarian one. The world is God's creation, not his Son. Man is God's image, not his Son. The history of the world is God's passion, not the process of his self-realization. It is only in fellowship with the first-born of creation that the world will be drawn into the trinitarian life of God; it is only in fellowship with the first-born of many brethren that men and women are drawn into that life. It is the trinitarian statements about the eternal generation and birth of the Son which bring about the christological concentration of cosmology and anthropology.

The Father who generates and brings forth communicates everything to the eternal Son – everything except his fatherhood. The Father communicates to the Son his divinity, his power and his glory, but not his fatherhood; otherwise the Son for his part would be a second Father. The Son therefore receives in eternity divinity and his being as Person from the Father. He does not for his part, however, become an 'origin of the Godhead'; otherwise there would be two such origins within the triune God. This difference in the characters of the Father and the Son is important for the dispute about the *Filioque*; for it already excludes the idea that the Spirit could proceed 'from the Father and the Son' in the sense of the Son's being a 'second origin' of the divinity of the Holy Spirit, in competition with the Father. The Father is the 'origin' of the Son and communicates to him his whole essence, with the sole exception of the capacity for being himself the 'origin' or 'source' of the Godhead.[72]

The generation and birth of the Son come from the Father's *nature*, not from his will. That is why we talk about the *eternal* generation and birth of the Son. The Father begets and bears the Son out of the necessity of his being. Consequently the Son, like the Father, belongs to the eternal constitution of the triune God. In Christian terms, no deity is conceivable without the eternal Father of the Son and without the eternal Son of the Father. Tradition distinguishes between the eternal birth of the Son from the Father, and the sending of the Son through the Father in time: the temporal sending issues from the liberty of the Father and the Son; the eternal birth springs from necessity of being.

A difficult question often arises at this point: the question whether a reason can be given – given not merely *a posteriori*, on the basis of the experience of salvation, but *a priori* too, out of the eternal constitution of the Trinity – why it was the eternal Son who had to become man in order to suffer and to die, and not just 'any one of the Persons of the Trinity'. Is there something in the eternal generation of the Son through the Father which from eternity, potentially and in tendency, destines the Son for incarnation – the Son, but not the Father, and not the Spirit either? This 'speculative' question is seldom answered. In the framework of the doctrine of the Trinity which we have developed here, it can be said that the Father's love, which generates and brings forth, reaches potentially and in tendency beyond the responding and obedient love of the eternal Son. The love of the Father for the Son, and the love of the Son for the Father are not the same – are not even congruent – simply because they are differently constituted. They do not stand in an equal reciprocal relationship to one another. The Father loves the Son with engendering, fatherly love. The Son loves the Father with responsive, self-giving love. The love of the Father which begets and brings forth the Son is therefore open for further response through creations which correspond to the Son, which enter into harmony with his responsive love and thereby fulfil the joy of the Father. Hence the love of the Father which brings forth the Son in eternity becomes creative love. It calls created beings into life, beings made in the image of the Son, who in fellowship with the Son return the Father's love. Creation proceeds from the Father's love for the eternal Son. It is destined to join in the Son's obedience and in his responsive love to the Father, and so to give God delight and bliss.

On the other hand, the Son's sacrifice of boundless love on Golgotha is from eternity already included in the exchange of the essential, the consubstantial love which constitutes the divine life of the Trinity. The fact that the Son dies on the cross, delivering himself up to that death, is part of the eternal obedience which he renders to the Father in his whole being through the Spirit, whom he receives from the Father. Creation is saved and justified in eternity in the sacrifice of the Son, which is her sustaining foundation.

(c) Who is the Holy Spirit?

Whereas according to biblical testimony clear personal concepts are associated with the names of the Father and the Son, the 'third Person' of the Trinity has a certain anonymity.[73] It is not always clear from the New Testament that the Holy Spirit is not merely a divine energy, but a divine subject too. On the other hand we read in the Gospel of John that 'God is spirit' (4.24). Spirit is therefore also a description of the divine existence, similar to the statement that 'God is love'. The attribute 'holy', too, does not describe any unique feature of the third Person of the Trinity, for the triune God himself is holy. Thomas Aquinas consequently thought that the third Person of the Trinity had no name of his own, but that he was only given the name 'Holy Spirit' because of biblical usage[74] – that is to say, on the basis of the economy of salvation to which the Bible testifies: the Spirit is holy because he himself sanctifies.

In Christian art – both Western and Eastern – the Trinity has therefore generally been represented by two Persons and a bird, the dove. Rublev's ikon is a notable exception. To depict the Spirit as a dove between the Persons of the Father and the Son expresses a duality rather than a Trinity.

The concept of the Holy Spirit's origin is difficult as well. As the source of the Godhead and as the Father of the Son, God breathes out the Holy Spirit in eternity. The Spirit proceeds in eternity from the Father, but from the Father inasmuch as he is 'the origin of the Godhead'. It is lacking in inner logic to understand the procession of the Spirit only from 'the Father'; for the first Person of the Trinity is only 'Father' in relation to the Son. The Spirit is 'breathed out' (*spiratio*) not begotten (*generatio*). So the Spirit cannot be a second Son of the Father. He proceeds from the Father. He does not equally proceed from the Son. If this were so, the Son would be the second Father and there would be two different 'origins' for the divine Spirit. This idea, which some Orthodox theologians find in the Western church's *Filioque*, would destroy God's unity and nullify the personal distinctions between the Father and the Son. We can therefore only say about the origin of the Spirit that: 1. He is not without origin, like the Father; 2. He is not generated, like the Son; 3. His procession from the Father (ἐκπόρευσις) is a relationship peculiar to himself, the factor determining him alone. His unique character is therefore defined negatively rather than positively.

Western theology ever since Augustine has suggested with a certain reserve that the Holy Spirit issues from the mutual love of the Father and the Son, and that the Spirit is the *vinculum amoris*, the bond of love which brings the Father and the Son to the truth in one another and with one another; that is to say, that the Spirit is the trinitarian Person who both truly distinguishes and truly unites the Father and the Son in their relation to one another. But that means that the inner-trinitarian efficacy of the Holy Spirit is only presented by and in the mutual relationship of the Father and the Son.

The concept of the Holy Spirit really has no organic connection with the doctrine of God the Father and the Son. Consequently it often simply seems like an appendix, either because of the biblical testimony, or for the sake of a 'trinity' in which the duality is brought to unity. But the inner coherence immediately becomes perceptible when we understand the Son as *the Word* (Logos). The

Father utters his eternal Word in the eternal breathing out of his Spirit. There is in God no Word without the Spirit, and no Spirit without the Word. In this respect the uttering of the Word and the issuing of the Spirit belong indissolubly together. It is even difficult to perceive that the second Person has any priority over the third Person of the Trinity. Word and Spirit, Spirit and Word issue together and simultaneously from the Father, for they mutually condition one another. The difficult thing then is only to call the common origin of the Word and the Spirit 'Father'.

The real problems about the knowledge and description of the immanent Trinity lie in the integration of these two different patterns: the logic of the Father and the Son, and the logic of the Word and the Spirit. Inasmuch as the Son of the eternal Father is at the same time the eternal Word of God, the eternal procession of the Spirit is bound up with him.

If the Spirit, together with the eternal Word, proceeds from the Father as 'origin of the Godhead', then we must also say that the Spirit is not created, but that he issues from the Father out of the necessity of the Father's being and is of the same essence or substance as the Father and the Son. In experiencing the Holy Spirit we experience God himself: we experience the Spirit of the Father, who unites us with the Son; the Spirit of the Son, whom the Father gives; and the Spirit who glorifies us through the Son and the Father.

According to John 15.26, 'the Spirit of truth proceeds from the Father' but is 'sent' by Christ the Son. According to John 14.26, the Father 'sends' the Spirit in Christ's name. If, according to the experience of salvation, the Holy Spirit is 'sent' by the Father *and by the Son*, then does not the perception of doxology tell us that he is then also bound to 'proceed' from the Father *and from the Son*? Can we – without destroying the truth of God himself – assume anything about the economy of salvation which does not originally correspond to something in the actual Trinity itself? But if – because the Spirit is sent from the Father and from the Son in time – we assume that the Spirit proceeds from the Father and from the Son in eternity, are we not then destroying the unity of the triune God? This is the double dilemma of the dispute over the *Filioque*, which we shall be discussing later.

2. The Life of the Trinity

(a) Person and Relation

The word persona (πρόσωπον) originally meant 'mask' and comes from the language of the theatre. What is meant is the mask disguising the actor's features, through which his voice is heard (*personare*).[75] In modern speech this corresponds exactly to the sociological concept of the 'role'. 'Role sociology' has also borrowed this term from the theatre and applied it to the social functions of men and women.[76] In Latin theology the concept of person was used first of all in Sabellian modalism: one God in three masks. In the anthropology of role sociology, man becomes *homo absconditus*, 'the man without qualities' in a 'world of qualities without man'. That is anthropological modalism in its extreme form.[77]

In Greek theology, on the other hand, the term *hypostasis* was used quite early on, parallel to the term *prosopon*, in the doctrine of the Trinity. Hypostasis does not mean the mask or mode of appearance; it means the individual existence of a particular nature. If the Latin term 'person' is to be used to cover the same content, then the concept of person has to be changed – which means deepened ontologically. It must no longer describe the interchangeable mask or role; on the contrary, it must describe the non-interchangeable, untransferable individual existence in any particular case. This is what Boethius's classic definition means: '*persona est rationalis naturae individua substantia.*'[78] For Boethius nature consisted of substance and accident. Consequently a person cannot be constituted of accidents but only out of substance. As individual substance, the person is characterized by substantiality, intellectuality and incommunicability. If we take Boethius' definition, the trinitarian Persons are not 'modes of being'; they are individual, unique, non-interchangeable subjects of the one, common divine substance, with consciousness and will. Each of the Persons possesses the divine nature in a non-interchangeable way; each presents it in his own way.

But since the trinitarian Persons are unique, they cannot merely be defined by their relationship to their common nature. The limitation to three would then be incomprehensible. The personality which represents their untransferable, individual being with respect to their common divine nature, means, on the other hand, the character of relation with respect to the other Persons. They have the divine nature in common; but their particular individual nature is determined in their relationship to one another. In respect of the divine nature the Father has to be called '*individua substantia*', but in respect of the Son we have to call him 'Father'. The position is no different in the case of the Son and the Spirit. The three divine Persons exist in their particular, unique natures as Father, Son and Spirit in their relationships to one another, and are determined through these relationships. It is in these relationships that they are persons. Being a person in this respect means existing-in-relationship.

This relational understanding of the person was pre-eminently introduced by Augustine. It expands and takes us beyond the 'substance' thinking of Boethius. It permits the differentiation: the three divine Persons possess the same individual, indivisible and one divine nature, but they possess it in varying ways. The Father possesses it of himself; the Son and the Spirit have it from the Father. There are three relations in the Trinity: fatherhood, sonship, the breathing of the Spirit (*paternitas, filatio, spiratio*). The inner being of the Persons is moulded by these relationships in accordance with the relational difference. The three Persons are independent in that they are divine, but as Persons they are deeply bound to one another and dependent on one another. But this relational understanding of the Persons has as its premise the 'substantial' interpretation of their individuality; the one does not replace the other.

Here there is a difference between the Orthodox and the Western trinitarian doctrine. It is a difference that became clear at the Council of Florence. It is impossible to say: person *is* relation;[79] the relation constitutes the person. It is true that the Father is defined by his fatherhood to the Son, but this does not constitute his existence; it presupposes it. Certainly, fatherhood is a relation, a 'mode of being'. But the fact that God *is* the Father says more than merely that: it adds to the mode of being, being itself. Person and relation therefore have to be understood in a reciprocal relationship. Here there are no persons without relations; but there are no relations without persons either. The reduction of the concept 'person' to the concept 'relation' is basically modalistic, because it suggests the further reduction of the concept of relation to a self-relation on God's part. But is person merely a 'concrete and really existing relation of God to himself'?[80] If it were, then God in the three Persons would be thrice himself, and the Persons would be nothing more than the triple self-repetition of God. This modalistic view not only dissolves the trinitarian concept of person; it does away with the interpersonal concept of relation as well. Moreover the number 'three' becomes incomprehensible.

But on the Orthodox side it is no less one-sided to say: the relations only *manifest* the persons. For that presupposes the constitution of the Persons simply in themselves, and without their relations. Then the relations would only express the difference in kind of the Persons, but not their association, their fellowship. But if, as we are maintaining here, personality and relationships are *genetically connected*, then the two arise simultaneously and together. The constitution of the Persons and their manifestation through their relations are two sides of the same thing. The concept of substance reflects the relations of the Person to the common divine nature. The concept of relation reflects the relationship of the Persons to one another. These are two aspects which have to be distinguished from one another. The trinitarian Persons *subsist* in the common divine nature; they *exist* in their relations to one another.

The doctrine of *the Trinity of love* carried on the development of the concept of Person, and took it one step further. This doctrine was evolved in the West from the time of Augustine and Richard of St Victor and was pursued right down to the Idealistic theology of the nineteenth century. According to Richard of St Victor, being a person does not merely mean subsisting; nor does it mean subsisting-in-relation. It means *existing*. He proposed as improvement of the old definition: 'A divine Person is a non-interchangeable existence of the divine nature.'[81] By the word 'existence' – *eksistentia* – he meant: existence, in the light of another. It is true that in the first place he related this other to the divine nature. But it can be related to the other Persons too. Then existence means a deepening of the concept of relation: every divine Person exists in the light of the other and in the other. By virtue of the love they have for one another they ex-ist totally in the other: the Father ex-ists by virtue of his love, as himself entirely in the Son; the Son, by virtue of his self-surrender, ex-ists as himself totally in the Father; and so on. Each Person finds his existence and his joy in the other Person. Each Person receives the fullness of eternal life from the other.

Hegel then picked up this idea and deepened it. It is the nature of the person to give himself entirely to a counterpart, and to find himself in the other most of all. The person only comes to himself by expressing and expending himself in others.[82]

The substantial understanding of person (Boethius) and the relational understanding of person (Augustine) was now expanded by the historical understanding of person (Hegel). The Persons do not merely 'exist' in their relations; they also realize themselves in one another by virtue of self-surrendering love.

This brings a third term into the doctrine of the Trinity, in addition to the concept of person and the concept of relation; and this makes it possible to perceive the living changes in the trinitarian relations and the Persons which come about through the revelation, the self-emptying and the glorification of the triune God. We have termed it the history of God, which takes place in the Trinity itself, and have in this sense talked about God's passion for his Other, about God's self-limitation, about God's pain, and also about God's joy and his eternal bliss in the final glorification.

Only when we are capable of thinking of Persons, relations, and changes in the relations *together* does the idea of the Trinity lose its usual static, rigid quality. Then not only does the eternal life of the triune God become conceivable; its eternal vitality becomes conceivable too.

(b) Perichoresis and Transfiguration

If the concept of person comes to be understood in trinitarian terms – that is, in terms of relation and historically – then the Persons do not only subsist in the common divine substance; they also exist in their relations to the other Persons. More – they are alive in one another and through the others in each several case.

This idea found expression in the early church's doctrine about the *immanentia* and *inexistentia* of the trinitarian Persons: *intima et perfecta inhabitatio unius personae in alia.*

John Damascene's profound doctrine of the eternal περιχώρησις or *circumincessio* of the trinitarian Persons goes even further.[83] For this concept grasps the circulatory character of the eternal divine life. An eternal life process takes place in the triune God through the exchange of energies. The Father exists in the Son, the

Son in the Father, and both of them in the Spirit, just as the Spirit exists in both the Father and the Son. By virtue of their eternal love they live in one another to such an extent, and dwell in one another to such an extent, that they are one. It is a process of most perfect and intense empathy. Precisely through the personal characteristics that distinguish them from one another, the Father, the Son and the Spirit dwell in one another and communicate eternal life to one another. In the perichoresis, the very thing that divides them becomes that which binds them together. The 'circulation' of the eternal divine life becomes perfect through the fellowship and unity of the three different Persons in the eternal love. In their perichoresis and because of it, the trinitarian persons are not to be understood as three different individuals, who only subsequently enter into relationship with one another (which is the customary reproach, under the name of 'tritheism'). But they are not, either, three modes of being or three repetitions of the One God, as the modalistic interpretation suggests. The doctrine of the perichoresis links together in a brilliant way the threeness and the unity, without reducing the threeness to the unity, or dissolving the unity in the threeness. The unity of the triunity lies in the eternal perichoresis of the trinitarian persons. Interpreted perichoretically, the trinitarian persons form their own unity by themselves in the circulation of the divine life.

The unity of the trinitarian Persons lies in the circulation of the divine life which they fulfil in their relations to one another. This means that the unity of the triune God cannot and must not be seen in a general concept of divine substance. That would abolish the personal differences. But if the contrary is true – if the very difference of the three Persons lies in their relational, perichoretically consummated life process – then the Persons cannot and must not be reduced to three modes of being of one and the same divine subject. The Persons themselves constitute both their differences and their unity.

If the divine life is understood perichoretically, then it cannot be consummated by merely one subject at all. It is bound to consist of the living fellowship of the three Persons who are related to one another and exist in one another. Their unity does not lie in the one lordship of God; it is to be found in the unity of their tri-unity.

Finally, through the concept of perichoresis, all subordinationism in the doctrine of the Trinity is avoided. It is true that the Trinity is constituted with the Father as starting point, inasmuch as he is understood as being 'the origin of the Godhead'. But this 'monarchy of the Father' only applies to the *constitution* of the Trinity. It has no validity within the eternal circulation of the divine life, and none in the perichoretic unity of the Trinity. Here the three Persons are equal; they live and are manifested in one another and through one another.

There is another, analogous process to the circulation of the divine life through the trinitarian Persons in their relations: the process of the mutual manifestations of the Persons through their relations in the divine glory. The expression and presentation of the divine life in the glory that characterizes it, is part of that divine life itself. The trinitarian Persons do not merely exist and live in one another; they also bring one another mutually to manifestation in the divine glory. The eternal divine glory is for its part displayed through the trinitarian manifestation of the Persons. From all eternity the Father is 'the Father of glory' (Eph. 1.17), the eternal Word is 'the reflection of glory' (Heb. 1.3) and the Holy Spirit is 'the spirit of glory' (I Peter 4.14).[84] The Persons of the Trinity make one another shine through that glory, mutually and together. They glow into perfect form through one another and awake to perfected beauty in one another.

In all eternity the Holy Spirit allows the Son to shine in the Father and transfigures the Father in the Son. He is the eternal light in which the Father knows the Son and the Son the Father. In the Holy Spirit the eternal divine life arrives at consciousness of itself, therein reflecting its perfect form. In the Holy Spirit the divine life becomes conscious of its eternal beauty. Through the Holy Spirit the eternal divine life becomes the sacred feast of the Trinity.

In Orthodox theology the doctrine of the trinitarian manifestations actually stands at the point where the theology of the Western church talks about the trinitarian relations. But this doctrine of the manifestation of the perichoresis of the divine life in the divine glory goes even further. And it is only this doctrine that corresponds doxologically to 'the glorification of the Spirit' in the experience of salvation.[85]

3. The Unity of the Trinity

The unity of the Trinity must be understood in a trinitarian sense, not monadically. Otherwise the unity would abolish the triple character of the Persons.

The tradition of the Western church liked to see the unity of the Trinity in the one, fundamental divine substance, in which the divine hypostases subsist. Tertullan's formula, '*una substantia – tres·personae*', already suggests this interpretation. But if the one divine substance is to represent the unity of the Trinity, then the three-in-oneness of the Persons is secondary in comparison. The threeness then contains no inherent unity in itself, and is easily reduced to the fundamental unity of the divine substance, as its threefold character. What can be said 'de Deo uno' is perceived by the light of natural reason. It is only what is perceived 'de Deo trino' that is supposed to be due to revelation. If the doctrine of God is built up in two parts like this, then God's unity has to be dealt with twice. In the past this has meant that the unity of the trinity receded behind the natural recognition that God *is*, and that he is one.

One arrives at similar conclusions if one thinks about God as subject and no longer as substance. Then too, the underlying premise is a non-trinitarian unity of the God-subject, and the Trinity is reduced to the threefold character of this one, identical subject. The unity of the three-in-one then no longer finds expression. The one lordship and the one self-communication of the One God now merely have a threefold structure.

If we follow the concepts described here for the constitution and the eternal life of the Trinity, then we have to talk about the unity of the triune God in three respects.

In respect of the constitution of the Trinity the Father is the 'origin-without-origin' of the Godhead. According to the doctrine of the two processions, the Son and the Spirit take their divine hypostases from him. So in the constitution of the Godhead, *the Father* forms the 'monarchial' unity of the Trinity.

But in respect of the Trinity's inner life, the three Persons themselves form their unity, by virtue of their relation to one another and in the eternal perichoresis of their love. They are concentrated round *the eternal Son*. This is the perichoretic unity of the Trinity.

Finally, the mutual transfiguration and illumination of the Trinity into the eternal glory of the divine life is bound up with this. This uniting mutuality and community proceeds from *the Holy Spirit*.

The unity of the Trinity is constituted by the Father, concentrated round the Son, and illumined through the Holy Spirit. So, summing up, we can say the following.

In the history and experience of salvation this illumination is perceived through the Spirit first of all. It is in the power of the Spirit that doxology begins. The perichoretic unity of the triune God is perceived in salvation history and reflected in salvation history. Lastly, the monarchy of the Father is perceived in the Trinity because everything in the history of salvation comes from him and strives towards him. To throw open the circulatory movement of the divine light and the divine relationships, and to take men and women, with the whole of creation, into the life-stream of the triune God: that is the meaning of creation, reconciliation and glorification.

§4 DOES THE HOLY SPIRIT PROCEED FROM THE FATHER 'AND FROM THE SON'?

> Et in Spiritum Sanctum,
> Dominum et vivificantem,
> qui ex Patre (Filioque) procedit,
> qui cum Patre et Filio simul
> adoratur et glorificatur,
> qui locutus est per prophetas.
>   (*Symbolum Nicaeno-Constantinopolitanum*)

1. The State of the Modern Discussion about the Filioque

The inclusion of the *Filioque* in the text of the Niceno-Constantinopolitan Creed of 381 (first of all in Spain, then through Charlemagne, and finally through Pope Benedict VIII) led to the schism in the church in 1054. In addition, the defence of the Filioque by theologians of the Western church, contrary to the denial of it by Eastern theologians, led to a one-sided trinitarian doctrine in the West, and hindered the development of a trinitarian pneumatology. The overcoming of the ecclesiastical dispute about the late inclusion of the Filioque into the confessional text of an ecumenical council, must therefore go hand in hand with the theological development of a more comprehensive doctrine of the Trinity. Consequently the new ecumenical conversations on the subject have at least three essential aims: 1. to clear up the dispute about the early council tradition; 2. to arrive at a common theological declaration about the relationship of the Son to the Holy Spirit; and 3. in the West, to achieve a more open-minded insight into the trinitarian independence of the Holy Spirit, in the fullness of his energies and influence in salvation history and in his eternal glorification of the Son and the Father.

The Councils of Lyons in 1274 and Florence in 1438–1445 were impeded by different political and church-political power groups: the more powerful West, under the leadership of Rome, tried to force the Filioque on the East, which had been weakened by the struggle against Islam. These attempts proved unsuccessful theologically and left bitterness behind them in the East.

It is curious that after their separation from Rome the Protestant churches made no serious attempt to take up conversations with the Orthodox Church again by returning to the original text of the creed, i.e., by renouncing the Filioque. The arguments that were put forward in the correspondence between Tübingen Protestant theologians and the theologians of the Patriarch Jeremiah II of Constantinople between 1573 and 1581, for example, were the ones familiar from mediaeval times.[86] They offered no new points of view. Protestant theologians continued to cling to the Filioque.[87] Consequently Orthodox theologians also merely went on repeating the objections to Augustine put forward by Photius and Gregorius Palamas. The trinitarian pneumatology of the orthodox Lutherans and Calvinists in no way differed from the ideas of their models, Augustine and Anselm. But this means that the Reformation saw itself as a Reformation of the *Western* church, with the schism of 1054 as its premise.

Old Catholic theology, on the other hand, sought contact with the Orthodox Church immediately after its separation from Rome in 1871 (which was brought about by the First Vatican Council); and as early as 1874/75 it held 'union conferences' on the subject in Bonn. Anglican and German Protestant theologians also took part in these, even if not as official representatives of the churches. Old Catholic theologians thought from the very beginning that the Filioque had been introduced in an illegitimate way in the West.

But it is only in recent years that liturgical and canon-law conclusions have been drawn from this: the Old Catholic church is the first church in the West that has officially struck out the 'Filioque' addition from the creed. And Old Catholic theology is the furthest advanced in developing a new formulation of trinitarian doctrine, in the tradition of the Western church, but without the Filioque.[88]

It is not only on the Western side that the fronts have begun to move in this matter, which for so long could only be described as tangled. In 1898 the *Revue Internationale de théologie* published in No. 24 'Theses on the Filioque: by a Russian theologian'.[89] The author was the famous church historian Boris Bolotov. It is true that these theses are a matter of dispute between Russian Orthodox and Greek Orthodox theologians.[90] But they intuitively indicate the direction in which an understanding between Western and Eastern traditions can be sought and achieved. Bolotov adheres to the procession of the Holy Spirit, 'from the Father alone'. But he sees the Son in such close proximity to the Father that the Son becomes the logical 'presupposition' and the factual 'condition' for the procession of the Spirit from the Father and to some extent involved in it. Consequently the Son is not removed from the procession of the Spirit from the Father, and is not uninvolved in it. Whereas Photian and Palamitic neo-Orthodoxy lays its main stress on the strict division between the generation of the Son through the Father, and the procession of the Spirit from the Father,[91] we find in Bolotov a theological approximation to the truth which the West tried to express through the Filioque – even if in an inappropriate way. Though it must be noted that Bolotov firmly rejects the Filioque in the procession of the Spirit from the Father. It is therefore not yet possible to judge Bolotov's 'theses' as being representative of the Eastern church's views; but they can certainly be acknowledged to be the most accommodating suggestion from the side of Orthodox theology in the direction of reconciliation with the West in this question.[92]

2. The Creed and its Theological Interpretation

As far as the official teachings of the church are concerned, the external, canonistic and liturgical problem can be solved if the Western churches acknowledge – in so far as they have not already done so – that the Filioque is a later addition to the credal text of an ecumenical council which was itself only recognized as such at a late stage. The Filioque was not originally intended as a polemical attack on the Eastern church. Its aim was simply to interpret and define the trinitarian statement of the creed more clearly. In the East too, the creed's statement was interpreted analogously (though in the opposite direction) through the interpretative 'ἐκ μόνου τοῦ πατρός'. In actual fact, therefore, whatever the intention may have been in secular and in ecclesiastical politics, what were at issue were really interpretative formulas, not attempts at a unilateral correction of the common creed. And if this is so, then the addition can be withdrawn and treated as what it is: an interpretation of the original text made in a particular situation of theological conflict. The actual theological discussion about the 'filioquistic' and the 'monopatristic' interpretation of the Trinity is unaffected by this. By withdrawing the Filioque a schism in the church can be ended; but a common discussion about the doctrine of the Trinity must be begun at the same time. The one is impossible without the other.

The creed itself avoids any comment about the participation of the Son in the procession of the Spirit from the Father. Nor does it say anything about the relationship between the Son and the Spirit. This silence may be understandable in the light of the struggle against the Pneumatomachians of the time, who understood the Spirit as a created being and subordinated him to the Son. At all events, it is impossible to interpret this silence as meaning a dogmatic decision of the Fathers of the council against a participation of the Son in the procession of the Spirit from the Father. They talked only about the procession of the Holy Spirit *from the Father* because they wanted to stress the Spirit's full divinity. Earlier formulations by Cappadocian theologians certainly talk about the Son's relationship to the Holy Spirit, so that they are able to interpret the Spirit as being also 'the Spirit of the Son' and 'the Spirit of Christ'. Dogmatically, however, it must be seen as a deficiency that the question of the participation of the Son in the procession of the Holy Spirit from the Father, or his participation in the form of the Spirit, did not receive any binding formulation either in the creed of 381 or later. Many Eastern and Western theologians have therefore called the creed's statements about the Holy Spirit incomplete and have proposed an attempt at a new, common formulation.

The real root of the theological differences between the Eastern church's triadology and the trinitarian doctrine of the Western church can be found in the question left open in 381. Consequently the schism in the church cannot be overcome simply by a return to the original text of the Niceno-Constantinopolitan Creed. The schism can only be healed if we find a common answer to the question about the relationship of the Son to the Holy Spirit and of the Holy Spirit to the Son.

3. The Procession of the Spirit from the Father of the Son

The Holy Spirit proceeds from the Father (John 15.26). The Father eternally 'breathes out' the Holy Spirit. The Holy Spirit does not proceed from the Son. Consequently it is a correct interpretation to say that the Holy Spirit proceeds 'solely' from the Father. This 'solely' is intended to denote the unique mode of the Spirit's procession from the Father, and aims to fend off any blurring or confusion of the inner-trinitarian relationships. The uniqueness of the procession of the Spirit from the Father (and therefore the 'sole causality' of the Father in respect of the Spirit) has in fact never been disputed by theologians of the Western church. Although their Filioque has given rise to this misunderstanding, they have in spite of it never seen the Son as 'competing' with the Father as regards the issuing of the Holy Spirit; there has never been any question of two sources for the Godhead. Consequently the Filioque could also be interpreted as *per Filium*. The Filioque was never directed against the 'monarchy' of the Father, even though this formula was supposed to ward off tendencies towards subordinationism in trinitarian doctrine, as well as trends towards a subordinationist dissolution of the Trinity in its own economy of salvation. It has never been denied in the West that the Son (John 16.27) and the Holy Spirit (John 15.26) proceed from the Father, each in his own way; and that therefore the Father is – in different ways – the 'origin' of them both; or that the Son and the Spirit glorify the Father in all eternity. The Father, being himself without origin, was always the first Person in the Trinity. And whereas he was called '$\alpha\dot{\upsilon}\tau\dot{o}\theta\varepsilon o\varsigma$', it proved impossible in the West too to describe the Son and the Holy Spirit in the same way. Consequently we have to assent to the formula about the Spirit's proceeding from the Father, without the addition 'Filioque'.[93]

But the exclusive addition ' "solely" from the Father' must be understood in the sense that it only refers to the *proceeding* of the Spirit – that is to say to his divine existence (hypostasis), and not also to his inner-trinitarian form in his relations to the Father and to the Son. This is shown by the Eastern church's argument in favour of the interpretitive addition of ' μόνου ': the Father brings forth the Spirit inasmuch as he is the sole origin, the sole ground and the sole source of the Godhead, not inasmuch as he is the Father of the Son. This argument only after all tells us that the Holy Spirit has his divine *existence* and divine substance solely from 'the source of the Godhead', who is the Father. It does not as yet tell us anything about the *relation* of the Father as *'proboleus'* or 'breather' to what he brings forth or breathes out – the Spirit. Nor is anything as yet stated about the relational and perichoretic *form* which the Holy Spirit takes on in his relationship to the Son. The Filioque was and is disputed, not because of the fatherhood of the first Person of the Trinity, but because of his monarchy – and rightly so at this point, provided that the Filioque is moved to this point at all. We have to distinguish between the constitution of the Trinity and the Trinity's inner life. This is admittedly difficult if, like Augustine and Aquinas, one now only understands 'person' in a relational sense and hence identifies the two levels of 'constitution' and 'relation'.

The creed tells us that the Holy Spirit 'proceedeth from the Father'. The first Person of the Trinity is the Father, but only in respect of the Son – that is to say, in the eternal generation of the Son. God the Father is always *the Father of the Son.*

He is not to be called Father because he is the Sole Cause, and because all things are dependent on him. God shows himself as the Father solely and exclusively in the eternal generation of the eternal Son. In salvation history he is exclusively 'the Father of Jesus Christ', and it is through Christ the Son and in the fellowship of this 'first-born' among many brothers and sisters that he is our Father too. In order to preserve this distinction – which is an important one in every sense – we would suggest deliberately talking about 'the Father of the Son'.

The Father is in all eternity solely the Father of the Son. He is not the Father of the Spirit. The procession of the Spirit from the Father therefore has as its premise the generation of the Son through the Father in eternity, for it is only in this that the Father manifests himself as the Father and *is* the Father. Just as 'Son' is a theological concept, not a cosmological one (as became clear in the Arian dispute), so 'Father' too is a theological concept, not a cosmological one. The doctrine of the Trinity makes this unmistakably clear.

> The Spirit is the third hypostasis of the Holy Trinity. His being presupposes the existence of the Father and the existence of the Son, because the Holy Spirit proceeds from the Father, and because the Father is the Father of the Son alone. Consequently, as soon as God *proboleus tou pneumatos* is called *Father*, he is thought of as having a Son.[94]

If, then, God as Father breathes out the Holy Spirit, then the Spirit proceeds from *the Father of the Son*. His procession therefore presupposes, firstly, the generation of the Son; secondly, the existence of the Son; and thirdly, the mutual relationship of the Father and the Son. The Son is the logical presupposition and the actual condition for the procession of the Spirit from the Father; but he is not the Spirit's origin, as the Father is. The procession of the Spirit from the Father must therefore be essentially distinguished from the generation of the Son through the Father, and yet it is connected with that generation relationally.

And if the Holy Spirit does not proceed from the Father only because he is the source of the Godhead, but because he is the Father of the only begotten Son, then he does after all issue from the fatherhood of God, which is to say from the Father's relationship to the Son. This makes the inner-trinitarian relationship between Word (Logos) and Spirit clear. The two 'processions' are simultaneous and in common. Although it is erroneous to conclude from this that the Spirit proceeds from the Father 'and the Son' we must none the less adhere to the fact that the Spirit proceeds from the Father in the eternal presence of the Son, and that therefore the Son is not uninvolved in it: 'Le Fils éternel n'est pas étranger à la procession du Saint Esprit' (P. Boris Bobrinskoy). The Son is eternally with and in the Father. The Father is never without the Son and nowhere acts without him, just as he is never without, and never acts without, the Spirit.

> Since the Holy Spirit proceeds from the Father during the existence of the Son, *hyparchontos tou hyou*, and since the Father

and the Son are through of as being directly 'contiguous', as
tangential, the moment of the eternally present procession of
the Holy Spirit is thought of as so taking place that the Holy
Spirit who proceeds from the Father is already received by the
Son as a complete hypostasis . . . The Holy Spirit who proceeds
from the Father as complete hypostasis, comes through the Son,
appears through the Son, reveals through the Son the essence
which he has from the Father. He shines through the Son and
interpenetrates in his light through him.[95]

Both Orthodox and Western theologians ought to be able to assent
to these remarks of Bolotov's, for they preserve the procession of
the Spirit 'from the Father alone', and yet move the Son into such
close proximity to the Father that the relationship of the Son to
the Spirit becomes directly intelligible. This leads us to the suggestion that in interpreting the creed we should talk about:
The Holy Spirit who proceeds from the Father of the Son.

4. What the Holy Spirit receives from the Son

According to the ideas we have developed up to now, it is only
possible to talk indirectly about a participation of the Son in the
procession of the Spirit from the Father, in the sense that this
participation is mediated by way of the Father's fatherhood. We
cannot yet declare that there is a direct relationship between the
Son and the Spirit. Statements according to which the Son is 'not
alien' to the procession of the Spirit from the Father, or 'not
uninvolved' in it, paraphrase with the help of double negations
what cannot yet be positively expressed, or what it is the intention
to avoid saying. But this remains unsatisfactory.

In order to get away from indirect paraphrases and to arrive at
direct statements, let us go back to Epiphanius' famous dictum,
according to which the Holy Spirit 'proceeds' from the Father and
'receives' from the Son. We understand this statement in inner-
trinitarian terms, and not as meaning that the Spirit 'proceeds'
from the Father in an eternally primordial way and only 'receives'
from the Son in a temporal sense.

If we understand the proposition as a description of the primordial relationships in the Trinity, then we have to ask: what in the
Holy Spirit proceeds from the Father, and what does he receive

from the Son? Our proposed answer would be: the Holy Spirit has from the Father his perfect, divine existence (*hypostasis*, *hyparxis*) and receives from the Son his relational form (*eidos*, *prosopon*). Although the procession of the Holy Spirit's divine existence must emphatically be ascribed to the Father *alone*, yet it must be equally firmly recognized that this form or visage is moulded by the Father *and by the Son*. That is why he is also called 'the Spirit of the Son'. The hypostatic procession of the Spirit from the Father must be clearly distinguished from his relational, perichoretic form with respect to the Father and the Son. By the very fact of declaring that the Holy Spirit proceeds from the Father 'alone', because he is the 'source of the Godhead', we have confined our statement as yet to the divinity of the hypostasis of the Holy Spirit, compared with any divine creation. We have not as yet said anything about his inner-trinitarian, interpersonal, perichoretic form.

The distinction which we are introducing between hypostasis and *prosopon* (or *eidos*) – which corresponds in Latin to the difference between *persona* and *facies* – may seem surprising at first sight. But the distinction can help us to differentiate between the relationship of the Holy Spirit to the being of the Godhead, and his relationship to the Father and to the Son in the process of the divine life itself.

The tradition of the Western church has developed this differentiation in the doctrine of the trinitarian relations. According to this doctrine, the relations and the persons are to be understood as complementary: the relations consist in the persons and the persons in the relations. The relations form the basis for the eternal perichoresis.

The tradition of the Eastern church has approached the complex that has to be considered here in two doctrines: the doctrine of the inner-trinitarian transfiguration of the triune God; and the doctrine of the inter-trinitarian energies. These post-Nicean doctrines certainly do not belong on the same level, but we should draw on their insights for a clarification of our problem.

We understand *hypostasis* and *hyparxis* in this context as bringing to expression the *being* of the Holy Spirit in respect of his divine origin, whereas the terms *prosopon* and *eidos* express his *form* in the trinitarian process of eternal life and eternal glory. Whereas hypostasis is an ontological term, form is an aesthetic one. They therefore do not compete with one another; they are complementary.

Pure form is supreme beauty, for beauty lies in perfect form, in so far as this is the expression of the inner nature, and if it is an expression that arouses love. Form comes to appearance when it is illumined and reflects the light. Then form is transfigured. For Paul, the object of a transfiguration of this kind is often the face (*prosopon*). The glory of God shines 'in the face of Christ' (II Cor. 4.6). The glory of the Lord is reflected on us all 'with unveiled face' (II Cor. 3.18). And one day we shall see God 'face to face' (I Cor. 13.12). When we talk about the *form* of the Holy Spirit, we mean his face as it is manifested in his turning to the Father and to the Son, and in the turning of the Father and the Son to him. It is the Holy Spirit in the inner-trinitarian manifestation of glory.

Objectively speaking, the procession of existence preceeds the reception of form in the relations we have described, for the existence of the receiver logically preceeds the reception. Consequently procession and reception are not the same thing. If the procession means the unique relationship of the Holy Spirit to the Father as 'the source of the Godhead', then the reception means the form of the Holy Spirit with respect to the Father and the Son. In the formulation of the relational, perichoretic form of the Holy Spirit, the Filioque has its justification. But it must be kept well away from the procession of the Holy Spirit. The Syrian-Orthodox Church of South India has formulated this point with especial clarity in the church's Whitsun prayer:

> When we say 'Father', the Son and the Holy Spirit come from him. When we say 'Son', the Father and the Holy Spirit are known through him. When we say Ruho (Spirit), the Father and the Son are perfect and complete in him. The Father is the Creator, not begotten; the Son is begotten, not begetting; the Holy Spirit (Ruho) proceeds from the Father, taking the person and the nature of the Father from the Son.[96]

We would therefore propose that we interpret the text of the creed by saying:

The Holy Spirit, who proceeds from the Father of the Son, and who receives his form from the Father and the Son.

§5. THE TRINITARIAN PRINCIPLE OF UNIQUENESS

The 'begetting' of the Son through the Father and the 'procession' of the Spirit from the Father are two different processes. If we sum them up under the heading of *processio*, and talk about 'two processions', the danger of an abstraction of this kind makes itself felt at once. The specific and particular character of the Son in relation to the Father, and the special character of the Spirit in relation to him, are obscured and passed over. It is then only too easy to interpret the Spirit as 'a second Son' or the Son as 'another Spirit'. Consequently, at this point we must not take any general heading at all to cover the generation of the Son through the Father and the issuing of the Spirit from the Father. We must remain concrete, and take time to relate the one after the other.

The 'issuing' of the Spirit from the Father and the 'reception' of his relational, perichoretic form from the Father and from the Son are two different processes. The Western church's Filioque blurs this difference. It all too easily suggests that the existence of the Holy Spirit has 'two origins' in the Father and the Son. So we must not add things together here, as the formula 'and from the Son' does, leaving unsettled what comes from the Father and what from the Son. We must remain specific and can only tell of the relationship between the Father and the Holy Spirit, and between the Son and the Holy Spirit, one after the other.

Orthodox theologians based their justifiable rejection of the undifferentiated Filioque formula on the Father's monarchy; but this, in its turn, is undifferentiated too. By introducing the Aristotelian concept of cause or origin (ἀρχή, αἰτία) into the doctrine of the Trinity, as the Cappadocians did (and this was not undisputed in the early church either), the uniqueness of the Father over against the Son and the Holy Spirit can certainly be emphasized. But if the Father is only named as the 'origin' of the divinity of the Son and the divinity of the Holy Spirit, then the specific difference between the generation of the Son and the procession of the Spirit is blurred.

The Father 'breathed out' the Holy Spirit in eternity as *the Father of the Son*, not as the monarch of the Godhead. The introduction of the concept of origin is understandable, as a defence against the non-differentiated doctrine of the Filioque. But contains a similar danger within itself as the position against which it is directed. By its means, God's universal relationship to the world – namely, his universal monarchy – is all too easily transferred to the inner trinitarian life of God. But we cannot expel the dangerous 'Filioqueism' from the doctrine of the Trinity by a 'monopatrism' without getting entangled in similar difficulties. Even the concept of the Father as sole origin threatens to blur the concrete inner-trinitarian relationships. The concept of origin can therefore only be used in a transferred sense. It is not a general heading covering both generation and breathing out.

Basically, according to the Cappadocian doctrine of the Trinity, both the Godhead and relationships of the persons coincide in the first Person of the Trinity. The first Person must guarantee both the unity of the Godhead and the threefold character of the Persons. If we do not keep these different meanings strictly apart, either the Trinity crumbles away into tritheism, or it is reduced by a subordinationist process to monotheism. It would therefore be helpful to remove the concept of the First Cause from trinitarian doctrine altogether, and to confine oneself to an account of the interpersonal relationships. For out of these the logical priority of the Father emerges all by itself.

The doctrine of the three hypostases or Persons of the Trinity is dangerous too, because it applies one and the same concept to the Father, the Son and the Holy Spirit. This suggests that they are homogeneous and equal, namely hypostases, persons or modes of being. But the heading hypostasis, person or mode of being blurs the specific differences between the Father, the Son and the Holy Spirit. This became particularly clear to us from the difficulty of understanding the Holy Spirit as 'Person' and as 'third Person' at that – that is to say, the difficulty of understanding him in the same way as the Son and the Father. The 'three Persons' are different, not merely in their relations to one another, but also in respect of their character as Persons, even if the person is to be understood in his relations, and not apart from them. If we wanted to remain specific, we should have to use a different concept in each case when applying the word 'person' to the Father, the Son and the Spirit.[97] The Holy Spirit is not a person in the same, identical sense as the Son; and neither of them is a person in the same, identical sense as the Father. Their description as divine Persons in the plural already shows a tendency towards modalism in itself. For the generic term hypostasis or person stresses what is the same and in common, not what is particular and different about them.

Finally, it is clear how much the doctrine of the substance of the Godhead, of which all three hypostases or Persons partake, threatens to obscure the trinitarian differences in a Sabellian, modalistic and ultimately unitarian sense. Ever since Thomas Aquinas, the doctrine of the Godhead's single substance has taken precedence in the West, logically and epistemologically, over the doctrine of the Trinity. But inherent in this procedence is the danger of depriving the doctrine of the Trinity itself of its function. The premise of the uncompounded nature of the Divine Being made the idea of the triune God questionable. That is why in the Western church trinitarian doctrine has almost without exception a tendency to modalism. This can only be changed if the indispensible idea of God's unity is expressed in trinitarian terms, and no longer in pre-trinitarian ones. The unity of God is to be found in the triunity of the Father, the Son and the Holy Spirit. It neither precedes that nor follows it.

From this brief account of the dangers inherent in the introduction of over-riding headings into the doctrine of the Trinity, we have to conclude that no summing-up, generic terms must be used at all in the doctrine of the Trinity. For in the life of the immanent Trinity everything is unique. It is only because everything in God's nature is unique that in the ways and works of God it can be recognized as the origin of other things. In considering the doctrine of the immanent Trinity, we can really only tell, relate, but not sum up. We have to remain concrete, for history shows us that it is in the abstractions that the heresies are hidden. The foundations of orthodoxy, on the other hand, are to be found in narrative differentiation. At the centre of Christian theology stands the eternal history which the triune God experiences in himself. Every narrative needs *time*. For the narrative in which he praises the triune God, man needs his time too. That is more appropriate for the eternal divine present than the abstractions in which time is dissolved.

VI

The Kingdom of Freedom

§1 CRITICISM OF POLITICAL AND CLERICAL MONOTHEISM

The functional problem of the doctrine of the Trinity lies in its relationship to the doctrine of the kingdom. How are God's Trinity and his kingdom related to one another? Is the doctrine of the Trinity the appropriate interpretation of the one divine lordship (Barth's view), or does the history of the kingdom of God reveal the divine life of the Father, the Son and the Spirit? Does the divine Trinity act only inwardly in its threefold nature, acting outwardly 'without division' (as Augustine taught)? Or are the 'works of the Trinity' defined in a trinitarian sense as well? The more we stress the economy of salvation and the lordship of God, the more we are compelled to stress God's unity, for this divine rule would seem only capable of being exercised by a single, identical subject. But the further doxology is developed, the more it is possible already to perceive the triunity in the history of salvation and in the lordship that makes us free; and the more this will be praised to all eternity.

We have developed the doctrine of the Trinity in the context of the surmounting of religious monotheism, monotheistic Christianity and Christian monotheism. We must therefore now go on to see its bearings on the criticism of political and clerical monotheism as well. We have said that monotheism is monarchism. The question: does God exist? is an abstract one. Theology is never concerned with the actual *existence* of a God. It is interested solely in the *rule* of this God in heaven and on earth. The notion of a divine monarchy in heaven and on earth, for its part, generally provides the justification for earthly domination – religious, moral, patriarchal or political domination – and makes it a hierarchy, a 'holy rule'. The idea of the almighty ruler of the universe everywhere requires abject servitude, because it points to complete dependency in all spheres of life.

The doctrine of the Trinity which evolves out of the surmounting of monotheism for Christ's sake, must therefore also overcome this monarchism, which legitimates dependency, helplessness and servitude. This doctrine of the Trinity must be developed as the true theological doctrine of freedom. Religiously motivated political monotheism has always been used in order to legitimate domination, from the emperor cults of the ancient world, Byzantium and the absolute ideologies of the seventeenth century, down to the dictatorships of the twentieth. The doctrine of the Trinity which, on the contrary, is developed as a theological doctrine of freedom must for its part point towards a community of men and women without supremacy and without subjection.

1. *Political Monotheism*

What is the relationship between the religious ideas of any given era and the political constitution of its societies? That is the question asked by political theology.[1]

The originally Stoic concept of political theology[2] presupposes the unity of politics and religion because it was the polis itself which exercised the public practice of religion. Political theology dealt with the sacred rites and sacrifices which the polis had to offer to the gods. To reverence the gods counted as the highest function of the state, for it was the gods who secured the peace and welfare of the whole community. The correspondence between the community's religious ideas and its political constitution counted as being one of life's self-evident premises.

When the churches took on an independent function in the practice of religion, and as differentiations increased in the sphere of both religion and politics, it became increasingly difficult to sum up the relation between religion and politics in any given situation by means of a single definition. The two modern theories about this relationship also prove inadequate in the face of the complex realities of the modern world. The *reflection theory*, according to which economic interests and political relationships are merely reproduced in the superstructure of religion, is only applicable to a limited degree;[3] while it is only in a very few cases that the contrary *theory of the secularization of religious ideas* can clearly demonstrate that religion has actually determined politics and economics.[4] Causal reductions and deductions are only very rarely realistic. Reciprocal influence and conditioning is much more frequent. Generally alliances between religious ideas and political options can be discovered, alliances evoked by particular situations and the interests of those involved. Within these alliances one can then discover affinities, correspondences, interdependencies and, occasionally, contradictions as well. Today's political theology, therefore, which enquires into the relationship between religious and political ideas, must note and define the situation and the constellations of interests in which these correspondences and contradictions appear and make themselves felt. This applies to historical situations, and to the present even more.

It was the Christian apologists of the ancient world who developed one of the first forms of political monotheism.[5] Since it meant discipleship of the Jesus who had been crucified by the power of the Roman state, early Christianity was felt to be hostile to the state and godless, and it was because of this that it was persecuted. Consequently it was all-important for the Christian apologists to present their faith as the truly reasonable religion, and hence as the divine worship which really sustained the state. Following Josephus, they linked biblical tradition about the one rule of the one God with philosophical monotheism. Philosophical monotheism was already associated with the cosmological doctrine of the single, hierarchical world order. The universe itself has a monarchical structure: one deity – one Logos – one cosmos. The fusing of biblical and cosmological monarchism gave rise to the notion of the single, universal pyramid: the one God is Creator, Lord and possessor of his world. His will is its law. In him the world has its unity and its peace. By distinguishing between Creator and creature, the biblical doctrine of creation (compared with Aristotelian and Stoic cosmology) accentuated the idea of God's power of disposal and the dependency of everything on his will.[6] Stoic pantheism was heightened into Christian theism. The universal monarchy was understood in absolutist terms: the world is not the visible 'body' of the invisible deity (Seneca's view); it is the 'work' of God the Creator.

The ready convertibility of political into cosmological ideas can already be perceived in Aristotle. His *Metaphysics*, Book 12, expounds the view that the deity is one, indivisible, immovable, impassible and hence perfect. The universe is ruled by the deity through *entelechy* and *eros*. All finite beings are directed towards, and are dependent upon, the infinite divine being. That is why the world has a monarchical constitution. This constitution can be perceived in the hierarchical gradations of inorganic, organic, unconscious, conscious and animate beings. Aristotle closes his remarks on cosmology with the famous statement: 'Being refuses to be badly administered. The rule of the many is not healthy; *let there be only one ruler*.'[7] The world must be understood as the ordering lordship of the one, perfect Being over the multiplicity of imperfect and finite things. But this statement is a quotation. It comes from the *Iliad*. And there it was meant politically. Agamemnon unites the divided and mutually hostile Greek cities against the Trojans with this cry: 'Let there be only one ruler!' The question whether Aristotle understood his hierarchical cosmology as a background legitimating the universal empire of Alexander the Great may be left on one side here. But if political rule was legitimated in the ancient world by an appeal to its correspondence with the gods, then polytheism corresponds to the multiplicity of cities and states, whereas cosmological monotheism calls for analogy in a universal imperium that unites the cities and states. This is the only way in which the notion of the correspondence of political and religious ideas can be maintained and used as a legitimation of rule.

The idea of theocracy was very much alive among the martyrs, during the Christian persecutions, and among the theological apologists of Christianity in the first three centuries. Consequently, from a very early period there was a Christian preference for the Roman empire. Remembrance of the Emperor Augustus's peaceful empire outshone even the remembrance of the Christ crucified by Pontius Pilate.[8] The justification of this political choice in favour of the Roman empire ran as follows: The polytheism of the heathen is idolatry. The multiplicity of the nations (which is bound up with polytheism, because polytheism is its justification) is the reason for the continuing unrest in the world. Christian monotheism is in a position to overcome heathen polytheism. Belief in the one God brings peace, so to speak, in the diverse and competitive world of the gods. Consequently Christendom is the one universal religion of peace. In place of the many cults it puts belief in the one God. What political order corresponds to this faith in the one God and the organization of his worship by the one church? It is the Emperor Augustus's kingdom of peace, seen as Rome's enduring obligation and commitment, and as the common hope of the nations.

This political theology was widespread from Origen right down to Eusebius of Caesarea.[9] True, it was not the common stock of the churches. Nor did it convince the Roman Caesars. But it makes it easy to understand why Constantine the Great tried to make out of Christianity a permitted and then a state religion, instead of a persecuted one. The doctrine of sovereignty suggested by Christian monotheism is, as we have seen, more absolutist than the theories based on Aristotle or the Stoics: the one almighty emperor is to a pre-eminent degree *the visible image* of the invisible God. His 'glory' reflects God's glory. His rule represents God's rule. Hence the one God is venerated in him. He is not merely the regent; he is the actual lord and possessor of the imperium. The law which applies to all does not bind him; his will is law, makes laws and changes them. He is ultimately in duty bound to extend the imperium to all peoples, in order to allow everyone to enjoy the peace uniting them: 'The one God, the one heavenly king and the one sovereign nomos and logos corresponds to the one king on earth.'[10] The idea of unity in God therefore provokes both the idea of the universal, unified church, and the idea of the universal, unified state: one God – one emperor – one church – one empire.

We may leave on one side here the millenarian expectations which some theologians associated with the 'Constantinian turn of events' and may proceed to modern absolutism, in order to investigate the theological and political doctrine of sovereignty which we find there too. 'All that the European Enlightenment left of Christian belief in God was the monotheism which is just as questionable in its theological content as it is in its political results.'[11] What are these political results? We may take as an example the seventeenth-century Huguenot doctrine of the state as it developed in France, the country of absolutism. After the unhappy outcome of the Huguenot struggles – with the fall of the fortress of La Rochelle in 1628 – many Calvinists turned away from the resistence doctrines of the monarchomachists and adopted Jean Bodin's absolutist theory of the state, in order to survive in Lous XIV's kingdom.[12] They condemned the execution of Charles I by Cromwell and developed their own, modern *raison d'état*. Samuel Borchart declared that the king was above the community of men because he occupied the place of God on earth.[13] For Moyse Amyraut, the image of God shines more brightly in the king than in other people, because God impresses on the king the character of his own majesty.[14] It follows from this: '*Summus princeps est autonomous et a solo Deo pendet.*'[15] He rules by divine right (*jure divino*) and is therefore responsible to no one but God. The seventeenth-century French Calvinists thought that this fundamental ἀνευθυνία (non-accountability towards anyone else) on the sovereign's part was the complete reflection or 'portrait' of the majesty of God. 'Our sole care must be to beseech of God that, just as He has given us a portrait of His majesty in the king's sovereignty, so He may also grant us an image of His righteousness in what the king doeth.'[16] It was only the ties of the sovereign with God, they believed, that protected his subjects from arbitrariness and tyranny. In this way they were going back to Calvin's theology of sovereignty, but they took from it only the nominalist features in his picture of God. Jean Bodin saw the ancient Roman maxim as authoritative: *Princeps legibus solutus est*. This maxim crops up in the nominalist description of *potentia divina absoluta* in slightly different form: *Deus legibus solutus est*. It is impossible to conceive of any law which is above God, for by the very nature of his being God himself embodies the highest law. If this divine sovereignty is made the prototype of the sovereignty of the sate, what emerges is a hitherto unknown absolutism of power. Theoretically, the union of the highest power and the highest law in God excludes earthly tyranny; but in actual practice the ruler's lack of accountability to anyone else puts him outside the law and 'above the constitution'. All that remains is John Hobbes' brutal principle: *Auctoritas, non veritas facit legem.*[17]

The European absolutism of the Enlightenment period was the final form of political monotheism in its religiously legitimated form. It was also the last attempt to establish a state based on religious unity. Through the French Revolution, the contrary idea of popular sovereignty then became the basis of the modern democratic state. The absolutist idea of sovereignty only continued to be cultivated by the people whom Carl Schmitt calls 'the state philosophers of counter-revolution' – Bonald, de Maistre and Donoso Cortes and – on the Protestant side – Friedrich Julius Stahl and Abraham Kuyper. If we trace its history further, as the history of a particular tradition, this absolutist view was then passed on to the modern anti-democratic and anti-Communist ideology of dictatorship.[18] Admittedly, for modern military dictatorships religious legitimation formulas have become superfluous altogether. The terror of naked force is enough to keep the friend–enemy alternative alive in a permanent civil war.

The expansion of the doctrine of the Trinity in the concept of God can only really overcome this transposition of religious into political monotheism, and the further translation of political monotheism into absolutism, by overcoming the notion of a universal monarchy of the one God. Historically speaking, however, the doctrine of the divine monarchy did not in fact 'run aground' on trinitarian dogma, as Erik Peterson maintains, because in the early church trinitarian dogma left this particular dogma untouched. As long as the unity of the triune God is understood monadically or subjectivistically, and not in trinitarian terms, the whole cohesion of a religious legitimation of political sovereignty continues to exist. It is only when the doctrine of the Trinity vanquishes the monotheistic notion of the great universal monarch in heaven, and his divine patriarchs in the world, that earthly rulers, dictators and tyrants cease to find any justifying religious archetypes any more.[19]

How must a doctrine of the Trinity be formulated if it is to have this intention?

(*a*) The Christian doctrine of the Trinity unites God, the almighty Father, with Jesus the Son, whom he delivered up and whom the Romans crucified, and with the life-giving Spirit, who creates the new heaven and the new earth. It is impossible to form the figure of the omnipotent, universal monarch, who is reflected in earthly rulers, out of the unity of this Father, this Son and this Spirit.

(*b*) If we see the Almighty in trinitarian terms, he is not the archetype of the mighty ones of this world. He is the Father of the Christ who was crucified and raised for us. As the Father of Jesus Christ, he is almighty because he exposes himself to the experience of suffering, pain, helplessness and death. But what he *is* is not almighty power; what he *is* is love. It is his passionate, passible love that is almighty, nothing else.

(*c*) The glory of the triune God is reflected, not in the crowns of kings and the triumphs of victors, but in the face of the crucified Jesus, and in the faces of the oppressed whose brother he became. He is the one visible image of the invisible God. The glory of the triune God is also reflected in the community of Christ: in the fellowship of believers and of the poor.

(*d*) Seen in trinitarian terms, the life-giving Spirit, who confers on us the future and hope, does not proceed from any accumulation of power, or from the absolutist practice of lordship; he proceeds from the Father of Jesus Christ and from the resurrection of the Son. The resurrection through the life-quickening energy of the Holy Spirit is experienced, not at the spearheads of progress, but in the shadow of death.

A political theology which is consciously Christian, and is therefore bound to criticize political monotheism, will ask what is in accord with God – what his correspondences on earth are – which means among other things: in the political constitution of a community? Attempts to restore the unity of religion and politics are mistaken. The result would be the engulfing of the church by the state. But we must ask which political options are in accord with the convictions of the Christian faith, and do not contradict them. We have said that it is not the monarchy of a ruler that corresponds to the triune God; it is the community of men and women, without privileges and without subjugation. The three divine Persons have everything in common, except for their personal characteristics. So the Trinity corresponds to a community in which people are defined though their relations with one another and in their significance for one another, not in opposition to one another, in terms of power and possession.

The monotheistic God is 'the Lord of the world'. He is defined simply through his power of disposal over his property, not through personality and personal relationships. He really has no name – merely legal titles. But the triune God represents an inexhaustible life, a life which the three Persons have in common, in which they are present with one another, for one another and in one another. What the doctrine of the Trinity calls *perichoresis* was also understood by patristic theologians as *the sociality* of the three divine Persons. Two different categories of analogy have always been used for the eternal life of the Trinity: the category of the individual person, and the category of community.[20] Ever since Augustine's development of the psychological doctrine of the Trinity, the first has taken precedence in the West; whereas the Cappadocian Fathers and Orthodox theologians, down to the present day, employ the second category. They incline towards an emphatically social doctrine of the Trinity and criticize the modalistic tendencies in the 'personal' trinitarian doctrine of the Western church. The image of the family is a favourite one for the unity of the Triunity: three Persons – one family.[21] This analogy is not just arbitrary. What it means is that people are made in the image of God. But the divine image is not the individual; it is person with person: Adam and Eve – or, as Gregory of Nazianzus declared, Adam and Eve and Seth – are, dissimilar though they are, an earthly image and parable of the Trinity, since they are consubstantial persons.[22] Whatever we may think about the first human family as trinitarian analogy, it does point to the fact that the image of God must not merely be sought for in human individuality; we must look for it with equal earnestness in human sociality.

The Christian doctrine of the Trinity provides the intellectual means whereby to harmonize personality and sociality in the community of men and women, without sacrificing the one to the other. In the Western church's doctrine of the Trinity the concept of Person was developed with particular emphasis. This had a strongly formative effect on Western anthropology. If today we understand person as the unmistakable and untransferable individual existence, we owe this to the Christian doctrine of the Trinity. But why was the concept of the perichoresis – the unity and fellowship of the Persons – not developed with equal emphasis? The disappearance of the social doctrine of the Trinity has made room for the development of individualism, and especially 'possessive individualism', in the Western world: everyone is supposed to fulfil 'himself' but who fulfils the community? It is a typically Western bias to suppose that social relationships and society are less 'primal' than the person.

If we take our bearings from the Christian doctrine of the Trinity, personalism and socialism cease to be antitheses and are seen to be derived from a common foundation. The Christian doctrine of the Trinity compels us to develop social personalism or personal socialism. For, right down to the present day, the Western cult of the person has allied itself with monotheism, whereas the basis of the socialism of the Eastern countries, if we look at it from a religious viewpoint, is not so much atheistic as pantheistic. That is why Western personalism and Eastern socialism have not hitherto been reconcilable. The human rights of the individual and the rights of society fall apart. Today it is vitally necessary for the two to converge in the direction of a truly 'humane' society; and here the Christian doctrine of the Trinity can play a substantial role. In this respect the new ecumenical conversations about questions of trinitarian doctrine in the Western and Eastern churches has a trend-setting importance for the future.

2. Clerical Monotheism

We find another form of monarchical monotheism in the church's doctrine of authority, by which we mean the doctrine and practice of the monarchical episcopate and its further development in the teachings about papal sovereignty.[23]

In the period of the apostolic Fathers, Christianity spread rapidly in Asia Minor. New congregations sprang up everywhere. The church's apostles vied with the free prophets. Consequently the unity of the church, and unity within the different congregations, was a burning issue. It was at that time that Ignatius of Antioch formulated the principle of the episcopate which has remained valid in many churches until the present day: one bishop – one church. He founded this episcopal unity of the church by means of the following theological hierarchy: one God – one Christ – one bishop – one church. The bishop represents Christ to his church just as Christ represents God. This representative derivation of divine authority is obviously monarchical monotheism. The church's hierarchy is supposed to correspond to and represent the divine monarchy.[24] The doctrine of the monarchical episcopate certainly brought unity into the Christian churches, but it did so at the cost of eliminating the charismatic prophets. The Spirit was now bound to the office. God's grace became the grace of the office. If the bishop guarantees the unity of the church through his sovereignty (because for the church he represents Christ), this unity is preserved even if there is no unity in the Christian community in the senses of a consensus. If the consensus collapses, the result is either subjugation or excommunication.

In the middle ages and in the nineteenth century the doctrine of the monarchical episcopate was developed further in the theology of the papacy.[25] The legitimation of the papal authority in questions of faith and morals, and its commissioning for 'the ministry of unity' is derived from the representative sequence: one church – one pope – one Peter – one Christ – one God. Papal authority guarantees the unity of the church. That authority is itself guaranteed by the Petrine apostolic succession. Peter's authority, in turn, is guaranteed by the words of the historical Jesus (Matt. 16.18) and the historicity of the conferring of the keys on Peter. From this the formula follows: 'Ubi Petrus – ibi Ecclesia.'[26]

In the context of this progression, the 'vicar of Christ' on earth possesses graduated divine authority, and his 'ex cathedra' declarations are therefore infallible, with an infallibility that can in fact only be enjoyed by the truth itself.[27] This theological justification of papal authority and the unity of the church it guarantees is visibly dominated by the monotheistic way of thinking. According to Thomist theology, indeed, the unity of highest power and total truth is peculiar to God, so that nobody should assent to the divine revelation without his own perception of, and insight into, the truth. And if this is true even of God's truth, how much more does it apply to the truth of the church and the papal definitions! Yet nominalism put the power of God above his truth and righteousness. Its absolutist interpretation of God's sovereignty has, understandably enough, also evoked a corresponding interpretation of papal sovereignty. It will be difficult to reduce the theological-ecclesiastical doctrine of authority again to the unity of power and truth in God himself, and to correct the bias in the historical development. It is more easily possible to expose the one-sidedness of the whole existing complex of ideas which is used to justify papal sovereignty and its guarantee of unity.

To base a justification of the church's unity and the pope's 'ministry of unity' on Matthew 16 is not only dubious and fraught with assumptions historically; it is also theologically weak. It would be just as legitimate to draw a line of historical continuity from the historical Jesus to the historical Peter, and then to the historical popes, even if Jesus had never risen. His resurrection plays no part at all in this justificatory complex of ecclesiastical authority. Yet according to the New Testament Christ's death and resurrection are the central mystery of the divine revelation.

But there is another, different justification for the church's unity – a trinitarian one. We find it in Jesus' High Priestly prayer in John

17.20f.: 'That they may all be one; even as thou, Father, art in me, and I in thee, that they also may be in us, so that the world may believe that thou hast sent me.' Here the unity of the Christian community is a trinitarian unity. It *corresponds* to the indwelling of the Father in the Son, and of the Son in the Father. It *participates* in the divine triunity, since the community of believers is not only fellowship *with* God but *in* God too. This unity of the church is already given through the prayer of Jesus, which the church can be sure was heard by the Father.

The trinitarian justification for the unity of the church is not merely more profound theologically than the monotheistic justification of the monarchical episcopate; it also defines the unity of the community of Christians differently. The universal and infallible authority of the pope represents *God as almighty*, and it is this almighty power which is experienced in the recognition of papal authority. But it is *God as love* who is represented in the community of believers and who is experienced in the acceptance of one person by another, as they have both been accepted by Christ. Monarchical monotheism justifies the church as hierarchy, as sacred dominion. The doctrine of the Trinity constitutes the church as 'a community free of dominion.'[28] The trinitarian principle replaces the principle of power by the principle of concord.[29] Authority and obedience are replaced by dialogue, consensus and harmony. What stands at the centre is not faith in God's revelation on the basis of ecclesiastical authority, but faith on the basis of individual insight into the truth of revelation. The hierarchy which preserves and enforces unity is replaced by the brotherhood and sisterhood of the community of Christ. The presbyterial and synodal church order and the leadership based on brotherly advice are the forms of organization that best correspond to the doctrine of the social Trinity. Of course most churches will in actual fact have mixed forms, with episcopal and synodal elements. But the trinitarian justification of the church's unity put forward here shows what the priorities are for a credible, a convincing church: 'that the world may believe'.

§2 THE TRINITARIAN DOCTRINE OF THE KINGDOM

If political and clerical monotheism is to be superseded, we are faced with the question of a positive theological doctrine of freedom. The theological doctrine of freedom must grow up out of a new understanding of the lordship and kingdom of God. Otherwise the doctrine of freedom cannot be a theological one. Ernst Bloch remarked that 'Where the great Lord of the universe reigns, there is no room for liberty, not even the liberty of the children of God, or the mystically democratic image of the kingdom which belonged to the millenarian hope'.[30] In saying this, Bloch is pointing on the one hand to the foundation of modern atheism, which started from the assumption that a God ruling in omnipotence and omniscience would make human liberty impossible. Consequently the denial of a God like this is the necessary presupposition for human liberty. On the other hand, Bloch reminds us of the Pauline liberty of the children of God, and the messianic hope for the kingdom of freedom. What interpretation of God and his rule is implicit in the Christian experience of liberation and the messianic hope for freedom?

1. Joachim of Fiore's Doctrine of the Kingdom

If we want to overcome the monotheistic interpretation of the lordship of God by the trinitarian understanding of the kingdom, then we must go back to Joachim of Fiore, and rediscover the truth of his trinitarian view of history.[31] Joachim counted as an 'Enthusiast' and an outsider. But in fact, ever since the middle ages, there is hardly anyone who has influenced European movements for liberty in church, state and culture more profoundly than this twelfth-century Cistercian abbot from Calabria, who believed that in his visions he had penetrated the concordance of the Old and New Testaments, and the mystery of the Book of Revelation. In the field of dogmatics, Thomas Aquinas's opinion of Joachim has generally simply been handed on – that he dissolved the doctrine of the Trinity in history, because he expected a special era of the Spirit.[32] This judgment is unfounded. His genuine writings were never condemned as heretical, even though they were – and are – more than revolutionary.

Joachim succeeded in uniting two different eschatologies, both of them belonging to the Christian tradition. The first goes back to Tyconius and was developed by Augustine: God created the world in seven days. Accordingly world history has seven ages. Six ages of toil and labour will be followed by the seventh age of rest.

This is the sabbath of world history, before the end of the world. When the seventh day of world history comes to an end, Augustine thought, the eternal day of God will begin – the kingdom of endless glory.

Joachim took over the other eschatology from the Cappadocian theologians. They already (even if only in passing) distinguished between the kingdom of the Father, the kingdom of the Son and the kingdom of the Spirit; and it was in this sequence that they conceived of the history of the divine rule. They thought here of different periods and modes of revelation conferred by the Father, the Son and the Spirit. The starting point was the promise of the Paraclete in the Gospel of John. Ever since Phrygian prophecy and montanism, this promise has continually awakened the expectation of a special period of revelation belonging to the Holy Spirit. The one kingdom of God therefore takes on particular forms in history corresponding to the unique nature of the trinitarian Persons.[33] It is the one kingdom of God, but it displays the separate impress of Father, Son and Spirit, each in his own way. Of course the Spirit and the Son are no more excluded from the Father's kingdom than is the Father from the kingdom of the Son and the Spirit. But the subject of sovereignty changes from the Father to the Son and to the Spirit. Neither the Cappadocians nor Joachim thought of there being any 'dissolution' of the Trinity in world history. It was rather a question of appropriating to the different Persons of the Trinity the forms which the kingdom took in the different eras of world history.

Joachim's great idea was to identify the seventh day of world history with the kingdom of the Spirit. The great 'sabbath' of history, before the end of the world, and the kingdom of the Spirit mean the same thing:

> The mysteries of Holy Scripture point us to three orders (states, or conditions) of the world: to the first, in which we were under the Law; to the second, in which we are under grace; to the third, which we already imminently expect, and in which we shall be under a yet more abundant grace . . . The first condition is therefore that of perception, the second that of partially perfected wisdom, the third, the fullness of knowledge.
>
> The first condition is in the bondage of slaves, the second in the bondage of sons, the third in liberty.

The first in fear, the second in faith, the third in love.
The first in the condition of thralls, the second of freemen, the third of friends.
The first of boys, the second of men, the third of the aged.
The first stands in the light of the stars, the second in the light of the dawn, the third in the brightness of day . . .
The first condition is related to the Father, the second to the Son, the third to the Holy Spirit.[34]

The first form of the kingdom is *the kingdom of the Father*. This is the creation and preservation of the world. In this kingdom God rules over all things through his power and providence. His lordship over men and women is determined by his law and the fear it evokes.

The second form of the kingdom is *the kingdom of the Son*. It is the redemption from sin through the servitude of the Son. In this kingdom God rules through the proclamation of the gospel and the administration of the sacraments of the church. Through their fellowship with the Son, people become the children of God instead of slaves under the Law. Their fear of God is transformed into trust in God.

The third form of the kingdom is *the kingdom of the Spirit*. It is the rebirth of men and women through the energies of the Spirit. It brings the *intelligentia spiritualis*. In this kingdom God rules through direct revelation and knowledge. Through the experience of the indwelling Spirit people turn from being God's children into his friends. The form of life lived in the kingdom of the Spirit is a charismatic one. Here no one will have to teach the other, for in the Spirit everyone perceives the divine truth directly, and everyone does what is good just because it *is* good. This is the full 'day of God'; this is the 'eternal sabbath'; this is 'the day of liberty'.

According to Joachim, the times and forms of the kingdom are so entwined with one another that the one is already pregnant with the next, and presses forward towards it. The kingdom of the Spirit is already implicit in the kingdom of the Son, just as the kingdom of the Son was already prepared for in the kingdom of the Father. It is true that Joachim likes to date these eras in biblical terms of salvation history, stating, for example, that the kingdom of the Father lasts until Zechariah. But although this chronology had an enduring effect on his followers' sense of time, it is not the main feature of his doctrine of the Trinity. Its main characteristic is the account of the qualitative *transitions*. Just as the kingdom of the Father and the kingdom of the Son press forward to the kingdom of the Spirit, in order to be perfected in it, so *the liberty* of men and women in history thrusts forward to *its* own kingdom: the servants of God will become his children, and his children will become his friends. These are steps of liberty in relation to God. They mean transitions in the form of qualitative leaps, not as continuous developments.

'Friend of God' is an old Gnostic and mystical expression for the person who has been perfected. Friendship with God is an accurate description of the intimacy of this relationship. Joachim explains that it is only the era of the Holy Spirit which will be the era of 'God's friends'. Wherever groups of 'God's friends', influenced by him, cropped up in the middle ages, it was this particular messianic claim which they asserted. For Joachim, therefore, friendship with God is also the highest stage of freedom. Moreover, the kingdom of freedom can only be the kingdom of the Spirit. Joachim continually appealed to II Corinthians 3.17: 'Where the Spirit of the Lord is, there is freedom.'

The enduring effect of Joachim's doctrine of the three eras (or three empires) of world history on the religious, cultural and political messianism of Europe has been often enough described.[35] To take only a few examples of this influence: in Germany, Lessing's *Gedanken über die Erziehung des Menschengeschlechts* ('Thoughts on the Education of Mankind') had a formative influence on the interpretation of the Enlightenment. Lessing quite deliberately picked up Joachim's ideas. Auguste Comte's teaching about the law of the three stages of the spirit is a reflection of Joachim. And when Karl Marx declares that communism is the final transition from the realm of necessity to the realm of liberty, then here too the far-off echoes of Joachim's influence can be heard.[36]

What interests us here is what the theological tradition of the church made out of Joachim's doctrine of the kingdom. Astonishingly enough, even orthodox Lutheran and Calvinist theologians are familiar with what we have called 'a trinitarian history of the kingdom'. For in the doctrine of Christ's kingly office they distinguished between the *regnum naturae*, the *regnum gratiae* and the *regnum gloriae*[37] – the kingdoms of nature, grace and glory.

The kingdom of nature is the kingdom of God's power (*regnum potentiae*). It comprises creation and the general universal rule of God through his almighty power and providence.

The kingdom of grace is God's spiritual kingdom. Here God rules over the church through word and sacrament.

The kingdom of glory is also called the kingdom of heaven. Here God rules through the blissful contemplation of his countenance in the company of the redeemed.

What is the difference between this theology of the three kingdoms, as the church recognized it, and Joachim's trinitarian doctrine of the kingdom?

Joachim taught that the three kingdoms were eras and stages in history. The kingdom of the Spirit is the final historical era – the sabbath day of world history. It is therefore history's completion; but not its end. The forms and eras of the kingdom of the Father, the Son and the Spirit again point beyond themselves to that kingdom of glory which replaces this history. Joachim interpreted the history of the kingdom in trinitarian terms, and the consummation of the kingdom in eschatological ones. That is to say he in fact developed a doctrine of *four* kingdoms: the kingdoms of the Father, the Son and the Spirit will be consummated in the triune God's kingdom of glory. This fact is often overlooked.

The orthodox Protestant doctrine about the threefold kingly rule of Christ, on the other hand, only talked about two historical kingdoms – the kingdom of nature and the kingdom of grace. The third kingdom of glory was thought of eschatologically. But this simply means that orthodox Protestantism – if we compare it with Joachim's doctrine – left out 'the kingdom of the Spirit', or combined it with the kingdom of the Son in 'the kingdom of grace'. Its christological theory of the threefold royal rule of Christ is much narrower than Joachim's trinitarian doctrine of the kingdom. As far as history and the human problems involved in it are concerned, orthodox Protestantism kept to the doctrine of the two kingdoms. God's general rule over the world and his particular will towards salvation are related only to one another, not to a third, future kingdom of the Spirit.

If we express this diagramatically, the difference appears as follows:

Joachim:

| The kingdom of the Father | → | the kingdom of the Son | → | the kingdom of the Spirit: | the kingdom of glory |

Orthodox Protestantism:

| Regnum naturae | → | regnum gratiae: | | regnum gloriae |

This difference had important consequences for the history of European thought. Mediaeval theology already concentrated the theological problems connected with liberty on the dialectic of nature and grace. At the beginning of the Enlightenment, 'nature' was interpreted by Hobbes, Leibniz and Malebranche as 'the realm of necessity'.[38] This meant that the old, ontological concept of nature was replaced by the new, scientific one. Nature now became the quintessence of what is ordered according to law, what is necessary; and so it also became the quintessence of what was unfree. It followed from this that 'the kingdom of grace' had to be remodelled and given a new form, as the realm of freedom, which was then conceived of as being man's morality and his self-determination. Necessity and freedom therefore arrive at an antinomy which is no longer resolvable in history. Even for the late Marx there was no hope of attaining the 'realm of freedom' from 'the realm of necessity' through the miracle of 'the leap'. Consequently he broke up the two kingdoms into two different spheres which he called the basis and the superstructure. 'This always remains a realm of necessity. Beyond it begins the development of human power which is its own end, the true realm of freedom which, however, can flourish only upon that realm of necessity as its basis.'[39] The secularized doctrine of the two kingdoms of necessity and freedom knows no separate and individual kingdom of the Spirit in which the antinomy of the others is abolished – it is not even aware of anything corresponding to this. And because it also lost the eschatological gaze forward to 'the kingdom of glory', what remains is only the tragedy of the irresolvable contradiction of history.

But is it a sufficient definition of freedom if the definition is merely a negative one, designed to distinguish it from a realm of necessity? How should we distinguish liberty from arbitrary licence if liberty can only be described as what transcends necessity, compulsion and bondage?

Drawing on some of Joachim of Fiore's ideas, let us try to develop a trinitarian doctrine of the kingdom which will get over the dualism of the church's doctrine of the two kingdoms, without destroying the useful distinction it contains. We shall not take over Joachim's modalistic attempt to divide the history of the kingdom chronologically into three successive eras, however. We shall instead interpret the history of the kingdom in trinitarian terms: the kingdoms of the Father, the Son and the Spirit mean continually present strata and transitions in the kingdom's history. Just as the kingdom of the Son presupposes and absorbs the kingdom of the Father, so the kingdom of the Spirit presupposes the kingdom of the Son and absorbs that. In developing a doctrine of the kingdom of God which is differentiated in a trinitarian sense, we are also searching for a theology of the history of human freedom.

2. The Trinitarian Doctrine of the Kingdom

The kingdom of the Father consists of the creation of a world open to the future, and the preservation both of existence itself and of its openness for the future of the kingdom of glory.[40] Joachim and the teachers of the church unanimously described the kingdom of the Father as *regnum naturae* or *regnum potentiae* – the kingdom of nature or the kingdom of almighty power. We are expanding this definition by *the dimension of the future*; for the goal of the creation of the world is the glorification of the triune God. A world which is created for this end has to be understood as an 'open system'.[41] It is only in the kingdom of glory that creation will be perfected, for the inner ground of creation is to be found in glory, not in covenant. Creation 'in the beginning' can only be the commencement of God's creative activity – an activity which also includes creation's continuance (*creatio continua*) and the new creation of heaven and earth (*creatio nova*). The interpretation of providence must be expanded correspondingly: providence and the general universal government of God does not merely mean the continuing preservation of creation from destruction. It also means that God keeps the world's true future open for it through the gift of time, which works against all the world's tendencies to close in on itself, to shut itself off. This must be understood as *the divine patience*. God has patience with his world because he has hope for it. God's hope is manifested in his readiness to endure the apostasy of the men and women he has created, their self-withdrawal and closed-in-ness. In the patience of his love he keeps the world's future open for it. It is wrong simply to see the kingdom of the Father as a 'kingdom of power'. Self-limitation, self-emptying and the patience of love already begin with the creation of the world, and it is these things that mark out God's whole government of the world, and his providence, as being the kingdom of the Father. Particularly if we understand the creation of the world in trinitarian terms as a self-restricting activity of the Father through the Son in the power of the Spirit (see Ch. IV, §2), then creation is the first stage on the road to liberty. Where it is the Father of Jesus Christ who reigns, and not 'the great Lord of the universe', the liberty of created things is given space. Where it is the Father of Jesus Christ and not 'the great Lord of the universe' who preserves the world through his patience, the liberty of created beings is given space and allowed time, even in the slavery they impose on themselves. The Father 'rules' through the creation of what exists and by opening up the eras of time.

The kingdom of the Son consists of the liberating lordship of the crucified one, and fellowship with the first-born of many brothers and sisters. The Son liberates men and women from servitude to sin through his own servitude (Phil. 2). He redeems men and women from death through his own surrender of himself to death. In this he consummates the Father's patience. He leads people into the glorious liberty of the children of God by making them like himself, in fellowship with him. In this he anticipates the kingdom of the Spirit. If creation is designed in such a way that its future is open for the kingdom of glory, then men and women are created as the image of God in order that they may become God's children. They are open for this future in which their destiny will be fulfilled. So turning away from the Creator to a life that contradicts God always means, in addition, being imprisoned in one's own existing being, and closed against the future (*incurvatio in seipsum*). This imprisonment, this closed-in-ness, means the death of every 'open system'. Liberation from it – liberation for primal openness – cannot come about through superior strength or compulsion, but only through vicarious suffering and the call to that liberty which vicarious suffering alone throws open. That is why both Joachim and the teachers of the church called the kingdom of the Son '– the servant's form of the kingdom'.[42]

Hark, hark, the wise eternal Word

>Like a weak infant cries.
>In form of servant is the Lord,
>And God in cradle lies.[43]

This must not be understood merely as if it were a limitation of God's power; it also has to be seen as a de-limitation of God's goodness. In the history of sin and death the kingdom of freedom takes on the form of the crucified Christ. It becomes a Christoform kingdom. Yet, like the kingdom of the Father, the kingdom of the Son is also directed towards the eschatological kingdom of glory. The Son will make us free for freedom. People are called and justified by him for glory. If unfree, closed, introverted people are opened for this future of theirs in God, they achieve an unimagined liberty. The Son therefore 'rules' through this surrender of himself to vicarious suffering and death, and through his resurrection into the glory that is to come. He 'rules' through 'the freedom for which he has made us free' (Gal. 5.1).

The kingdom of the Spirit is experienced in the gift conferred on the people liberated by the Son – the gift of the Holy Spirit's energies. That is the reason why the kingdom of the Spirit is as closely linked with the kingdom of the Son, as the kingdom of the Son is with the kingdom of the Father. In the experience of the Spirit we lay hold on the freedom for which the Son has made us free. Through the mediation of Christ we experience a kind of 'direct presence of God': God in us – we in God. The mystics were right to call this 'the birth of God in the soul'. Through faith and by listening to his conscience, a person becomes God's friend. In the powers of the Spirit, the energies of the new creation are experienced too. In the Spirit that new community comes into being which is without privileges and subjection, the community of the free. In the Spirit the new creation in the kingdom of glory is anticipated. As the beginning and 'earnest' or pledge of glory, the kingdom of the Spirit is directed towards the kingdom of glory; it is not itself already that kingdom's fulfilment. The New Testament says that the Holy Spirit 'descends' and that he 'indwells'. Through his descent, his 'condescension' – or so we could interpret it – the Spirit participates in his own way in the self-limitation of the Father and the self-emptying of the Son. Consequently the form the kingdom takes in the Spirit is not yet the kingdom's consummation. The indwelling of the Spirit (*inhabitatio spiritus sancti in corde*) is the anticipation of the eschatological indwelling of God's glory. If through the experience of the Spirit men and women in their physical nature become God's temple (I Cor. 6.13bff.), then they are anticipating the glory in which the whole world will become the temple of the triune God (Rev. 21.3).

The kingdom of the Spirit cannot well be identified with the kingdom of the Son, for the Son actually becomes man, while the Spirit's presence is merely an indwelling. There is no incarnation of the Spirit, and no servanthood of the Spirit.[44] Nor can the kingdom of the Spirit be identified with the eschatological kingdom of glory, for the Spirit is already experienced here and now, in history, in our bodily nature, through fellowship with Christ. The kingdom of the Spirit is historical. It presupposes the kingdom of the Father and the kingdom of the Son and, together with the kingdom of the Father and the kingdom of the Son, points in its own way towards the eschatological kingdom of glory.

Finally, the kingdom of glory must be understood as the consummation of the Father's creation, as the universal establishment of the Son's liberation, and as the fulfilment of the Spirit's indwelling. Creation is the material promise of glory, being full of the cyphers and signs of the beauty to come. The kingdom of the Son is the historical promise of glory, being full of the experiences and hopes of brotherhood and sisterhood, which is to say of love. Finally, the kingdom of the Spirit is the actual dawn of the kingdom of glory, even though it be still under the conditions of history and death. The trinitarian doctrine of the kingdom therefore sums up 'the works of the Trinity' (creation, liberation, glorification) and points them towards the home of the triune God. The kingdom of glory is the goal – enduring and uninterrupted – for all God's works and ways in history.

§3. THE TRINITARIAN DOCTRINE OF FREEDOM

Joachim already viewed the trinitarian history of the kingdom of God as the history of humanity's progressive and growing liberty. Let us take up the ideas which we developed in our critical discussion of Joachim earlier in the chapter, and develop them a little further.[45] We said that the kingdom of the Father is determined by the creation of the world and its preservation through God's patience. This constitutes the freedom of created things and preserves for them the necessary space in which to live. The kingdom of the Son is determined by the liberation of men and women, through suffering love, from their deadly withdrawal into themselves, their closed-in-ness. This restores the freedom of created beings and redeems them from self-destruction. The kingdom of the Spirit, finally, is determined by the powers and energies of the new creation. Through these powers and energies people become God's dwelling and his home. They participate in the new creation. This gives liberty its bearings and fills it with infinite hope. These three determinations of the history of God's kingdom point towards the eschatological kingdom of glory in which people will finally, wholly and completely be gathered into the eternal life of the triune God and – as the early church put it – be 'deified' ($\theta\acute{\epsilon}\omega\sigma\iota\varsigma$).

Let us now translate this doctrine of the kingdom of God into the doctrine of the freedom of men and women which necessarily corresponds to it.

1. Forms of Human Freedom

The realm of necessity determines human beings, like all other things, through laws and necessities. The realm of freedom begins when people grasp their dependencies on the forces of nature, understand them and learn to control them. Through science and technology people try to make themselves the lords of nature instead of its slaves. This is certainly the first step into the realm of freedom, for with the progressive liberation of men and women from dependency on nature and their progressive self-determination, the particular history of human beings with nature begins. So this first freedom means power over nature. But the actual acquiring of the power does not as yet determine whether it will be used for good or evil, constructively or destructively. *Liberation* from the realm of necessity can therefore only be viewed as the beginning; it is not yet the realm of freedom itself; otherwise freedom would mean nothing more than the end of necessity and would remain totally undefined in itself.

'The person who chooses has the torment of choice', says the German proverb. The realm of freedom would be this 'torment' and nothing more than that, if it were not for the realm of the Good, beyond necessity and freedom. The realm of the Good means the place from which moral purposes and values shine into the realm of freedom, so that freedom may be used properly – that is to say, for life's preservation and not for its destruction. Freedom's goal cannot be the mere increase of power. Consequently the moral purposes and values of the realm of the Good transcend the realm of freedom in quality. So initially we know two sides to freedom: the liberation from compulsion and necessity, and the striving for the realization of the Good.

What does the realm of the Good consist of? According to what we have just said, it must be freedom in its own, moral world, the world that is in correspondence with itself. It can no longer be this ambiguous world, in which freedom becomes the torment of choice; it must be that unequivocal world in which freedom consists of joy in the Good and in doing what is right simply as a matter of course. To do what is good as a matter of course is not yet a characteristic of the realm of freedom between the liberation from necessity and the striving for the good. Consequently the realm of freedom has to be interpreted as the history of freedom, the struggle for freedom, the process of freedom.

What we have described here as the realms of necessity, freedom and the Good are certainly not three ages; they are stages and transitions which are always present in the experience of freedom. We can therefore also interpret them as strata in the concept of freedom generally. People always live in the transition from necessity to freedom, and always, too, in the transition from freedom of choice to the free practice of what is good. At the same time, the tendency to the realm of the Good is inherent in the experience of freedom. The more power mankind acquires over nature, the more dangerous the human history of freedom becomes, and the more urgent the orientation towards the realm of the Good. Otherwise people could not acquire power over the power they have, and could make no free use of their liberty.

After this attempt to develop the general concept of 'the realm of necessity' and 'the realm of freedom', we must finally consider dimensions in the concept of freedom as it has historically evolved.

The first definition equates 'freedom' with 'rule'; this is a definition that is familiar to us from political history.[46] Because all previous history can be viewed as a permanent struggle for power and still more power, it is only the person who wins the struggle, and therefore rules, who is called free. The losers are subjected and exploited, and are called 'unfree'. The linguistic history of the word 'freedom' shows that it takes its origin from a slave-owning society. The only person who is free in a society of this kind is the master, the lord. The slaves and the women and children he rules over are not free. Paul uses this language too, when he talks about the conflicts which are abolished in the community of Christians: Jews and Gentiles, men and women, freemen and slaves. But the person who interprets freedom as lordship can only be free at the cost of other people. His freedom means oppression for others; his riches make other people poor; his power means the subjugation of his subjects, and of women and children.

The person who interprets freedom as rule is really only aware of himself and his own property.[47] He is not aware of other people as persons. Even when we say that a person is free to do and leave undone what he likes, we are interpreting freedom as lordship – as the person's mastery over himself. Even when we say that a person is free if he is not determined by any inner or outer compulsions, we are interpreting freedom as lordship: everyone is to be his own king, his own master, his own slave-owner. And in saying this we have simply 'internalized' external compulsions, transferring them to 'an inward compulsion'. The extent to which the interpretation of freedom as lordship is based on a male society is shown by the very words 'lord-ship' and 'master-y'.

In Western Europe, princely absolutism and feudalism were succeeded by middle-class liberalism; but this liberalism none the less went on clinging to the model of feudal lordship. Everyone who bears a human visage has the same right to liberty, say the liberals. This liberty of every individual only finds its limits where it infringes the liberty of others. Anyone who lays claim to his own freedom must respect the same freedom on the part of the other person. But that means that for this middle-class liberalism too, freedom means lordship. Everyone finds in the other person a competitor in the struggle for power and possession. Everyone is for everyone else merely the limitation of his own freedom. Everyone is free in himself, but no one shares in the other. In its ideal form this is a society of individuals who do not disturb one another but who are themselves solitary. No one determines the other, everyone determines himself. Freedom has then really become general. Everyone has the right to be free. But is this true freedom?

The other definition, which we know from social history, defines freedom not as lordship but as community. If we link this up with what we have just said about the desolateness of middle-class liberalism, we can say: the truth of freedom is love. It is only in love that human freedom arrives at its truth. I am free and feel myself to be truly free when I am respected and recognized by others and when I for my part respect and recognize them. I become truly free when I open my life for other people and share with them, and when other people open their lives for me and share them with me.[48] Then the other person is no longer the limitation of my freedom; he is an expansion of it. In mutual participation in life, individual people become free beyond the limits of their individuality, and discover the common room for living which their freedom offers. That is the social side of freedom. We call it love and solidarity. In it we experience the uniting of isolated individuals. In it we experience the uniting of things that have been forcibly divided.

'Divide and rule' is the old, familiar method of domination. As long as freedom means lordship, everything has to be separated, isolated, detached and distinguished, so that it can be dominated. But if freedom means community, fellowship, then we experience the uniting of everything that has hitherto been separated. The alienation of person from person, the division between human society and nature, the dichotomy between soul and body, and, finally, religious anxiety are abolished; liberation is experienced when people are again one: one with each other, one with nature, and one with God. Freedom as community is therefore a movement that counters the history of power and class struggles, in which freedom could only be viewed in terms of lordship.

Freedom as lordship destroys community. As lordship, freedom is a lie. The truth of human freedom lies in the love that breaks down barriers. It leads to unhindered, open communities in solidarity. It is only this freedom as community that can heal the wounds which freedom as lordship has inflicted, and still inflicts today.

Up to now we have interpreted freedom either in the relationship between subject and object, as lordship, or in the relationship between subject and subject, as community, fellowship. But there is a third dimension too: freedom in the relationship of subjects to a *project*.[49] Without this dimension freedom still cannot be comprehended. In relationship to the project of the future, freedom is a creative initiative. Anyone who transcends the present in the direction of the future in what he thinks, says and does is free. Seen theologically, this is the special dimension given by the experience of the Spirit. In the Spirit we transcend the present in the direction of God's future, for the Spirit is the 'earnest' or 'pledge of glory'.

Freedom in the light of hope is the creative passion for the possible. Unlike lordship, it is not merely directed towards what already exists. Nor, like love, is it only directed towards the fellowship of existing people. It is directed *towards the future*, in the light of the Christian hope for the future of the coming God. The future is the kingdom of not yet defined potentialities, whereas the past represents the limited kingdom of reality. Creative passion is always directed towards a project of a future of this kind. People want to realize new possibilities. That is why they reach forward with passion. In hope, reason becomes productive fantasy. People dream the messianic dream of the new, whole life that will at last be truly alive. They explore the future's possibilities in order to realize this dream of life. This future dimension of freedom has long been overlooked, theologically too, because the freedom of the Christian faith was not understood as being participation in the creative Spirit of God.

Freedom as the lordship of man over objects and subjects is a function of property. Freedom as community between people is a social function. Freedom as a passion for the future is a creative function. We might sum it up by saying that the first means having, the second being, and the third becoming.

In this historically developed dimension of freedom, there must be compromising adjustment. In bourgeois societies the category of having has overrun the category of being – being in a truly human sense – and its reduction is an urgent task; but under the conditions of this life, no total abolition of having in being is possible and desirable. The abolition of property by means of a society that has become personal and authentically social only loses its trend toward romantic regression when the project of the common future is historically understood, is desired, and when everyone accepts common responsibility for it. Freedom as lordship can only be abolished for the benefit of freedom as community, when freedom as initiative and the responsibility for a common future comes to the fore. So in these historical dimensions of freedom too, there is a recognizable trend towards freedom as initiative, as creativity, and as a passion for the future.

2. *Trinity and Freedom*

The experience of freedom always has a religious dimension. Consequently the concept of freedom has a theological dimension as well. This is shown by the atheistic justification of freedom in modern times. In order to affirm and desire the liberty of men and women, God has to be denied: either there is a God who rules and people are not free; or people are free – but then there must not be any God. In this crude alternative we have atheistic freedom on the one hand, over against monotheistic dependency on the other. And, conversely, the political world order that is allied with religion is contrary to man's freedom and self-responsibility.

In the doctrine of the Trinity which we shall be developing in this chapter, we shall be going along with Joachim of Fiore, though critically. It is a doctrine that overcomes monarchical dependency and provides the justification for human freedom in more dimensions than one. An immovable and apathetic God cannot be understood as the foundation of human freedom. An absolutist sovereign in heaven does not inspire liberty on earth. Only the passionate God, the God who suffers by virtue of his passion for people, calls the freedom of men and women to life. He gives human freedom its divine room for living. The triune God, who realizes the kingdom of his glory in a history of creation, liberation and glorification, wants human freedom, justifies human freedom and unceasingly makes men and women free for freedom. Trinitarian theology is directed towards the justification of a comprehensive, many-dimensioned doctrine of freedom. The conception we shall go on to develop is therefore the following:

The trinitarian doctrine of the kingdom is the theological doctrine of freedom. The theological concept of freedom is the concept of the trinitarian history of God: God unceasingly desires the freedom of his creation. God is the inexhaustible freedom of those he has created.

3. Freedom in the Kingdom of the Triune God

In the kingdom of the Father, God is the Creator and the lord of those he has created. Men and women are his created beings and are hence his property as well. In their naked existence human beings are completely and utterly dependent on their Creator and preserver. They can contribute nothing to what God creates, for they owe everything they are to God's creative activity. If God takes them into his service, becoming their master and lord, this is their exaltation and their mark of distinction. To be 'the servant of God' raises men and women above all the rest of God's creatures. To be used and needed by God the Lord, and therefore not to be useless and superfluous, gives their lives meaning. So to be the servant of God is not a humiliating title. It is a title conferring honour. Moses was looked upon as 'the Servant of God' who was chosen to lead his people into freedom. Isaiah 53 promises the 'new Servant of God' who bears the sins of the world. According to Philippians 2, the Son of God took upon himself the form of a servant and was obedient even unto death on the cross. The apostles viewed themselves as slaves of God and servants of the kingdom. In this very fact they found the freedom that raised them above the world. For the person who is a servant of the Most High is indeed utterly dependent on his master; but he is completely free from other things and other powers. He fears God alone and nothing else in the world. He belongs to his Lord alone and to no one else. He hears his voice alone and no other voice at all. The sole lordship of God, which the first commandment proclaims, is the foundation for the extraordinary freedom of having to have 'no other gods' beside him. This is what Paul means too when he explains freedom with the help of the theological hierarchy of property: 'All things are yours and you are Christ's and Christ is God's' (I Cor. 3.22f.).

In the kingdom of the Son, the freedom of being God's servants is preserved outwardly, but its inward quality is changed. The servants of the Lord became the children of the Father. In the fellowship of the Son people enter into a new relationship with God. The freedom of God's children does not evolve out of the freedom of God's servants. It only becomes possible where the Son appears. Knowledge of the Father and free access to him are the characteristics which place the freedom of God's children above the freedom of his servants. Children belong to the family. They cannot be dismissed like servants. They are one with the father. They are not the father's property. On the contrary, they are joint owners of the father's property. They are his heirs. The liberty of the children of God therefore lies in their personal and intimate relationship to the Father and, on the other hand, in their participation in the Father's kingdom. Their relationship to one another also distinguishes them from servants: servants obey the master's commands, each for himself. What binds them together is merely sharing the same social position. But the children of God are bound together because they are brothers and sisters. The liberty of the children of God lies not least in the free access to each other which people find in the love that binds them and in the joy they find in one another.

In the kingdom of the Spirit the sovereign freedom towards the world of God's servants, and the intimate freedom of his children are both preserved; but again the inward quality of these things is changed. The servants of the Lord and the children of the Father become God's friends: 'No longer do I call you servants, for the servant does not know what his master is doing; but I have called you friends, for all that I have heard from my Father I have made known to you' (John 15.15). By virtue of the indwelling of the Holy Spirit, people enter into this new 'direct' relationship with God. The freedom of God's friends does not evolve out of the freedom of God's children. It only becomes possible when people know themselves in God and God in them. That is the light of the Holy Spirit. As John 15 shows, Jesus saw his disciples not only as brothers but as his friends as well. This friendship too is born out of Christ's giving of himself: 'Greater love has no man than this, that a man lay down his life for his friends. You are my friends if you do what I command you' (John 15.13f.).

The title 'friend of God' was widespread in the ancient Greek world. The truly wise are 'the friends of the gods'. The Hellenistic Jews called Moses 'the friend of God'. The New Testament Epistle of James (2.23) declares: 'Abraham believed God, and it was reckoned to him as righteousness; and he was called the friend of God.' Otherwise Abraham is considered as being 'the father of believers'. Here he is the first of God's friends. Friendship with God finds its pre-eminent expression in prayer. In obeying God's command a person feels himself to be the Lord's servant. In faith in the gospel he sees himself as being the child of his heavenly Father. As God's friend he talks to God in prayer, and his prayer becomes a conversation with his heavenly friend. Friendship with God means the assurance that his prayer is heard. Of course 'praying' and 'hearing' are still expressions belonging to the language of servants and children. In friendship the distance enjoined by sovereignty ceases to exist. The friend knows that his friend is listening to him. God 'can be conversed with'.[50] God listens to his friends. By virtue of friendship with God in the Spirit, we have the chance to influence God and to participate in his rule. God does not want the humility of servants or the gratitude of children for ever. He wants the boldness and confidence of friends, who share his rule with him. Kant said that friendship combines affection with respect. God makes men and women his friends by inclining affectionately towards them and by listening to them. He makes people his friends by letting them find themselves and by respecting their responsibility. People draw near to God by praying without begging and by talking to him in a way that shows they respect his liberty. The prayer of the friend is neither the servility of the servant nor the importunity of the child; it is a conversation in the freedom of love, that shares and allows the other to share. Friendship is 'the concrete concept of freedom'.[51]

The freedom of servants, the freedom of children and the freedom of God's friends correspond to the history of the kingdom of God. They are stages on a road, as it were, but without being stages in a continuous development. Freedom is defined qualitatively here, not quantitatively. Consequently it is misleading to date these stages on the road, either chronologically or in salvation history, as Joachim admittedly did. It is better to think of *strata in the concept of freedom*. Then these transitions are present in every experience of freedom. In the experience of freedom, we experience ourselves as God's servants, as his children, and as his friends; and in this way we perceive the stages for ourselves. To be God's servant therefore remains just as much a dimension of freedom as being God's child, even if friendship with God goes beyond both. Yet there is also a *trend* in the experience of freedom – a trend from being a servant to being a child, and then to being a friend of God's. This can be called 'growth', if by growth in faith we do not mean the further development of a unique experience, but

ABBREVIATIONS

CD   Karl Barth, *Church Dogmatics*, ET T. & T. Clark, Edinburgh and
      Eerdmans, Grand Rapids, Michigan 1936–69
ET   English translation
EvTh *Evangelische Theologie*, Munich
IKZ   *Internationale kirchliche Zeitschrift*, Bern
KuD   *Kerygma und Dogma*, Göttingen
LThK *Lexikon für Theologie und Kirche*, Freiburg
MPG   Migne, *Patrologia Graeca*, Paris
MPL   Migne, *Patrologia Latina*, Paris
NF   Neue Folge (New Series)
NTD   Das Neue Testament Deutsch
PhB   Philosophische Bibliothek, Leipzig
PTSt Patristische Texte und Studien, Berlin
RE   *Realencyklopädie für protestantische Theologie und Kirche*, 3rd
      ed. Gotha 1896–1913
RGG   *Religion in Geschichte und Gegenwart*, 3rd ed. Tübingen 1956–
      65
ThEx Theologische Existenz heute, Munich
TDNT *Theological Dictionary of the New Testament*, ET Grand Rapids,
      Michigan 1964–76
ZKG   *Zeitschrift für Kirchengeschichte*, Stuttgart
ZThK *Zeitschrift für Theologie und Kirche*, Tübingen

NOTES

I Trinitarian Theology Today

1. P. Melanchthon, *Loci Communes*, 1521, *Melanchthons Werke* II, ed. R. Stupperich, Gütersloh 1952, p. 7.

2. K. Rahner already complains about this. Cf. 'Remarks on the Dogmatic Treatise *De Trinitate*', *Theological Investigations* IV, ET Darton, Longman & Todd, London 1966, pp. 77ff.

3. F. Schleiermacher, *Glaubenslehre*, 2nd ed. §§ 3 and 4.

4. Ibid. § 170.

5. J. Sobrino pointed to this dialectic. Cf. 'Theologisches Erkennen in der europäischen und der lateinamerikanischen Theologie' in *Befreiende Theologie*, ed. K. Rahner, Stuttgart 1977, pp. 123ff., with reference to the dialectical principle of knowledge 'sub specie contrarii' as treated in J. Moltmann, *The Crucified God*, ET SCM Press 1974, pp. 25ff.

6. Cf. here now C. Lasch, *The Culture of Narcissism. American Life in an Age of Diminishing Expectations*, New York 1978.

7. I. Kant, *Der Streit der Fakultäten*, PhB 252, p. 33.

8. Ibid. p. 34.

9. Cf. G. Gutiérrez, ET *A Theology of Liberation*, Orbis Books, New York 1973, SCM Press 1974, p. 11.

10. I. Kant, *Critique of Pure Reason*, preface to the second edition.

11. Thomas Aquinas, *Summa Theologiae*, I qu. 2 a 3.

12. J. Seiler, *Das Dasein Gottes als Denkaufgabe. Darlegung und Bewertung der Gottesbeweise*, Lucerne 1965, pp. 60f.

13. H. Denzinger, *Enchiridion Symbolorum*, 26th ed., Freiburg 1957, 1785.

14. Ibid. 2071.

15. R. Descartes, *Discours de la méthode*, PhB 26 a, esp. pp. 25ff. For the investigation and presentation of the modern metaphysics of subjectivity, cf. especially W. Schulz, *Der Gott der neuzeitlichen Metaphysik*, 6th ed., Pfullingen 1978, and his great work *Ich und Welt. Philosophie der Subjektivität*, Pfullingen 1979.

16. F. Nietzsche, 'Der tolle Mensch' in *Die fröhliche Wissenschaft*, no. 125.

17. Augustine, *Soliloquia*, I, 2 and II, 1. Cf. M. Grabmann, *Die Grundgedanken des Heiligen Augustinus über Seele und Gott* (1929), Darmstadt 1967.

18. R. Descartes, 3. *Meditation*, PhB 27, p. 42.

19. R. Bultmann, 'What Does it Mean to Speak of God?' in *Faith and Understanding*, SCM Press 1969, p. 63.

20. Cf. K. Rahner, 'Remarks on the Dogmatic Treatise *De Trinitate*' (see n. 2 above), pp. 77ff.; H. Mühlen, *Der Heilige Geist als Person*, 2nd ed., Münster 1963; C. Heitmann and H. Mühlen, *Erfahrung und Theologie des Heiligen Geistes*, Hamburg and Munich 1974, especially H. Mühlen, 'Soziale Geisterfahrung als Antwort auf eine einseitige Gotteslehre', pp. 253ff., and G. Wagner, 'Der Heilige Geist als offenbarmachende und vollendende Kraft', pp. 214ff.

21. So the influential textbook by C. I. Nitzsch, *System der christlichen Lehre* (1829), 6th ed., Bonn 1851, p. 184. The standard work on the history of the doctrine of the Trinity up to the nineteenth century is still F. C. Baur, *Die christliche Lehre von der Dreieinigkeit und Menschwerdung Gottes in ihrer geschichtlichen Entwicklung*, I–III, Tübingen 1843.

22. R. Rothe, *Theologische Ethik* I, 2nd ed., Wittenberg 1867, § 34; F. H. R. Frank, *System der christlichen Wahrheit*, 1878–80, 3rd ed. 1893, § 14; I. A. Dorner, *System der christlichen Glaubenslehre*, I, Berlin 1879, § 31 and §32.

23. R. Musil, *The Man without Qualities*, ET Secker & Warburg 1953–60, vol. I, p. 175.

II *The Passion of God*

1. O. Dreyer, *Untersuchungen zum Begriff des Gottgeziemenden in der Entwicklung der antiken Gottesvorstellung*, Göttingen 1966.

2. J. K. Mozley, *The Impassibility of God. A Survey of Christian Thought*, Cambridge 1926, is the classic and most comprehensive treatment of the subject. Cf. also W. Maas, *Unveränderlichkeit Gottes*, Munich, 1974; Chung Young Lee, *God suffers for us. A Systematic Inquiry into the Concept of Divine Passibility*, The Hague 1974; J. Woltmann, Ἀπαθὲς ἔπαθεν *Apathie als metaphysisches Axiom und ethisches Ideal und das Problem der Passion Christi in der Alten Kirche*, Diss. Erlangen 1972; W. McWilliams, 'Divine Suffering in Contemporary Theology' *Scottish Journal of Theology*, 33, 1980, pp. 35–54.

3. G. C. Stead, *Divine Substance*, Oxford 1977.

4. These questions are treated in detail in W. Elert, *Der Ausgang der altkirchlichen Christologie. Eine Untersuchung über Theodor von Pharan und seine Zeit*, Berlin 1957. The more modern German contributions to the problem start from the dogmatic difficulties which Elert pointed out: H. Mühlen, *Die Veränderlichkeit Gottes als Horizont einer zukünftigen Christologie. Auf dem Wege zu einer Kreuzestheologie in Auseinanderset-*

zung mit der altkirchlichen Christologie, Münster 1969; H. Küng, *Menschwerdung Gottes. Eine Einführung in Hegels theologisches Denken als Prolegomena zu einer künftigen Christologie*, Freiburg 1970; J. Moltmann, *The Crucified God. The Cross of Christ as the Foundation and Criticism of Christian Theology*, ET SCM Press and Harper & Row, New York 1974; E. Jüngel, *Gott als Geheimnis der Welt. Zur Begründung der Theologie des Gekreuzigten im Streit zwischen Theismus und Atheismus*, Tübingen 1977.

5. According to Irenaeus the *Deus impassibilis* has become *passibilis*. According to Melito 'the One who cannot suffer, suffers'. In his famous treatise Gregory Thaumaturgus describes 'the Suffering of Him who cannot suffer'. Cf. H. Crouzel, 'La passion de l'impassibile' in *L'homme devant Dieu* I, Paris 1964, pp. 269–279, and L. Abramowski, 'Die Schrift Gregor des Lehrers "Ad Theopompum" und Philoxenus von Mabbug', *ZKG* 89, 1978, pp. 273–290. Out of the abundance of typical titles we may mention here G. Stanihurstius' cumbersome *Historia von dem heiligen Leiden des unsterblichen Gottes im sterblichen Leibe*, Kempten 1678. The last great treatment of the subject by B. R. Brasnett is also entitled *The Suffering of the Impassible God*, London 1928.

6. D. Merezhkovsky makes this double meaning of the word 'passion' the guiding idea of his incomparable meditation *Tod und Auferstehung*, Leipzig 1935: 'It is astonishing, and can doubtless only be explained by two thousand years of custom, that we no longer find it surprising that the church (which calls every "passion" sinful and "lack of passion" holy) has the courage to call its holy of holies "the passion" ' (pp. 8f.). Heinrich Heine wrote: 'Eternal renown is due to the symbol of that suffering God, the Saviour with the crown of thorns, whose blood was, as it were, the healing balm which ran down into the wounds of mankind' (*Zur Geschichte der Religion und Philosophie in Deutschland*, Book I, Insel edition, 4.55).

7. H. de Lubac, *Histoire et esprit. L'intelligence de l'Écriture d'après Origène*, Paris 1950; Maas, op. cit., pp. 136ff.

8. Origen, *Commentary on Romans* (VII. 9; MPG 14.1129 A).

9. *Selecta in Ezechielem* (c. 16; MPG 13.812 A).

10. *Homilia VI in Ezechielem* (MPG XIII, 714 f).

11. I am here taking up and developing ideas which I have already expressed in *The Crucified God*, especially in ch. 6.

12. A. Heschel, *Die Prophetie*, Cracow 1936, and in more detail in *The Prophets*, New York 1962, especially pp. 221ff.

13. Ibid., ch. 12: 'The Theology of Pathos', pp. 221ff.

14. This is stressed by K. Woollcombe, 'The Pain of God', *Scottish Journal of Theology* 20, 1967, pp. 129–148, who thereby carries on the English discussion on the passibility of God.

15. Heschel, *The Prophets*, pp. 232ff.

16. Ibid., ch. 18: 'Religion of Sympathy', pp. 307ff.

17. Cf. P. Lapide and J. Moltmann, *Jüdischer Monotheismus – christliche Trinitätslehre. Ein Gespräch*, Munich 1979; Moltmann, pp. 32ff., and Lapide, pp. 54ff.

18. P. Kuhn, *Gottes Selbsterniedrigung in der Theologie der Rabbinen*, Munich 1968; A. M. Goldberg, *Untersuchungen über die Vorstellung von der Shekhinah in der frühen rabbinischen Literatur*, Berlin 1969; Gershom Scholem, *Von der mystischen Gestalt der Gottheit*, Zürich 1962, pp. 135ff.

19. Kuhn, op. cit., pp. 89ff.; Scholem, op. cit., pp. 144f.

20. Scholem, op. cit., pp. 145ff.

21. G. Scholem, *Die jüdische Mystik in ihren Hauptströmungen*, Frankfurt 1957, p. 253. (This book is based on the 3rd US edition of *Major Trends in Jewish Mysticism*; New York 1954, London 1955.)

22. F. Rosenzweig, *Der Stern der Erlösung*, III, 3rd ed., Heidelberg 1954, pp. 192ff.

23. Ibid., p. 194.

24. Scholem, *Die jüdische Mystik*, pp. 253f.

25. Scholem, *Von der mystischen Gestalt*, p. 146. Cf. also E. Wiesel's moving book about Auschwitz, *Night*, New York and London, 1960 (with a foreword by F. Mauriac), p. 76, and the comments in Moltmann, *The Crucified God*, pp. 273f.

26. J. K. Mozley, op. cit., p. VIII:

27. C. E. Rolt, *The World's Redemption*, London 1913, p. 95.

28. B. H. Streeter's own work on the subject was interrupted by Rolt's book. He therefore published a summing up of his own and Rolt's ideas under the title 'The Suffering of God', *The Hibbert Journal*, 47, April 1914, pp. 603–611.

29. Rolt, op. cit., p. 95.

30. Ibid., p. 35.

31. Ibid., p. 27. In Germany Karl Barth and H. Urs von Balthasar were the first to demand that the being of God and the cross of Christ be considered together, and to try to do so. Cf. Barth, *Church Dogmatics* II/2, and von Balthasar, *Mysterium Salutis*, ed. J. Feiner and M. Löhrer, III/2, Einsiedeln and Cologne 1969, pp. 133ff.

32. Canon V. F. Storr, *The Problem of the Cross*, (1919) 2nd ed., London 1924, said that God did not rest in an Olympian heaven, but suffered himself when Jesus suffered on earth: 'The Divine Love revealed in and mediated by Jesus, eternally suffers from our sin.' George Campbell Morgan, *The Bible and the Cross*, London 1909, also sees the cross against the background of God's eternal suffering. C. A. Dinsmore, *Atonement in Literature and Life*, London, Boston and New York 1906, writes: There was a cross in the heart of God before there was one planted on the green hill outside of Jerusalem. And now that the cross of wood has been taken down, the one in the heart of God abides, and it will remain so long as

there is one sinful soul for whom to suffer.' References in Mozley, op. cit., pp. 148ff.

33. H. Bushnell, *The Vicarious Sacrifice*, London 1866, p. 35.

34. J. Hinton, *The Mystery of Pain*, London 1866, p. 40.

35. Rolt, op. cit., p. 247: 'God is a Trinity because He is perfect Love.'

36. Ibid., p. 95.

37. Ibid., pp. 203f.

38. Ibid., p. 119.

39. Ibid., p. 124.

40. Ibid., p.126. This is basically Barth's doctrine about nullity; cf. *CD* II/2 pp. 122ff., III/3 pp. 289ff. Barth too talks about the 'shadow-world of Satan' which only exists by virtue of the divine denial.

41. Rolt, op. cit., p. 127.

42. Ibid., p. 246. This idea about the 'experience' which God has to go through on his 'passage' through history is otherwise only to be found in mysticism. It corresponds to the Jewish-kabbalistic doctrine about the wanderings of the divine Shekinah through the dust of this world's streets. Cf. also P. Tillich, *Systematic Theology* III, Chicago 1963, reissued SCM Press 1978, p. 405: 'The Divine Life is the eternal conquest of the negative; this is its blessedness.'

43. G. A. Studdert Kennedy, *The Hardest Part*, London 1918.

44. Ibid., p. 14.

45. Ibid., p. 95. Similarly p. 98: 'Men are turning to God in Christ, even as they curse the Christian God. They do not, and will not, believe in the Monarch on the throne; they do, and will, believe in the Servant on the Cross.'

46. Ibid., p. 42. K. Kitamori and D. Bonhoeffer formulated similar ideas during the horrors of World War II; cf. Kitamori, *Theology of the Pain of God*, ET SCM Press and John Knox Press, Richmond, Va. 1966; Bonhoeffer, *Letters and Papers from Prison*, ET, 3rd enlarged edition, SCM Press and Macmillan, New York 1971. Similar experiences gave their stamp to the shared theological insight.

47. Madrid 1912; *The Tragic Sense of Life in Men and Nations*; references are to ET Selected Works, vol. 4, Routledge & Kegan Paul and Princeton University Press 1972 but quotations have been retranslated.

48. Cf. the extensive monograph by R. Garcia Mateo, *Dialektik als Polemik. Welt, Bewusstsein, Gott bei Miguel de Unamuno*, Frankfurt 1978; also E. Rivera, *El tema de Dios en M. de Unamuno*, Cuadernos Salamancinos de Filosofia V, 1978, pp. 315–335.

49. R. Schneider, *Verhüllter Tag*, Cologne 1954, p. 65.

50. Unamuno *The Tragic Sense of Life*, p. 17.

51. M. de Unamuno, *The Agony of Christianity*, ET Selected Works, vol. 5, Routledge & Kegan Paul and Princeton University Press 1972.

52. Quoted in Garcia Mateo, op. cit., p. 156.

53. Unamuno, *The Agony of Christianity*, pp. 9f.

54. Unamuno, *The Tragic Sense of Life*, p. 184.

55. Ibid., p. 224.

56. Ibid., p. 224.

57. Ibid., p. 228.

58. The quotation comes from *Christmas Eve*, V, lines 23–25.

59. *The Tragic Sense of Life*, p. 223.

60. Ibid., p. 223.

61. Ibid., p. 227.

62. Ibid., p. 229.

63. Ibid., p. 227. S. Kierkegaard already wrote similarly (*Papirer* XI, Copenhagen 1970, I A 422): 'Christianity is: what God has to suffer with us human beings ... Now there is, if one may so put it, in God the contradiction which is the source of all torment: he is love and yet he is unchangeable ... When Christ cried, "My God, my God, why hast thou forsaken me" – that was terrible for Christ, and this is the way it is commonly represented. But it seems to me that it was still more terrible for God to hear his cry ... to be unchangeable and then to be love: infinite, profound, unfathomable grief!' On this see H. Deuser, *Dialektische Theologie. Studien zu Adornos Metaphysik und dem Spätwerk Kierkegaards*, Munich, Mainz 1980.

64. Following R. Schneider, *Unamunos Briefwechsel. Nachwort*, Nuremberg 1955, pp. 332f.

65. *The Tragic Sense of Life*, p. 223.

66. Ibid., p. 162.

67. Ibid., p. 225.

68. Ibid., p. 224.

69. Ibid., p. 225.

70. These remarks are a reference to the agreement which R. Garcia Mateo (op. cit., pp. 157ff.) has detected between what Unamuno says about the suffering God and my own theology of the cross.

71. For a general characterization cf. P. Evdokimov, *Christus im russischen Denken*, Trier 1977, pp. 191ff.

72. N. Berdyaev, *The Meaning of History*, ET Geoffrey Bles and Scribner's 1939. Cf. also his *Spirit and Reality*, ET Bles and Scribner's 1939 and 1946.

73. Berdyaev, *The Meaning of History*, p. 58.

74. Berdyaev, *Spirit and Reality*, 1946 edition p. 115: 'Christianity does away with fate, with insoluble destiny. But tragedy survived in the Christian world, although its character was transformed. Christian tragedy is a tragedy of freedom as distinct from a tragedy of fate.' Cf. here C. Hartshorne, 'Whitehead and Berdyaev. Is there Tragedy in God?' in *Whitehead's Philosophy. Selected Essays, 1935–1970*, Lincoln 1972, pp. 183ff.

75. *The Meaning of History*, p. 57 (altered).

76. Ibid., p. 55 (altered).

77. Ibid., p. 45 (altered). Cf. F. W. J. Schelling, *Philosophie der Offen-barung* (1841/42), ed. stw. 181, esp. XVI: 'The Trinity, pointing to a further development of the theogonic process.' Cf. here M. Welker, *Der Vorgang Autonomie*, Neukirchen 1975, pp. 91ff.

78. In fact what is really meant is probably the Western metaphysics that followed Parmenides and Plato.

79. *The Meaning of History*, p. 46.

80. Ibid., p. 47.

81. Ibid., p. 47.

82. Ibid., p. 47 (altered).

83. Ibid., p. 48.

84. Ibid., p. 48 (altered). On the mystical doctrine of 'the divine thirst' cf. also Lady Julian of Norwich, *Revelations of Divine Love*, 31: 'The same desire and thirst that He had upon the Cross (which desire, longing and thirst, as to my sight, was *in him from without beginning*) the same hath he yet, and shall, unto the time that the last soul that shall be saved is come up to his bliss . . . The ghostly thirst is lasting in Him as long as we be in need, drawing us up to His bliss.' Quoted in Woollcombe, op. cit., p. 135.

85. *The Meaning of History*, p. 51 (altered).

86. Ibid., p. 48.

87. *Spirit and Reality*, 1946 edition, p. 98.

88. Ibid., p. 106.

89. G. Büchner, *Dantons Tod*, Act III.

90. O. Kirn, article 'Tod', *RE*[3], 19, pp. 801–5.

91. Cf. B. Albrecht, *Gott und das Leid der Menschen*, Meitinger Klein-schriften 52, Freising 1976.

92. Cf. here M. Welker (ed.), *Diskussion über J. Moltmanns Buch 'Das gekreuzigte Gott'*, Munich 1979, especially H. H. Miskotte's contri-bution, 'Das Leiden ist in Gott', pp. 74ff., and my reply, pp. 168ff.

93. K. Barth, *CD* II/2, p. 166. On Barth's doctrine of freedom, cf. the closely differentiating study by G. S. Hendry, 'The Freedom of God in the Theology of Karl Barth', *Scottish Journal of Theology*, 31/3, 1978, pp. 229–244. Hendry shows that Barth's criticism of Hegel – that he made God 'his own prisoner' – is a superficial one. He also points to Barth's use of the doctrine of emanation, which is in contradiction to his (Barth's) nominalism.

94. *CD* IV/2, p. 346.

95. Ibid., II/2, p. 10.

96. H. H. Martenson, *Christian Dogmatics*, ET T. & T. Clark, Edin-burgh 1866, § 51, pp. 99ff. esp. p. 101. As solution Martenson proposes: 'The only way to solve this contradiction, is to assume that God has a two-fold life – a life in himself of unclouded peace and self-satisfaction, and a life in and with his creation, in which He not only submits to the

conditions of finitude but even allows His power to be limited by the sinful will of man.'

97. Cf. n. 94.

98. F. von Hügel, 'Suffering and God', *Essays and Addresses*, II, London 1926 quoted in B. R. Brasnett, *The Suffering of the Impassible God*, p. 124: 'Perfect liberty excludes choice.'

99. Barth, *CD* II/1 §28.

100. On the modern concept of freedom under the spell of possessive individualism, cf. C. B. Macpherson, *The Political Theory of Possessive Individualism*, Oxford 1962: 'Freedom is a function of possession' (p. 3).

101. J. Moltmann, *Menschenwürde, Recht und Freiheit*, Stuttgart 1979.

102. Augustine, *De trin.* VII, 12.14:

> Immo vero vides trinitatem,
> si vides caritatem . . .
> Ecce tria sunt, amans
> et quod amatur, et amor.

For this section cf. E. Sartorius, *Die Lehre von der Heiligen Liebe. 1. Abt. Von der ursprünglichen Liebe und ihrem Gegensatz*, Stuttgart 1842; also the profound meditative writings, *Im Banne der Dreieinigkeit*, Regensburg 1934, and *Im Geheimnis*, Regensburg 1951, ed. F. Kronseder, SJ.

103. I. A. Dorner, *Die Unveränderlichkeit Gottes*, Leipzig 1883, p. 355.

104. N. Berdyaev, *The Meaning of History*, p. 48.

105. E. Troeltsch, *Glaubenslehre. Nach den Heidelberger Vorlesungen aus den Jahren 1911 und 1912*, ed. M. Troeltsch, Munich and Leipzig, 1925, § 14: 'Gott als Liebe', pp. 218ff.

III The History of the Son

1. A. von Harnack, *What is Christianity?*, ET Harper Torchbooks 1957, p. 193. Cf. also pp. 124ff. 'The Gospel and the Son of God, or the Christological question'.

2. Ibid., p. 125.

3. Ibid, p. 144. One must however also notice the sentence at the end of the whole section: 'It is not a mere factor that he is connected with the Gospel: *he was its personal realization and its strength, and this he is felt to be still.*' (p. 145)

4. I. Kant, *Der Streit der Fakultäten*, A 50, 57.

5. F. Schleiermacher, *The Christian Faith*, § 170, ET of 2nd ed., T. & T. Clark, Edinburgh 1928.

6. K. Barth *CD* I/1 § 8, pp. 295ff.

7. Ibid, pp. 299ff.

8. Ibid, p. 349: 'We may unhesitatingly equate the lordship of God, to which we found the whole of the biblical concept to be related, with what

the vocabulary of the early Church calls the essence of God, the *deitas* or *divinitas*, the divine οὐσία, *essentia, natura,* or *substantia.* The essence of God is the being of God as divine being. The essence of God is the Godhead of God.' Cf. also O. Weber, *Grundlagen der Dogmatik* I, 2nd ed. 1957, p. 397: 'God is this sole God as *the Lord* who acts on us. His unity is μοναρχία'.

9. Barth, *CD* I/1, p. 350.

10. Ibid, p. 354.

11. Here I am following A. Schlatter, *Johannes der Täufer,* Basle 1956; W. Wink, *John the Baptist in the Gospel Tradition,* London 1968; W. Bieder, *Die Verheissung der Taufe im Neuen Testament,* Zürich 1966; F. Lentzen-Deis, *Die Taufe Jesus nach den Synoptikern,* Frankfurt 1970. Cf. also F. Mussner, 'Ursprünge und Enfaltung der neutestamentlichen Sohneschristologie' in *Grundfragen der Christologie heute,* ed. L. Scheff-czyk, Questiones Disputatae 72, Freiburg 1975, pp. 77–113.

12. L. Goppelt, *Theologie des Neuen Testaments,* 3rd ed., Göttingen 1978, p. 92.

13. Ibid., p. 249.

14. J. Jeremias, *New Testament Theology* I, ET SCM Press and Scrib-ner, New York, 1971, pp. 53f.; and for criticism, F. Hahn, *The Titles of Jesus in Christology,* ET Lutterworth Press and World Publishing Co., New York, 1969, pp. 295ff.; M. Hengel, *The Son of God,* ET SCM Press and Fortress Press, Philadelphia 1976, p. 66.

15. Cf. here F. Hahn, op. cit., pp. 308ff.; J. Jeremias, op. cit., pp. 56ff L. Goppelt, op. cit., pp. 251ff.; also G. von Rad, *Wisdom in Israel,* ET SCM Press and Abingdon Press, Nashville, 1972, esp. pp. 144ff.; G. Foh-rer, article ' σοφία', *TDNT* VII, pp. 465ff. on Job 28 and Prov. 8.

16. Contrary to L. Goppelt, op. cit. p. 251, who talks about a 'mutual knowing between God and man'.

17. Cf. here J. Jeremias, *Abba,* Göttingen 1966, pp. 15–67, and *NT Theology,* pp. 61ff.

18. M. Hengel is more cautious in his judgment: 'Even if Jesus probably did not designate himself "Son of God" in so many words, the real root of the post-Easter title lies in the relationship to God as Father', op. cit., p. 63.

19. J. Jeremias, op. cit., p. 180. If the revelation of the Father is as central for Jesus as Jeremias has shown (in my view rightly), then we should no longer talk about 'the [kingly] reign of God' (pp. 31ff.), but rather about God's fatherly rule.

20. W. Kramer, *Christ, Lord, Son of God,* ET SCM Press and A. R. Allenson, Naperville, Ill., 1966, pp. 111ff.; W. Thüsing, *Per Christum in Deum. Studien zum Verhältnis von Christozentrik und Theozentrik in den paulinischen Hauptbriefen,* 2nd ed., Münster 1969, pp. 115ff.; E. Käsemann, *The Epistle to the Romans,* ET SCM Press and Eerdmans, Grand Rapids, 1980, pp. 217ff. Even when we consider the christological

'sending' formulations, we should think of the sending of the divine Wisdom: 'Send her forth out of the holy heavens, And from the throne of thy glory bid her come' (Wisd. 9.10). F. Christ, *Jesus Sophia. Die Sophia-Christologie bei den Synoptikern*, Zürich 1970.

21. J.-A. Bühner, *Der Gesandte und sein Weg im 4. Evangelium*, Tübingen 1977.

22. For the interpretation cf. D. S. Merezhkovsky, *Tod und Auferstehung*, Leipzig 1935; E. Schweizer, *Das Evangelium nach Markus*, NTD 2, 5th ed. 1978.

23. E. Vogelsang, *Der angefochtene Christus bei Luther*, Berlin 1932, esp. pp. 44ff.

24. Ibid., p. 45.

25. O. Michel, *Der Brief an die Hebräer*, 12th ed., Göttingen 1966, p. 132.

26. D. S. Merezhkovsky, op. cit., p. 322; A. von Harnack, *Probleme im Text der Leidensgeschichte Jesu*, Berlin 1901.

27. O. Michel, op. cit., p. 74: 'Χωρις θεοῦ has textual preference. God leads Christ into suffering (2.10), but at the same time accentuates this suffering through the trial of God-forsakenness (Mark 15.34).' Michel considers the canonical reading 'χάριτι θεοῦ ' to be 'probably a substitution and correction'.

28. H. Gese, 'Psalm 22 und das Neue Testament' in *Vom Sinai zum Zion, Alttestamentliche Beiträge zur biblischen Theologie*, Munich 1974, pp. 180–201.

29. D. S. Merezhkovsky, op. cit., p. 320. W. Kasper in *Jesus the Christ*, ET Burns and Oates, London and Paulist Press, New York 1976, thinks on the other hand that the use of Psalm 22 proves that 'Jesus' faith did not give way.' Anyone who uses Jesus' faith on the cross for a christology that makes him a human pattern, is thereby losing sight of Jesus' experience of being cursed on the cross, with its saving efficacy for all sinners. The modern psychological considerations, according to which Jesus 'broke down' or just 'did not break down' (W. Kasper, p. 120) on the cross, fail to grasp anything of the reality of the event that took place between Jesus and his Father, or between the Father and his Son. The heroic phrases which R. Bultmann uses when he talks about Jesus' 'foundering' on the cross, may be applicable to heroes like Leonidas at Thermopylae. At the cross they are utterly out of place.

30. W. Popkes, *Christus Traditus. Eine Untersuchung zum Begriff der Dahingabe im Neuen Testament*, Zürich, Stuttgart 1967, esp. pp. 153ff., 371ff. Cf. also K. Kertelge, *Der Tod Jesus. Deutungen im Neuen Testament*, Questiones Disputatae 74, Freiburg 1976.

31. Cf. also further reflections in H. Mühlen, *Die Veränderlichkeit Gottes als Horizont einer zukünftigen Christologie*, 2nd ed., Münster 1976.

32. So already B. Steffen, *Das Dogma vom Kreuz. Beitrag zu einer staurozentrischen Theologie*, Gütersloh 1920, p. 152.

33. This astonishing sentence comes from Patriarch Philareth of Moscow; quoted in P. Evdokimov, *Christus in russischen Denken*, Trier 1977, pp. 64 and 227.

34. Cf. here Adrienne von Speyr, quoted in B. Albrecht, *Eine Theologie des Katholischen. Einführung in das Werk Adrienne von Speyrs*, vol. II, Einsiedeln 1973, p. 156: 'In the ties of nature that bind the Father with ... the Son in Christ's suffering because of sin and his experience of sin, the God who is spirit already has an experience – if we may so put it – which belongs essentially to the redemption of the world. This "experience" is expanded at the death of the Lord. In the night of the cross that fell between the Father and the Son, God himself experienced the surrender in the form of sinful death. He had a new experience, unknown to him in his eternal life. He therefore gathered death into eternal life ... Through this reception into eternal life, the death of sin was destroyed; what remained was only death as a form and vessel for the divine life. Every death that is died in Christ is therefore for the future a way to eternal life. This does not merely make it something different for us; the Trinity has a different relation to it as well. Death is no longer something alien to it. The Son tasted death in his estrangement from the Father, and hence the Father also tasted death in the separation from the Son. Even the source of life in God, the Holy Spirit, is touched and transformed by this separation of the Father from the Son. For during the duration of the separation this source was sealed up and closed, as it were. It only begins to flow again when the Son returns to the Father.' If according to biblical testimony the delivering up of the Son takes place 'through the Holy Spirit', this last statement cannot be maintained. In the experience of death and in the Son's descent into Hell, the source or 'well of life' rather flows into death and hell. The life which the Spirit creates is 'life from the dead' (Rom. 11.15).

35. Cf. J. Moltmann, *Theology of Hope*, pp. 172ff.; *The Crucified God*, pp. 160ff.; *The Church in the Power of the Spirit*, pp. 98ff.

36. U. Wilckens, *Resurrection*, ET St Andrew Press 1977; W. Thüsing, *Erhöhungsvorstellung und Parusieerwartung in der ältesten nachösterlichen Christologie*, Stuttgart 1969.

37. On the concept of *Vorschein* – pre-reflection, pre-figuration or fore-shadowing – cf. E. Bloch, *Das Prinzip Hoffnung*, Frankfurt 1959.

38. B. Klappert, *Die Auferweckung des Gekreuzigten*, Neukirchen 1971.

39. J. Jervell, *Imago Dei. Gen. 1.26f. im Spätjudentum, in der Gnosis und in den paulinischen Briefen*, Göttingen 1960; W. Thüsing, op. cit., pp. 115ff.; L. Goppelt, op. cit., pp. 405ff.; M. Hengel, op. cit., pp. 7ff.

40. The alternative which L. Goppelt sees here does not exist. The conclusion which he draws is a typically monotheistic and mistaken in-

terpretation: 'Paul does not aim to explain the inner structure of the deity, like the later doctrine of the Trinity; he wants to characterize the soteriological happening of the going-out-of-himself of the *one* God' (op. cit., p. 453).

41. O. Weber, op. cit., I, pp. 419ff.: Heilsgeschehen und Trinitätslehre ('The Event of Salvation and the Doctrine of the Trinity').

42. J. Moltmann, *The Crucified God*, pp. 256ff.; E. Schendel, 'Herrschaft und Unterwerfung Christi. 1. Kor. 15. 24–28' in *Exegese und Theologie der Väter bis zum Ausgang des 4. Jahrhunderts*, Tübingen 1971.

43. W. Thüsing, op. cit., p. 246.

44. Here we again have to distinguish between Christ's *messianic rule* over the dead and the living (Rom. 14.9) and his *chiliastic kingdom*, in which the dead (the martyrs) will be raised (I Cor. 15.23; Rev. 20.1–4). Both are provisional compared with *the kingdom of glory*.

IV *The World of the Trinity*

1. On Augustine cf. M. Schmaus, *Die psychologische Trinitätslehre des Hl. Augustinus*, Münster 1927, pp. 151ff.

2. K. Barth took these concepts over from early Protestant orthodoxy, as did E. Jüngel, 'Das Verhältnis von "ökonomischer" and "immanenter" Trinität', *ZThK* 72, 1975, p. 362.

3. G. von Rad, *Old Testament Theology*, I, ET SCM Press and Harper and Row, New York, 1962, pp. 136ff.; cf. also W. H. Schmidt, *Die Schöpfungsgeschichte der Priesterschrift*, 2nd rev. ed., Neukirchen 1967.

4. J. Moltmann, *Theology of Hope*, ET SCM Press and Harper and Row, New York, 1967.

5. G. von Rad, op. cit., I, p. 138.

6. L. Köhler, *Old Testament Theology*, Lutterworth Press, London, and Westminster Press, Philadelphia, 1957, p. 87.

7. J. Moltmann, 'Creation as an Open System' in *The Future of Creation*, SCM Press and Fortress Press, Philadelphia, 1979, pp. 115ff.; A. R. Peacocke, *Creation and the World of Science*, the Bampton Lectures 1978, Oxford 1979.

8. Here I am following G. von Rad, op. cit. II, ET SCM Press and Harper and Row, New York, 1965, pp. 243ff.

9. Cf. W. Pannenberg, *Jesus – God and Man*, ET SCM Press and Westminster Press, Philadelphia, 1968; 2nd ed. Westminster Press, Philadelphia, 1977, pp. 390ff. W. Kasper, *Jesus the Christ*, pp. 185ff.: 'The Son of God as the Fulness of Time'.

10. Cf. G. Fohrer and U. Wilckens, article 'σοφία, TDNT VII, pp. 465–529.

11. Cf. R. Bultmann, *The Gospel According to John*, ET Blackwell, Oxford 1971, pp. 13ff.; R. Schnackenburg, *The Gospel According to St*

John I, ET Burns and Oates 1980, pp. 221–81; H. Gese, 'Der Johannes-
prolog' in *Zur biblischen Theologie*, Munich 1977, pp. 192–201.

12. I am here picking up ideas which I expressed most recently in
'Theology of Mystical Experience' in *Experiences of God*, ET SCM Press
and Fortress Press, Philadelphia, 1980, pp. 55ff.

13. For a particularly one-sided example of a Christian-theistic doctrine
of creation cf. O. Weber, *Grundlagen der Dogmatik*, I, new ed. Neukirch-
en 1977, pp. 510ff.; he simply polemizes against the doctrine of emanation. A. R. Peacocke, op. cit., gives more comprehensive information about
the Christian doctrine of creation.

14. K. Barth, *CD*, III/1ff.

15. Cf. J. Moltmann, *Theology of Play*, ET Harper and Row, New
York, 1972, *Theology of Joy* SCM Press, 1973, 'The Theological Play of
the Goodwill of God', pp. 39ff.; For scientific parallels cf. now M. Eigen
and R. Winkler, *Das Spiel* 2nd ed. Munich 1976.

16. Cf. I. A. Dorner, *System der christlichen Glaubenslehre* I, Berlin
1879, p. 418.

17. The basis is Richard of St Victor's doctrine of the Trinity, *De
Trinitate*, which he developed as a doctrine of divine love. In the nineteenth
century, starting from this and from Hegel's dialectic, Sartorius, Twesten,
Nitzsch, Julius Müller, Liebner and also I. A. Dorner, each in his own
way, took the *ethical* approach to an exposition of the Trinity. Cf. especially T. A. Liebner, *Christologie oder die christologische Einheit des
dogmatischen Systems*, Göttingen 1849, esp. pp. 234ff. On 'panentheism'
on the basis of process philosophy cf. N. Pittenger, *Process-Thought and
Christian Faith*, Welwyn 1968.

18. Dorner finds this danger in W. Beyschlag, *Christologie des Neuen
Testaments*, 1866, pp. 249ff. Cf. *System der christlichen Glaubenslehre* II,
1, Berlin 1880, pp. 363f. This is also the reproach always levied against
Hegel by nineteenth-century theologians.

19. So Meister Eckehart, *Deutsche Predigten und Traktate*, ed. and tr.
J. Quint, 4th ed., Munich 1977, p. 185: 'The Father brings forth his Son
in the soul in the same way as he brings him forth in eternity and in no
other way. He must do so whether he will or no. The Father brings forth
his Son unceasingly and I will say more: he brings me forth as his Son and
as the same Son. I will say yet more: he brings me forth as himself, and
himself as myself, and me as his being and as his nature.' Cf. *Meister
Eckhart*, ET C. de B. Evans, London 1924, vol. I, Sermon 66, p. 164.
Similarly Angelus Silesius, *Der cherubinische Wandersmann* I: 'I know
that without me God cannot live an instant. If I become nothing he must
give up the ghost himself . . . I am as of much consequence for God as he
for me. I help him maintain his being as he helps me maintain mine.'

20. I. A. Dorner, op. cit., p. 358; 'The meaning can only be that God
did not create out of superfluity of being, which would be incompleteness
and disharmony or suffering; nor did he create in order to complement

himself; nor, finally, was he forced by creative intelligence and its will towards the world. He created out of the bliss and perfection of his love and out of the self-consistency of that love's free will, part of which is *the pleasure of self-communication.* And by creating we mean: led non-being out of the mere condition of being-thought – out of potentiality – into actuality. The world is a goodly purpose, in correspondence with God's love, not a fortuitous one.'

21. Augustine, *De trin.* XV, 1; 4, 7 laid the foundation for this formulation.

22. Here I am following Gershom Scholem's brilliant account of Luria's teachings in *Major Trends in Jewish Mysticism,* New York 1954, London 1955, pp. 244ff. Cf. also his 'Schöpfung aus Nichts und Selbsverschränkung Gottes', *Eranos Jahrbuch 1956,* pp. 87–119.

23. J. Emden, *Mitpachat Sefarim,* Lemberg 1870, p. 82, quoted in Scholem, *Trends,* p. 411. According to rabbinic doctrine God's 'self-humiliation' in history begins with creation. Cf. P. Kuhn, *Gottes Selbsterniedrigung in der Theologie der Rabbinen,* Munich 1968. These ideas were at least taken up by Nicholas of Cusa, F. Oetinger, A. von Oettingen; and by E. Brunner, *Dogmatics* II, London, Lutterworth Press 1952, p. 20: 'This however, means that God does not wish to occupy the whole of space Himself, but He wills to make room for other forms of existence. In so doing He limits Himself . . . The χένωσις which reaches its paradoxical climax in the cross of Christ, began with the creation of the world'. Cf. also Schelling, *Philosophie der Offenbarung,* op. cit. XII, p. 177: 'But now God at the same time suspends his act of existing, which is a necessary act, in order to put the being that differs from himself in the place of that first existing.'

24. So according to Jakob Böhme and of pioneer importance for Ernst Bloch's ontology of not-yet-being; Karl Marx, *Frühschriften,* ed. S. Landshut, Stuttgart 1953, p. 330: 'Among the characteristics which are innate in matter, movement is the first and most important – not merely as mechanical and mathematical movement, but even more as urge, the spirit of life, tension, as the torment of matter, to use Jacob Böhme's phrase.'

25. C. Olevian, *De substantia foederis gratuiti inter Deum et electos itemque de mediis, quibus ea ipsa substantia nobis communicatur,* Geneva 1585.

26. In line with this are the highly questionable words in the Easter Vigil of the Roman Missal:

> 'O certe necessarium Adae peccatum
> quod Christe morte deletum est!
> O felix culpa, quae talem ac tantum
> meruit habere Redemptorem.'

27. Cf. I. A. Dorner, *System der christlichen Glaubenslehre,* II/1, Berlin 1880, pp. 422ff.

28. F. Schleiermacher, *The Christian Faith,* op. cit., §89.

29. J. Müller, 'Ob der Sohn Gottes Mensch geworden sein würde, wenn das menschliche Geschlecht ohne Sünde geblieben wäre?' *Texte zur Kirchen- und Theologiegeschichte*, ed. J. Wirsching, Gütersloh 1968.

30. Cf. here J. Moltmann, *The Crucified God*, pp. 256ff., with criticism of Calvin, A. von Ruler and D. Sölle.

31. This has been specially stressed by P. Ricoeur in *Le Conflit des interprétations*, Paris 1969, pp. 393ff.

32. J. Jervell, *Imago Dei, Gen. 1.26f. im Spätjudentum, in der Gnosis und in den paulinischen Briefen*, Göttingen 1960.

33. J. Moltmann, *Der Mensch. Christliche Anthropologie in den Konflikten der Gegenwart*, GTB 338, 4th ed. Gütersloh 1979, esp. pp. 152ff.

34. U. Mauser has put this point impressively; cf. *Gottesbild und Menschwerdung*, Tübingen 1971.

35. J. Moltmann, *The Crucified God*, pp. 267ff.

36. Here I am taking up ideas expressed by H. G. Geyer in 'Anfänge zum Begriff der Versöhnung', *EvTh* 38, 1978, pp. 235ff., esp. pp. 247ff. Cf. also C. F. D. Moule, *The Origin of Christology*, Cambridge 1977, especially his concept of 'the corporate Christ'.

37. This is the outstanding christological idea underlying the *Confession de Fe* de la Iglesia Presbiteriana Reformada en Cuba of 1977 in Article I, 1.01: 'The church believes in Jesus Christ, the "Son of God", our "first-born brother".' Cf. also Article 1.A.06, 1.C.03, 1.C.07. This church proclaims that Jesus Christ is the incarnate Son of God and our risen Brother. It thereby testifies in socialist Cuba that the love that is prepared for sacrifice and is in solidarity with others is both divine and human "necessity".'

38. Cf. F. Hahn, 'Das biblische Verständnis des heiligen Geistes' in *Erfahrung und Theologie des Hl. Geistes*, ed. C. Heitmann and H. Mühlen, Hamburg, Munich 1974, pp. 131ff.; E. Schweizer, *The Holy Spirit*, ET SCM Press and Fortress Press, Philadelphia 1981, and his article '$\pi\nu\epsilon\tilde{\upsilon}\mu\alpha$', *TDNT* VI, pp. 332–451; G. W. H. Lampe, *God as Spirit*, Oxford 1977.

39. Cf. H. Schlier, 'Herkunft, Ankunft und Wirkungen des heiligen Geistes im Neuen Testament' in *Erfahrung und Theologie des Hl. Geistes*. op. cit., pp. 118ff.

40. J. Moltmann, *The Church in the Power of the Spirit*, ET SCM Press and Harper and Row, 1977, pp. 108ff.: 'The glory of Jesus and the "feast without end" '; H. Urs von Balthasar, *Herrlichkeit. Eine theologische Ästhetik*, I Einsiedeln 1961.

41. E. Käsemann, 'The Cry for Liberty in the Worship of the Church', in *Perspectives on Paul*, ET SCM Press 1971, pp. 122ff., esp. pp. 134ff.

42. K. A. Bauer, *Leiblichkeit – das Ende aller Werke Gottes*, Gütersloh 1971.

43. So F. Hahn, op. cit., pp. 143f.

44. J. Moltmann, 'The Trinitarian History of God' in *The Future of Creation*, pp. 80ff., esp. pp. 88ff.

45. G. Wagner, 'Der Heilige Geist als offenbarmachende und vollendende Kraft. Das Zeugnis der orthodoxen Tradition' in *Erfahrung und Theologie des Hl. Geistes*, op. cit., pp. 214ff., esp. pp. 217f. Cf. also 'Sohn and Geist. Die Frage der Orthodoxie', *Concilium* 15, 1979, pp. 499ff., with contributions by D. Ritschl, M. Fahey and T. Stylianopoulos (ET no. 128, *Conflicts about the Holy Spirit*, ed. H. Küng and J. Moltmann).

46. Cf. Ch. II: 'The Passion of God'.

47. I. A. Dorner, *Unveränderlichkeit*, op. cit., p. 361; 'Thus, out of the sphere of temporal history and of free creative beings, something results for God, something which according to his own, absolute judgment is of value, a satisfaction for the divine consciousness which it did not have before, a joy which it could not have of itself and without the world . . .

When the song of praise really one day sounds . . . (Rev. 19.6; 21.3), this will be for God too a truly new song, which did not sound for him in the same way through his foreknowledge or his eternal decree, as in the joyful feast that followed the creation of the world; but just as the acquiring of history in time is something real and valuable in itself, so it will also be for God, by virtue of the unalterability of his living love.'

48. Dante, *Il Paradiso*, Canto XXVII, II,4: 'Un riso dell'universo'.

V *The Mystery of the Trinity*

1. O. Weber, *Grundlagen der Dogmatik*, I, p. 405: 'There really is a kind of permanence in heresy.'

2. Schleiermacher did this in his own way: *Glaubenslehre* § 22. Cf. K.-M. Beckmann, *Der Begriff der Häresie bei Schleiermacher*, Munich 1959.

3. Cf. A. Gilg, *Weg und Bedeutung der altkirchlichen Christologie*, Munich 1955, pp. 12ff.

4. E. Peterson, 'Monotheismus als politisches Problem' in *Theologische Traktate*, Munich 1951, pp. 49ff., and for recent comment A. Schindler, *Monotheismus als politisches Problem. Erik Peterson und die Kritik der politischen Theologie*, Gütersloh 1978. For the concept of the One God in the ancient world cf. also E. Peterson, *EIS THEOS. Epigraphische, formgeschichtliche und religionsgeschichtliche Untersuchungen*, Göttingen 1926. On the concept of 'monarchianism' cf. A. von Harnack, article 'Monarchianismus' *RE³*, 13, 324.

5. Quoted in E. Peterson, 'Monotheismus', op. cit., pp. 70ff.

6. On the political theology of monotheism cf., as well as E. Peterson, H. Berkhof, *Kirche und Kaiser. Eine Untersuchung der Entstehung der byzantinischen und der theokratischen Staatsauffassung im vierten Jahrhundert*, Zürich 1947.

7. On the philosophical concept of the One, cf. the article 'Eine (das),

Einheit', *Historisches Wörterbuch der Philosophie*, ed. J. Ritter, II, Basle and Stuttgart 1972, 361ff. On the theological concept of unity in the early church cf. C. Stead, *Divine Substance*, Oxford 1977, pp. 157ff., esp. pp. 180ff. Because both in monotheism and in monarchianism the exclusive monadic concept of the One is used, but not the uniting concept of 'unity', I am using the term 'monotheism' where other people, following the ideas of the nineteenth century, talk about 'theism'. Cf. for example W. Pannenberg, 'Die Subjektivität Gottes und die Trinitätslehre', *KuD* 23, 1977, pp. 25ff.

8. H. Berkhof, *Theologie des Heiligen Geistes*, Neukirchen 1968, pp. 15ff.

9. F. Loofs, *Paulus von Samosata. Eine Untersuchung zur altkirchlichen Literatur- und Dogmengeschichte*, Leipzig 1924. Cf. also the more recent H. de Riedmatten, *Les actes du procès de Paul de Samosata*, Fribourg 1952.

10. I. A. Dorner, *System der christlichen Glaubenslehre*, I, Berlin 1879, p. 357.

11. A. Harnack, *Dogmengeschichte*, 4th ed. Tübingen 1905, p. 192 (ET *History of Dogma*, 1894–99).

12. Cf. here the extensive investigation by J. A. Heins, *Die Grundstruktuur von die modalistiese Triniteitsbeskouing*, Kampen 1953. Heins treats both the modalism of the early church and its modern form, and stresses particularly the problem of monism, which he demonstrates from the use of the terms *monas* and *monarchia*.

13. Cf. Heins, ibid., p. 34.

14. *Tertullian adversus Praxean*, ed. E. Kroymann, Tübingen 1907; cf. also the introduction, with its detailed account of the dogmatic history.

15. Cf. Heins, op. cit., pp. 49ff.

16. He uses for this the terms *platysmos*, *diastole*, *ekstasis* and *systole*.

17. W. Gericke, *Marcell von Ankyra*, Halle 1940. The interpretation of the divine *monas* as 'identical subject' derives from F. C. Baur, *Die christliche Lehre von der Dreieingkeit*, Tübingen 1841, I, p. 252; but it is in itself influenced by Hegel.

18. F. Schleiermacher, 'Über den Gegensatz zwischen der sabellianischen und der athanasianischen Vorstellung von der Trinität', *Theol. Zeitschrift*, 1882, now in *Friedrich Schleiermacher und die Trinitätslehre*, Texte zur Kirchen- und Theologiegeschichte 11, ed. M. Tetz, Gütersloh 1969.

19. Ibid., p. 82. Schleiermacher's interpretation anticipates modern Protestant theology of revelation: 'The Trinity, however, is the revealed God and every member of it is a way of revelation of its own; but the deity in each one of these members is not an other, but only the same One, which is not made known to us in itself but only as the One revealed in these three themselves'. Schleiermacher recognized that the problem of unity is the main problem of the doctrine of the Trinity. What he criticized

about the Athanasian doctrine of the Trinity was its incapacity to distinguish between the unity of the divine essence and the Person of the Father. The inner-trinitarian monarchy of the Father makes the Son and the Spirit subordinate and unequal. But his attempt to take up the Sabellian doctrine of the Trinity leads to an impossible position which he himself recognizes: the one God has to remain indefinably behind and in his three-fold manifestations, and in addition no reason can be given why he should manifest himself at all. The relationships between God *as* Father, *as* Son and *as* Spirit take on no importance, because each of these identifications can only be understood as a self-relationship of the unknown God. The difficulty of the Athanasian and the Sabellian views of the Trinity, which Schleiermacher recognized with great acuteness, can only be settled if the unity of God is equated neither with the essence nor with one person of the triune God.

20. I am here following the summing up given by E. Kroyman, op. cit., xxff. On Tertullian's concept of substance, cf. C. Stead, *Divine Substance*, op. cit., pp. 202ff.

21. I. A. Dorner maintained this thesis, impressively and in detail: *System der christlichen Glaubenslehre*, I, Berlin 1879, §32, p. 430: 'The absolute Personality in its relationship to the divine hypostases and attributes': 'In the trinitarian processes of the life and spirit of God, absolute personality is the eternally present result; so the self-conscious God, who desires and possesses himself, is also present in such a way in each of the divine distinctions that these – which would not in themselves and individually be personal – yet participate in the One of the divine personality, each in its own way. But as the absolute divine personality is the single constitution of the three divine modes of being which participate in it and has its understanding in them, as they have theirs in it, so this same divine personality which, in its ultimate relationship and according to its nature, is holy love, is also the single constitution and the highest power of all divine characteristics.' Barth took over the concept of 'modes of being' from Dorner.

22. So Karl Barth, *CD* I/1, p. 354: 'With the doctrine of the Trinity, we step on to the soil of Christian monotheism.' For a detailed justification cf. pp. 351ff. So also W. Pannenberg, 'Die Subjektivität Gottes und die Trinitätslehre', *KuD* 23, 1977, p. 39. n. 34: 'The doctrine of the Trinity, in the sense of patristic theology particularly, must be understood as the Christian form of monotheism. It must actually be interpreted as the positive condition for a consistent monotheism.' On the other hand he declares 'Christian theism' to be a heresy (p. 39). In this connection there is an important demonstration of the considerable similarity of Barth's doctrine of the Trinity with Hegel's, with impressive criticism of both, by L. Oeing-Hanhoff, 'Hegels Trinitätslehre', *Theologische Quartalschrift*, 159, 1979, pp. 287–303.

23. *Christlichen Dogmatik im Entwurf*, München 1927, p. 126.

24. Ibid., p. 127.
25. Ibid., p. 131.
26. Ibid., p. 132.
27. Ibid., p. 140.
28. Ibid., p. 151.
29. Ibid., p. 170. Cf. also p. 165, where Barth understands by 'person': 'One of the ways in which the one personal God and Lord, who thinks and wills for himself, grounding himself in himself, is God and Lord.' Similarly O. Weber, *Grundlagen der Dogmatik*, I, p. 417. He interprets the divine Persons as 'God himself' and hence understands the homousios not as participation in divine substance, but as a divine repetition – 'Him-self once more'. Similarly H. Berkhof, *Theologie des Hl. Geistes*, op. cit., pp. 133ff., who interprets Barth's 'modes of being' as modes of move-ment (*modus motus*): one God in a threefold movement. Berkhof has now developed a federal-theological doctrine, however, which comes close to the doctrine of the 'open Trinity' presented in this book. Cf. *Christian Faith. An Introduction to the Study of the Faith*, Grand Rapids 1979, pp. 330ff.: 'The Covenant as Tri(u)nity.'
30. *CD* I/1, pp. 304ff.
31. Ibid., p. 314.
32. Ibid., p. 332.
33. Ibid., p. 350. Also II/1, pp. 287ff.
34. Ibid., p. 358. Cf. similarly O. Weber, *Grundlagen der Dogmatik*, I, p. 419: 'The point is to state that God as He-himself lives, acts and rules *in* the actuality of his being-God, from eternity and hence also in his revelation, *in a threefold way as the One*.'
35. *CD* I/1, p. 359.
36. I. A. Dorner, *System der christlichen Glaubenslehre*, I, p. 371.
37. J. G. Fichte, *Die Anweisung zum seligen Leben oder auch Die Religionslehre* (1812), Stuttgart 1962, Zehnte Vorlesung, pp. 155ff. On the idea of the Spirit as the bond of fellowship in the deity, cf. also F. Hölderlin, *Fragment 'Über Religion'. Gesammelte Werke* IV, Stuttgart 1961, pp. 287ff., with his concept of the 'common' or 'joint Godhead'. Hölderlin's criticism of Fichte's 'ego' philosophy probably influenced He-gel's philosophy. Cf. D. Henrich, 'Hegel und Hölderlin' in *Hegel im Kontext*, ed. Suhrkamp 510, Frankfurt 1971, pp. 9–40.
38. This can be seen in an astonishing way in K. Barth, 'Das christliche Verständnis der Offenbarung', ThEx NF, 1948, pp. 3–4. It is only from p. 5 onwards that the speculatively acquired, general principles of 'God's self-revelation' are applied to 'revelation as Christians interpret it'. Inter-esting and topical in this connection is F. C. Baur's account and criticism of C. I. Nitzsch (*Dreieinigkeit*, op. cit., III, p. 943): 'God reveals simply himself, not something else not himself; he communicates himself. Now the One who reveals, who is communicated, is none other than the One who communicates; but the relationship between subject and object has

in this process of revelatory activity already come into being . . . With what right can it then be maintained that the Trinity of revelation must already have as presupposition an independent Trinity of essence?'

39. *CD* I/1, p. 332 (altered). Cf. also p. 480: 'The Holy Ghost is the love which is the essence of the relation between these two modes of being of God.'

40. L. Oeing-Hanhoff comes to this conclusion in *Hegels Trinitätslehre*, op. cit., pp. 395ff. He cites in its support F. von Baader's judgment: 'So many hold that they have gone to the root of the matter when they maintain that the Spirit is love, i.e., the unity of the Father and the Son; whereby, however, they deny the dogma or principle of the Trinity in that they set up a God who is two-in-one instead of three-in-one.'

41. *CD* I/1, p. 488.

42. Ibid., p. 487.

43. 'Tritheism' was the reproach levied against Christian belief in the Trinity from the very beginning. It was consequently continually rejected, from 260 (Pope Dionysius) onwards. It goes back particularly to the (Western church's) Athanasian creed: 'Non tres Dii, sed unus Deus.' Since that time the reproach of tritheism has belonged to the stock of Western trinitarian doctrines. Cf. M. Schmaus, article 'Tritheismus' in *LThK*, 2nd ed., X, pp. 365f.; W. Philipp, article 'Tritheismus' in *RGG*, 3rd ed., VI, 1043f. As the history of theology shows, there has never been a Christian tritheist. Even Barth does not name any, although he argues so vigorously against tritheism. Probably it is the triadology of the Eastern church that is meant. The standard argument against 'tritheism' practically serves everywhere to disguise the writer's own modalism. For a criticism of Barth's 'modalism', cf. L. Hodgson, *The Doctrine of the Trinity*, London 1943, p. 229; D. M. Baillie, *God was in Christ*, London 1947, p. 134.

44. *CD* I/1, pp. 306, 384ff.

45. U. Hedinger, *Der Freiheitsbegriff in der Kirchlichen Dogmatik K. Barths*, 1962; G. S. Hendry, 'The Freedom of God in the Theology of Karl Barth', *Scottish Journal of Theology*, 31, 1978, pp. 229–244.

46. K. Rahner, 'Remarks on the Dogmatic Treatise *De Trinitate*', *Theological Investigations* IV, ET Darton, Longman & Todd, London 1966, pp. 77–102; also his 'Der dreifaltige Gott als transzendenter Urgrund der Heilsgeschichte', *Mysterium Salutis* II, Einsiedeln 1967, pp. 317–401, and *Grundkurs des Glaubens*, Freiburg 1976, pp. 139ff.

47. K. Rahner, *Mysterium Salutis*, pp. 342f.

48. Rahner, *Grundkurs*, op. cit., p. 140.

49. Ibid. Cf. also K. Barth, *CD* I/1, p. 351: 'But in it [i.e. the doctrine of the Trinity] we are speaking not of three divine I's, but thrice of one divine I.'

50. This is the subject of criticism by H.-J. Lauter, *Die doppelte Aporetik der Trinitätslehre und ihre Überschreitung, Wissenschaft und Weisheit*, pp. 36–73, pp. 60ff., and F. X. Bantle, 'Person und Personbegriff in

der Trinitätslehre Karl Rahners' in *Münchner Theol. Zeitschrift*, 30, 1979, pp. 11–24. For the subject in the framework of the history of dogma, cf. S. Otto, *Person und Subsistenz*, Munich 1968.

51. *Mys. Sal.*, op. cit., p. 392.

52. Cf. the evidence in Bantle, op. cit., pp. 20ff. Cf. also E. J. Fortman, *The Triune God. A Historical Study of the Doctrine of the Trinity*, London 1972, pp. 295ff.

53. Evidence in Bantle, op. cit., p. 22.

54. *Mys. Sal.*, p. 366, n. 29.

55. Ibid., p. 387.

56. *Grundkurs*, op. cit., p. 141.

57. See *Theological Investigations* IV, op. cit., p. 89. For criticism cf. Bantle, op. cit., p. 15.

58. Cf. Ch. II §7.

59. J. W. v. Goethe, *Der west-östliche Diwan*, VIII, 21; ET by J. Whaley, two language, DTV edition, Munich 1979. Marx's ideal of 'the total, many-sided and profound person' corresponds to this; cf. K. Marx, *Frühschriften*, ed. S. Landshut, Stuttgart 1953, p. 243.

60. R. Rothe, *Theologische Ethik*, I, pp. 59ff. (1st ed.); *Theologische Ethik* I, 2nd ed., Wittenberg 1867, §34, pp. 136f.: 'As the absolute unity of the divine personality (the divine ego) and the divine nature, God is the absolute person.' For criticism cf. I. A. Dorner, *System der christlichen Glaubenslehre*, I, pp. 390ff.

61. I. A. Dorner, ibid., §32, pp. 430ff. Cf. quotation in n. 21.

62. M. Kähler, *Die Wissenschaft der christlichen Lehre*, 3rd. ed., Leipzig 1905, §372, p. 330. Similarly R. Grützmacher, *Der dreieinige Gott – unser Gott*, Leipzig 1910, p. 52: 'It is because – and only because – God develops himself into a threefold personality that there is an independent, self-sufficient and unified personal life in God. God is not also personality because the three Persons of the Father, the Son and the Spirit are added to him; the divine personality only comes into being by separating and closing again in the process of the threefold personal life.'

63. K. Barth, *CD*, II/2, p. 123; cf. also pp. 166ff. Orthodox theology is also familiar with the idea of the retroactive effect of the cross on the eternal Trinity. Cf. P. Evdokimov, *Christus im russischen Denken*, Trier 1977, pp. 62ff., 222f.

64. *The Crucified God*, ch. VI, 5, pp. 235ff.: 'Trinitarian Theology of the Cross'; also *Diskussion über 'Der gekreuzigte Gott'*, ed. M. Welker, Munich 1979.

65. Ibid., p. 227.

66. W. Kasper rightly notes this. Cf. his 'Revolution im Gottesverständnis?' in *Diskussion* (cf. n. 64 above), pp. 140ff.

67. Cf. Ch. IV.

68. This doxology is used by the Reformierte Kirche in Deutschland.

69. Cf. here the textbooks by F. Diekamp, *Katholische Dogmatik*, I,

12th ed., Münster 1957; E. J. Fortman, *The Triune God*, London 1972; *Mysterium Salutis. Grundriss heilsgeschichtlicher Dogmatik*, ed. J. Feiner and M. Löhrer, II, Einsiedeln 1967; H. Mühlen, *Der Heilige Geist als Person in der Trinität, bei der Inkarnation und im Gnadenbund: Ich-Du-Wir*, 2nd ed., Münster 1966; O. Weber, *Grundlagen der Dogmatik*, I, Neukirchen 1964; E. Schlink, article 'Trinität', *RGG*, 3rd ed., VI, 1032–1038. I am following the different positions put forward by tradition and am discussing them systematically.

70. J. W. von Goethe, 'Grenzen der Menschheit'. The German text reads as follows:

> Wenn der uralte heilige Vater
> mit gelassener Hand
> aus rollenden Wolken
> segnende Blitze
> über die Erde schickt,
> kuss ich den lezten Saum seines Kleides,
> kindliche Schauer treu in der Brust.

71. J. Denzinger, *Enchiridion Symbolorum*, 26th ed., Freiburg 1947, no. 276; Nec enim de nihilo, neque de aliaqua alia substantia sed de Patris utero, id est, de substantia ejus idem Filius genitus vel natus esse credendus est.' In this sense the trinitarian Father himself is 'Beyond God the Father' in the words of Mary Daly's basic feminist book (Boston 1973). T. A. Liebner also declares in his book, *Christologie oder die christologische Einheit des dogmatischen Systems,* Göttingen 1849, p. 205: 'In a similar way people have dared to call that divine act of self-generation and self-recognition in which God enjoys the assurance of himself, love towards itself, thereby inventing *the androgynous nature* of God, by taking sexual love as symbol.'

72. On this argument cf. V. Lossky, 'The Procession of the Holy Spirit in Orthodox Trinitarian Doctrine' in *In the Image and Likeness of God*, ET from French, Mowbray, London 1975, pp. 71ff.

73. This is Lossky's starting point too. Ibid., p. 74. Cf. also *Concilium* 15, 1979, no. 10: *Der Heilige Geist im Widerstreit*, esp. 'Sohn und Geist', with contributions by D. Ritschl, M. Fahey, T. Stylianopoulos, pp. 499–514 (ET no. 128, *Conflicts about the Holy Spirit*, ed. H. Küng and J. Moltmann). H. Mühlen's attempt in *Der Heilige Geist als Person*, pp. 100ff., to constitute the Spirit as We-Person from the I of the Father and the Thou of the Son, seems like a personalistic postulate, as long as the counterpart for that 'We' cannot be named in inner-trinitarian terms; for the first person plural, like the first person singular, is related to a counterpart, to the 'you'. If the Spirit forms the 'We' of the Triunity, then he himself is the perichoresis. The Tri-unity is then only a duality: I + Thou = We.

74. Thomas Aquinas, *Summa Theologiae* I, q 26,a.1.

75. W. Pannenberg, article 'Person' in *RGG*, 3rd ed., V, 230–235. For

criticism cf. also *Der kleine Pauly. Lexikon der Antike*, IV, Munich 1972, article 'persona', col. 657: 'The etymology (Etr. φersu?) is disputed. But at all events the derivation (held in both ancient and modern times) that it comes from the alleged function of the person as voice-amplifier ... cannot be maintained because of the difference of quantity between *persŏnare* and *persōna*.'

76. R. Dahrendorf, *Homo sociologicus*, ET Routledge and Kegan Paul, London 1973; ET originally published in *Essays in the Theory of Society*, 1968.

77. R. Musil, *The Man without Qualities*, ET Secker & Warburg, London 1953–60, I, p. 175.

78. Boethius, *Trin*, 3.1–5. MPL 64, 1343 C.

79. Thomas Aquinas, *Summa Theologiae* I, q 40, a.2: 'Persona est relatio.' K. Barth took up this proposition and its neo-scholastic interpretation and expressly made it his own. Cf. *CD* I/1, pp. 365f. For him it is an argument for no longer talking about 'persons' but about the 'three modes of being of the one God'.

80. O. Weber, op. cit., p. 418.

81. Richard of St Victor, *De Trinitate*, MPL 196, 887–992. New critical edition: P. Ribaillier, *Richard de Saint-Victor, De Trinitate. Texte critique avec introduction, notes et tables*, Paris 1958; G. Salet, *Richard de Saint-Victor, La Trinité*, Paris 1959.

82. G. W. F. Hegel, *Philosophie der Religion. Die absolute Religion*, PhB 63, pp. 61 and 71f.

83. John of Damascus, *De Fide Orthodoxa*, MPG 94, 789–1228. New critical edition: *Die Schriften des Johannes Damaskenos*, PTSt 12, vol. II, ed. B. Kotter, Berlin and New York 1973.

84. V. Lossky, op. cit., p. 94.

85. Cf. Ch. IV, §4.

86. *Acta et Scripta Theologorum Wirtembergensium, et Patriarchae Constantinopolitani D. Hieremiae: quae utrq; ab anno MDLXXVI. usque ad annum MDLXXXI. de Augustana Confessione inter se miserunt*, Wittenberg 1584; German: *Wort und Mysterium. Der Briefwechsel über Glauben und Kirche 1576–1581 zwischen den Tübinger Theologen und dem Patriarchen von Konstantinopel*, Witten 1958.

87. Cf. here F. C. Baur, *Die christliche Lehre von der Dreieinigkeit und Menschwerdung Gottes in ihrer geschichtlichen Entwicklung*, III, Tübingen 1843, pp. 389ff. The Würtemberg theologians held that without the Filioque, firstly, the unity and identity of being of the Father and the Son could not be preserved and, secondly, that the hypostatic connection between the Son and the Spirit could not be shown.

88. Cf. the work of Bishop Urs Küry, 'Die Bedeutung des Filioque-Streites für den Gottesbegriff der abendländischen und der morgenländischen Kirche' in *IKZ* 33, 1943, pp. 1–19; also his 'Grundsätzlich-theologische Erwägungen zur Filioque-Frage' (1969–70), *IKZ* 58, 1969,

pp. 81–108; also the 'Erklärung der internationalen altkatholischen Bischofskonferenz zur Filioque-Frage', *IKZ* 61, 1971, and the 'Glaubensbrief der internationalen altkatholischen Bischofskonferenz' *IKZ* 61, 1971, pp. 65–68. For the Anglican church cf. *Anglican-Orthodox Dialogue. The Moscow Statement agreed by the Anglican-Orthodox Joint Commission*, 1976, ed. K. Ware and C. Davey; also *The Report of the Lambeth Conference*, 1978.

89. *Revue Internationale de Théologie*, no. 24, 1898, pp. 681–712, and comment *Istina*, Paris 1972, pp. 3–4: 'La procession du Saint Esprit. Orient et Occident.'

90. Contrary to Bolotov, cf. V. Lossky, op. cit., pp. 72f.

91. A. Papadopoulou, *Gregor Palamas' Lehre vom Ausgang des Heiligen Geistes*, Thessaloniki 1971, pp. 70ff.

90. A working group of Faith and Order in the World Council of Churches has worked anew on the Filioque question and has taken up Bolotov's suggestions. The doctrine of the Trinity I have expounded here owes much to this working group.

93. Cf. here also G. S. Hendry, *The Holy Spirit in Christian Theology*, London 1965, pp. 30ff., with criticism of Barth's adherence to and new formulation of the Filioque. I. A. Heron gives an excellent summing up of the dogmatic history and makes a good dogmatic suggestion in ' "Who proceedeth from the Father and the Son": The Problem of the Filioque', *Scottish Journal of Theology* 24, 1971, pp. 149–166; A. M. Aagaard, *Helliganden sendt til Verden*, Aarhus 1973, pp. 207ff.

94. Bolotov, op. cit., p. 692.

95. Ibid., pp. 694f.

96. Quoted in N. J. Thomas, *Die syrisch-orthodoxe Kirche in südindischen Thomas-Christen. Geschichte – Kirchenverfassung – Lehre.* Würzburg 1967, p. 67. In Syrian the Greek word *ousia* is used for essence and the Syrian word *q'nomo* for person.

97. So also B. Lonergan, *Divinarum Personarum Conceptionem analogicam*, 2nd ed. Rome 1959, p. 236.

VI *The Kingdom of Freedom*

1. The term and the question both derive from the political theorist Carl Schmitt, *Politische Theologie. Vier Kapitel zur Lehre von der Souveränität*, Munich 1922, 2nd ed. 1934; *Politische Theologie II. Die Legende von der Erledigung jeder Politischen Theologie*, Berlin 1970. Cf. K.-M. Kodalle, *Politik als Macht und Mythos*, Stuttgart 1973. J. B. Metz began to work out a new theological definition of 'political theology' in *Theology of the World*, ET Burns and Oates, London, and Seabury Press, New York, 1973; he continued his attempt in *Glaube in Geschichte und Gesellschaft*, Mainz 1977. Cf. H. Peukert (ed.), *Diskussion zur 'politischen Theologie'*, Munich, Mainz 1969; also J. Moltmann, 'Theologische Kritik

der politischen Religion', in J. B. Metz, J. Moltmann and W. Oemüller, *Kirche im Prozess der Aufklärung*, Munich, Mainz 1970, pp. 11–52; *The Crucified God*, pp. 317ff.: 'Ways towards the Political Liberation of Man'. Cf. also D. Sölle, *Political Theology*, ET Fortress Press, Philadelphia 1974; S. Wiedenhofer, *Politische Theologie*, Stuttgart 1976; J. M. Lochman, *Perspektiven politischer Theologie*, Zürich 1971.

2. M. Pohlenz, *Die Stoa*, I, 3rd ed., Göttingen 1964; It was this concept which E. Peterson made the basis of his famous treatise, 'Monotheismus als politisches Problem' (1935) in *Theologische Traktate*, Munich 1951, pp. 48–147; the book views the question in the context of the history of theology. For an analysis and discussion of this essay, cf. A. Schindler (ed.), *Monotheismus als politisches Problem? Erik Peterson und die Kritik der politischen Theologie*, Gütersloh 1978. When he published his book in 1935, Peterson took up a critical position with regard to Carl Schmitt's 'political theology': 'The doctrine of the divine monarchy was bound to run aground on the doctrine of the Trinity. This is not merely the finish, theologically speaking, of monotheism as a political problem; it also means a final and fundamental breach with every "political theology" which misuses the Christian proclamation for the justification of a political situation' (p. 105). Does this mean 'every political theology' or merely affirmative political theology? C. Schmitt – as the sub-title of his *Politischen Theologie II* shows – assumes that the first is true, and the same applies to some of the writers in Schindler's collection of essays. But Peterson did not mean to dismiss every political theology. This is shown by his 'Preliminary Remarks': 'For the Christian, political action must always be subject to the premise of belief in the triune God' (p. 47).

3. E. Peterson uses it none the less, op. cit., p. 91: 'The concept of the divine monarchy, which was merely the reflection of the earthly monarchy in the *imperium romanum*. . . .'

4. So C. Schmitt, *Politische Theologie*, op. cit., 1934, p. 49: 'All the pregnant concepts of the modern theory of the state are secularized theological concepts. Not merely in their historical development, because they were carried over into constitutional theory from theology . . . but in their systematic structure as well, a knowledge of which is necessary for a sociological examination of these terms.'

5. Cf. E. Peterson, op. cit.; A. A. T. Ehrhardt, *Politische Metaphysik von Solon bis Augustin*, I, Tübingen 1959; H. Berkhof, *Kirche und Kaiser*, Göttingen 1947.

6. For the way Augustine took over and changed the stoic teaching about natural law, cf. E. Wolf, 'Naturrecht und Gerechtigkeit' in *Naturrecht oder Rechtspositivismus*, ed., W. Maihofer, Darmstadt 1962, pp. 52–72.

7. References in E. Peterson, op. cit., p. 49.

8. Ibid., pp. 98ff.

9. W. Elert, *Der Ausgang der altkirchlichen Christologie*, Berlin 1957,

pp. 26ff.: 'Das Problem des politischen Christus'; C. Gunton, 'The Political Christ', *Scottish Journal of Theology*, 32, 1979, pp. 521–540.

10. Quoted in E. Peterson, op. cit., p. 91.

11. E. Peterson, *Vorbemerkung*, op. cit., p. 47.

12. J. Bodin, *Les six livres de la République*, 2nd ed., Paris 1583. For comment cf. P. Hazard, *The European Mind 1680–1715*, ET Hollis and Carter, London 1953; C. Hill, *The Century of Revolution 1603–1714*, London 1961; A. A. van Schelven, *Het Calvinisme gedurende zijn Bloetijd*, I, Amsterdam 1951.

13. S. Borchart, 'De jure ac potestate Regium' in *Opera Omnia*, Leyden 1692, vol. 1, pp. 995ff., esp. p. 998, 1. Cf. also J. Moltmann, 'Prädestination und Heilsgeschichte bei M. Amyraut', *ZKG* 65, 1957, pp. 270–303.

14. M. Amyraut, *Discours de la souveraineté des Roys*, Saumur 1650.

15. S. Borchart, op. cit., p. 1018

16. A. A. van Schelven, op. cit., p. 241.

17. Cf. here G. Beyerhaus, *Studien zur Staatsanschauung Calvins. Mit besonderer Berücksichtigung seines Souveränitätsbegriffs*, Berlin 1910; J. Bohatec, *Calvins Lehre von Staat und Kirche unter besonderer Berücksichtigung des Organismusgedankens*, Breslau 1937, reprinted Aalen 1961, and *Budé und Calvin*, Graz 1950, pp. 330ff.: 'Die Autorität Gottes', p. 335: 'In the statement that God himself is the law, his authority appears as sovereignty, since it also expresses . . . God's superiority to natural law as well. Here Calvin is a forerunner of Bodin, the classic exponent of sovereignty, just as he would also subscribe to Hobbes's statement that "auctoritas facit legem" . . . According to Calvin the divine law is true because it has been promulgated by the divine authority.' On Hobbes cf. D. Braun, *Der sterbliche Gott oder Leviathan gegen Behemoth*, Zürich 1963.

18. C. Schmitt, *Politische Theologie*, op. cit., pp. 50ff., and *Die Diktatur. Von den Anfängen des modernen Souveränitätsgedanken bis zum proletarischen Klassenkampf*, 2nd ed., Munich 1928.

19. This was what A. N. Whitehead also had in mind with his criticism of theistical philosophy (cf. *Process and Reality. An Essay in Cosmology*, New York 1960, pp. 520f.). It was fateful idolatry when the church formed its idea of God on the model of worldly Egyptian, Persian and Roman rulers. 'The Church gave unto God attributes which belonged exclusively to Caesar.' The rise of 'theistic philosophy', which was completed with the emergence of Islam, led to the idea of God which was based on the model of the imperial ruler, on the model of personified moral energy, and on the model of the ultimate philosophical principle. It will be permissible to add that this 'theistic' philosophy represents a highly patriarchal one. Whitehead rightly draws attention to the difference from Christianity in its original form – a difference which it is impossible to overlook: 'There is, however, in the Galilean origin of Christianity yet another suggestion which does not fit very well with any of the three main

strands of thought. It does not emphasize the ruling Caesar, or the ruthless moralist, or the unmoved mover. It dwells upon the tender elements in the world, which slowly and in quietness operate by love; and it finds purpose in the present immediacy of a kingdom not of this world. Love neither rules, nor is it unmoved, also it is a little oblivious as to morals. It does not look to the future; for it finds its own reward in the immediate present.'

20. W. R. Matthews already noted this; cf. *God in Christian Thought and Experiences*, London 1930, p. 193.

21. Similarly the Anglican L. Hodgson, *The Doctrine of the Trinity*, London, and New York, 1944, p. 95; cf. also A. M. Allchin, *Trinity and Incarnation in Anglican Tradition*, Oxford 1977; Geervarghese Mar Osthathios, *Theology of a Classless Society*, London 1979, pp. 147ff.

22. *Gregor von Nazianz. Die fünf theologischen Reden. Text und Kommentar*, ed. J. Barbel, Düsseldorf 1963, p. 239 (Oratio V, 11).

23. Cf. the volume of essays *Papsttum als ökumenische Frage,* ed. the Arbeitsgemeinschaft der ökumenischen Institute, Munich, Mainz 1979.

24. The Pauline *kephale* theology of I Cor. 11.3 shows a corresponding derivation of male primacy over the woman: 'The head of every man is Christ, the head of a woman is her husband, and the head of Christ is God'; Eph. 5.22f.: 'The husband is the head of the wife as Christ is the head of the church.' The derivation in Heb. 12. 5–10 must also be called patriarchalist. Karl Barth, *CD* III/4, §54, developed a theory of female subordination out of Paul's *kephale* theology which rightly met with astonishment and opposition. Cf. C. Green, 'Karl Barth on Women and Man', *Union Theol. Quarterly Review*, 3/4 1974; I. A. Romero, 'K. Barth's Theology of the Word of God' in *Women and Religion*, Montana 1974; cf. L. M. Russell, *The Future of Partnership*, Philadelphia 1979; E. Moltmann-Wendel, 'Partnerschaft' in *Frauen auf neuen Wegen. Studien und Problemberichte zur Situation der Frauen in Gesellschaft und Kirche*, Gelnhausen 1978. For exegesis cf. F. Crüsemann and H. Thyen, *Als Mann und Frau geschaffen. Exegetische Studien zur Rolle der Frau,* Gelnhausen 1978.

25. K. Rahner and J. Ratzinger, *Episkopat und Primat*, Freiburg 1961; G. Schwaiger, *Papstgeschichte von den Anfängen bis zur Gegenwart*, 6th ed., Munich 1964; A. B. Hasler, *Wie der Papst unfehlbar wurde: Macht und Ohnmacht eines Dogmas*, Munich, Zürich 1979.

26. H. de Lubac, *Meditations sur l'Eglise*, 2nd rev. ed., Paris 1953, pp. 231ff., following a saying of Ambrose's. Peter is the centre of truth and Catholic unity, the one visible centre of all God's children.

27. H. Küng, *Infallible? An Enquiry*, ET Collins, London, 1971. For comment cf. K. Rahner (ed.), *Zum Problem der Unfehlbarkeit. Antworten auf die Anfrage von H. Küng*, Freiburg 1971; H. Küng (ed.), *Fehlbar? Eine Bilanz*, Einsideln 1973.

28. G. Hasenhüttl, *Herrschaftsfreie Kirche, Sozio-theologische Grundlegung*, Düsseldorf 1974.

29. P. Evdokimov, *L'Orthodoxie*, Paris 1965, p. 131. On this complex cf. also S. Harkianakis 'Can a Petrine office be meaningful in the Church?' in *Concilium* 7 no. 4, 1971, ET of Vol 4 no. 7 (reissued as no. 64, *The Petrine Ministry in the Church*, ed. Hans Küng), pp. 115–21: 'But these words (John 17.20ff) become even more meaningful perhaps if we remember that this exemplary mode of unity within the Trinity is the basic presupposition for the unity of the Church which we hope will be achieved.' (p. 118)

30. E. Bloch, *Das Prinzip Hoffnung*, Frankfurt 1959, p. 1413. On this chapter cf. esp. H.-J. Kraus's great outline of biblical theology, *Reich Gottes: Reich der Freiheit. Grundriss Systematischer Theologie*, Neukirchen 1975.

31. H. Grundmann, *Studien über Joachim von Floris*, Leipzig, Berlin, 1927; E. Benz, *Ecclesia Spiritualis*, Stuttgart 1934; A. Dempf, *Sacrum Imperium*, Munich 1929; H. Mottu, *La manifestation de l'Esprit selon Joachim de Fiore*, Paris 1977. For the material I am mainly following here E. Benz, 'Creator Spiritus. Die Geistlehre des Joachim von Fiore, *Eranos-Jahrbuch* 1956, pp. 285–355; Benz considers especially Joachim's two works *Concordia Novi ac Veteris Testamenti*, Venice 1519, and *Expositio in Apocalypsim*, Venice 1527.

32. Thomas Aquinas, *Summa Theologiae* II 1, q 106, a 4; also E. Benz, 'Thomas von Aquin und Joachim von Fiore', *ZKG* LIII, 1934, pp. 51–116.

33. Aquinas contested this, pointing to John 7.39 and putting Christ's glorification, resurrection and ascension on an equal footing.

34. *Concordia Novi ac Veteris Testamenti*, Venice 1519, Lib. V, 84, 112. Translation by E. Benz, *Eranos-Jahrbuch* 1956, pp. 314f. Joachim gives a similar summing up of his teaching in his *Expositio in Apocalypsim*, Venice 1527 (reprinted Frankfurt 1964), pp. 5ff. As far as I can see, Joachim talks about *tempus, aetas, status*, but does not actually use the word *regnum*.

35. K. Löwith, *Weltgeschichte und Heilsgeschichte*, 2nd ed. Stuttgart 1953, pp. 136ff.; cf. also F. Gerlich, *Der Kommunismus als Lehre vom tausendjährigen Reich*, Munich 1921.

36. This is especially true of Ernst Bloch: his messianic Marxism is Joachimite – that is to say mystical and democratic–socialism. Cf. J. Moltmann, 'Philosophie in der Schwebe des Messianismus' in *Im Gespräch mit Ernst Bloch*, Munich 1976, pp. 73–89.

37. H. Schmid, *Die Dogmatik der evangelisch-lutherischen Kirche. Dargestellt und aus den Quellen belegt*, 7th ed., Gütersloh 1893, pp. 266ff.; H. Heppe and E. Bizer, *Die Dogmatik der evangelisch-reformierten Kirche. Dargestellt und aus den Quellen belegt*, Neukirchen 1958, pp.

361; *Hutterus Redivivus oder Dogmatik der evangelisch-lutherischen Kirche*, 3rd. ed., Leipzig 1836, pp. 261ff.

38. References in L. Oeing-Hanhoff, 'Das Reich der Freiheit als absoluter Endzweck der Welt' in *Freiheit. Theoretische und praktische Aspekte des Problems*, ed. J. Simon, Munich 1977, pp. 55–83. I am indebted to him for many suggestions and have tried to answer his questions in my own way.

39. K. Marx, *Das Kapital*, Berlin 1949, III, pp. 873f., ET *Capital*, Chicago 1909, III, pp. 954f. For comment cf. I. Fetscher, *Die Freiheit im Lichte des Marxismus-Leninismus*, 4th ed., Bonn 1963.

40. Cf. Ch. IV § 2: 'The Creation of the Father'.

41. Cf. J. Moltmann, 'Creation as an Open System' in *The Future of Creation*, ET SCM Press and Fortress Press, Philadelphia, 1979, pp. 115–130.

42. Heppe and Bizer, *Dogmatik der evangelisch-reformierten Kirche*, op. cit., p. 557.

43. T. Pestel (*c*. 1584–*c*. 1659). Cf. Nikolaus Hermann's Christmas hymn:

> Er äussert sich all seiner G'walt,
> wird niedrig und gering
> und nimmt an sich ein's Knechts Gestalt:
> der Schöpfer aller Ding'.

44. Cf. here H. Mühlen, *Der Heilige Geist als Person*, op. cit., pp. 260ff.

45. On the theological concept of freedom used here cf. J. Moltmann, 'Die Revolution der Freiheit' in *Perspektiven der Theologie*, Munich 1968, pp. 189–211; W. Pannenberg, *The Idea of God and Human Freedom*, ET Westminster Press, Philadelphia 1973; also G. Gutiérrez, *Theology of Liberation*, ET Orbis Books, New York, 1973, SCM Press, 1974; P. C. Hodgson, *New Birth of Freedom. A Theology of Bondage and Liberation*, Philadelphia 1976; M. D. Meeks, 'Gott und die Ökonomie des Heiligen Geistes', *EvTh* 40, 1980, pp. 40–57.

46. Cf. H. Günther, *Freiheit, Herrschaft und Geschichte. Semantik der historisch-politischen Welt*, Frankfurt 1979.

47. C. B. Macpherson has shown in *The Political Theory of Possessive Individualism*, Oxford 1962, how since the beginning of the Englightenment and of capitalism freedom has increasingly been made 'a function of possession' (p. 3). This individualizes people. They are no longer defined through their social relationships but through their relationship to possession. The individual is free inasmuch as he is the owner of his person, his working capacity or his property. This transforms human society into a market of bartering relationships between owners. What makes a person a person is then certainly freedom; but freedom now means nothing other than being the owner of himself. For this Macpherson has coined the phrase 'possessive individualism'.

48. Hegel stresses this. Cf. *Philosophy of Right*, ET Oxford University Press 1952, § 21. For comment cf. L. Oeing-Hanhoff, 'Konkrete Freiheit' in *Stimmen der Zeit*, 1971, pp. 372ff., and 'Das Reich der Freiheit als absoluter Endzweck der Welt', op. cit., pp. 67f. Cf. also K. Marx, MEGA I, Abt. 3, pp. 546f., who calls this the true freedom: 'To have been for you the mediator between you and the species, i.e., to be known and experienced by you yourself as complement to your own being and as a necessary part of yourself – i.e., to know myself to be confirmed both in your thinking and in your love' (quoted in I. Fetscher, *Die Freiheit im Lichte des Marxismus–Leninismus*, 4th ed., Bonn 1963, p. 32).

49. For this term cf. R. Garaudy, *Das Projekt Hoffnung*, Vienna 1977.

50. K. Barth, *CD* III/3, p. 285.

51. G. W. F. Hegel, *Werke* VII, p. 60.

INDEX OF NAMES